THE ETHICS OF CARE

THE ETHICS OF CARE

Personal, Political, and Global

Virginia Held

OXFORD
UNIVERSITY PRESS

2006

OXFORD
UNIVERSITY PRESS

Oxford University Press, Inc., publishes works that further
Oxford University's objective of excellence
in research, scholarship, and education.

Oxford   New York
Auckland   Cape Town   Dar es Salaam   Hong Kong   Karachi
Kuala Lumpur   Madrid   Melbourne   Mexico City   Nairobi
New Delhi   Shanghai   Taipei   Toronto

With offices in
Argentina   Austria   Brazil   Chile   Czech Republic   France   Greece
Guatemala   Hungary   Italy   Japan   Poland   Portugal   Singapore
South Korea   Switzerland   Thailand   Turkey   Ukraine   Vietnam

Copyright © 2006 by Oxford University Press, Inc.

Published by Oxford University Press, Inc.
198 Madison Avenue, New York, New York 10016

www.oup.com

Oxford is a registered trademark of Oxford University Press

Library of Congress Cataloging-in-Publication Data

Held, Virginia.
The ethics of care: personal, political, and global / Virginia Held.
    p.   cm.
Includes bibliographical references and index.
ISBN-13 978-0-19-518099-2
ISBN-13 978-0-19-532590-4 (Pbk.)
1. Caring.   2. Feminist ethics.   I. Title.

BJ1475.H45 2005
177'.7—dc22   2005040551

Printed in the United States of America
on acid-free paper

For my grandchildren

Alexander, Owen, Madeleine, Kailey, and Nicolas

Acknowledgments

Since the publication of my book *Feminist Morality: Transforming Culture, Society, and Politics* in 1993, I became persuaded that the ethics of care I began to examine there merited further development. I wrote a series of papers on various aspects of care, presenting them at conferences and colloquia, discussing them, and publishing most of them. This book is based on many of those papers, though all have been rewritten, and much material is new.

I am very grateful to the many people who have given me their thoughts, reactions, criticisms, agreements, disagreements, and suggestions on these papers and on the arguments and observations in this book. I especially want to thank for their valuable comments Elizabeth Anderson, Barbara Andrew, Cheshire Calhoun, Richmond Campbell, Claudia Card, David Copp, Felmon Davis, Carol Gould, Kent Greenawalt, Mark Halfon, David Johnston, Alison Jaggar, Eva Kittay, Heidi Malm, Diana Meyers, Jennifer Nedelsky, Hilde Nelson, Martha Nussbaum, Rosamond Rhodes, Sara Ruddick, Susan Sherwin, Robert L. Simon, James P. Sterba, Nadia Urbinati, Jeremy Waldron, Iris Marion Young, and the anonymous reviewers of parts or all of the book.

For the opportunities they offered to present many of the ideas considered here and have them discussed, I thank the American Philosophical Association (Central and Pacific Divisions), the American Society for Value Inquiry, the City University of New York Graduate School, Columbia University, Dalhousie University, two IVR (Internationale Vereinigung Für Rechts-Und Sozialphilosophie) World Congresses, Kutztown University, the New Jersey Regional Philosophy Association, the State University of New York at Brockport, Suffolk Community College, Tufts University, Union College, the University of Delaware, the University of Toronto Law School, the University of Turku (Finland), and Vanderbilt University.

I thank the publishers for permissions to use revised versions or portions of the following papers they published. An earlier version of chapter 1 appears as "The Ethics of Care," in the *Oxford Handbook of Ethical Theory*, edited by David Copp (New York: Oxford University Press, 2006). An earlier version of chapter 2 appeared as "Taking Care: Care as Practice and Value," in *Setting the Moral Compass*, edited by Cheshire Calhoun (New York: Oxford University Press, 2004). Chapter 4 includes material from "Justice and Utility: Who Cares?" in *Philosophic Exchange* 26 (1995–96); "The Meshing of Care and Justice," *Hypatia* (spring 1995); and "The Contribution of Feminist Philosophy," *Associations* (1998). An earlier version of chapter 5, "Liberalism and the Ethics of Care," appeared in *On Feminist Ethics and Politics*, edited by Claudia Card (Lawrence: University Press of Kansas, 1999). An earlier version of chapter 6, "Caring Relations and Principles of Justice," appeared in *Controversies in Feminism*, edited by James P. Sterba (Lanham, MD: Rowman and Littlefield, 2001). A much shorter version of chapter 7, "Care and the Extension of Markets," was published in *Hypatia* 17(2) (spring 2002). Chapter 8 is based in part on "Rights and the Presumption of Care," in *Rights and Reason; Essays in Honor of Carl Wellman*, edited by Marilyn Friedman et al. (Dordrecht: Kluwer Academic Publishers, 2000, with kind permission of Springer Science and Business Media). Chapter 9 includes material from "Feminist Morality and Rights," in *Rechtstheorie*, Beiheft 19; "Rights," in *A Companion to Feminist Philosophy*, edited by Alison M. Jaggar and Iris Marion Young (Malden, Mass.: Blackwell, 1998); and "Feminism and Political Theory," in *Blackwell Guide to Social and Political Philosophy*, edited by Robert L. Simon (Malden, Mass.: Blackwell, 2002). Much shorter and earlier versions of chapter 10, "Care and Justice in the Global Context," appeared in *Associations* (2003) and *Ratio Juris* 17(2) (June 2004): 141–55.

I am enormously grateful to the City University of New York for the many years of steady employment, periodic sabbaticals, wonderful students, and committed colleagues that have made it possible for me to work as a philosopher aiming to affect the wider world and not just how philosophers think. My graduate teaching at the CUNY Graduate Center and undergraduate teaching at Hunter College have offered countless insights and arguments reflected in this book.

For steady companionship and a lighter touch, I thank my partner of many years, Robert L. Thompson, and my children, Julia and Philip, and their families. The balance they provide has been indispensable.

Contents

THE ETHICS OF CARE

Introduction

In the past few decades, the ethics of care has developed as a promising alternative to the dominant moral approaches that have been invoked during the previous two centuries. It has given rise to an extensive body of literature and has affected many moral inquiries in many areas. It is changing the ways moral problems are often interpreted and changing what many think the recommended approaches to moral issues ought to be.

With interest in normative perspectives expanding everywhere—from the outlines of egalitarian families and workplaces, to the moral responsibilities of parents and citizens, to the ethical evaluations of governmental and foreign policies—the ethics of care offers hope for rethinking in more fruitful ways how we ought to guide our lives.

It has the potential of being based on the truly universal experience of care. Every human being has been cared for as a child or would not be alive. Understanding the values involved in care, and how its standards reject violence and domination, are possible with the ethics of care.

It need not invoke religious beliefs that carry divisive baggage. It does not rely on dubious claims about universal norms of reason to which we must give priority in all questions of morality. Instead, it develops, on the basis of experience, reflection on it and discourse concerning it, an understanding of the most basic and most comprehensive values.

In part I of this book, I develop the ethics of care as a moral theory or approach to moral issues. In part II I explore the implications of the ethics of care for political, social, and global questions, considering also how such attempts to use the theory should allow in turn for improvements in it.

In chapter 1 I make the case that the ethics of care is a distinct moral theory or approach to moral theorizing, not a concern that can be added on to or included within other more established approaches, such as those of Kantian

moral theory, utilitarianism, or virtue ethics. The latter is the more controversial claim, since there are similarities between the ethics of care and virtue
ethics. But in its focus on relationships rather than on the dispositions of
individuals, the ethics of care is, I argue, distinct.

In chapter 2, I explore what care "is," or what we mean or should mean by
the term 'care.' I conclude that it is both a practice, or cluster of practices, and
a value, or cluster of values. It takes place in existing caring practices to some
extent, although existing practices are usually embedded in unsatisfactory
contexts of domination. And it provides standards by which to evaluate these
practices and to recommend better ones.

Since caring practices and values do require caring persons, I explore in
chapter 3 what the characteristics of a caring person should be. I conclude that a
caring person not only has the appropriate motivations in responding to others
or in providing care but also participates adeptly in effective practices of care.

In developing the ethics of care, contrasts have been drawn between care
and justice. In chapter 4 I examine contrasts between ethical theories based on
justice or on utility and those based on care. I consider the possible meshing
of care and justice, and the ways we might conceptualize how the pieces of a
satisfactory, comprehensive moral theory should fit together.

Chapter 5 contrasts the assumptions and implications of the ethics of care
with those of traditional liberalism and defends the ethics of care against liberal
critiques. Chapter 6 extends the discussion of universalization in moral theorizing and defends the ethics of care against the presumed requirement of the
dominant moral theories that universal principles of reason always be accorded
priority.

With chapter 7 I begin the examination of the implications of the ethics of
care for political and social issues, the focus of part II. I first address the political
question of whether market ways of conducting activities such as child care,
education, and health care should be expanded or limited, and I touch on the
implications of the issues for cultural activities. I show how dominant moral
approaches lack the resources to deal with this question, whereas the ethics of
care provides persuasive arguments for limiting markets.

In chapter 8 I discuss how actually respecting the rights we recognize as
important presupposes that persons are sufficiently interconnected to care
whether rights are respected. I also consider how the civil society to which
enormous attention has suddenly been paid in the past decade can be understood in terms of caring relations.

Chapter 9 examines arguments for limiting the reach of law and legalistic
thinking, rather than imagining that law can be a suitable model for all thinking
about morality. It also explains how the ethics of care has the resources to
recommend dealing with power and violence and need not and should not be
built on idealized images of family peace and harmony.

In chapter 10 I explore the implications of the ethics of care for relations
between states and for the possibilities of global civility. Once again, I suggest
how the ethics of care offers promise beyond that found in the more familiar
theories of justice.

In this book I try to present the hopeful potential of a new and developing moral approach. The ethics of care is only a few decades old, a very short time in the history of human attempts to evaluate how we should live our lives and to recommend what we ought to do. The ethics of care still has many weaknesses and lacunae, but its development is an ongoing, cooperative project. With this book I hope to contribute to its further improvement.

PART I

CARE AND MORAL THEORY

1

The Ethics of Care as Moral Theory

The ethics of care is only a few decades old.[1] Some theorists do not like the term 'care' to designate this approach to moral issues and have tried substituting 'the ethic of love,' or 'relational ethics,' but the discourse keeps returning to 'care' as the so far more satisfactory of the terms considered, though dissatisfactions with it remain. The concept of care has the advantage of not losing sight of the work involved in caring for people and of not lending itself to the interpretation of morality as ideal but impractical to which advocates of the ethics of care often object. Care is both value and practice.

By now, the ethics of care has moved far beyond its original formulations, and any attempt to evaluate it should consider much more than the one or two early works so frequently cited. It has been developed as a moral theory relevant not only to the so-called private realms of family and friendship but to medical practice, law, political life, the organization of society, war, and international relations.

The ethics of care is sometimes seen as a potential moral theory to be substituted for such dominant moral theories as Kantian ethics, utilitarianism, or Aristotelian virtue ethics. It is sometimes seen as a form of virtue ethics. It is almost always developed as emphasizing neglected moral considerations of at least as much importance as the considerations central to moralities of justice and rights or of utility and preference satisfaction. And many who contribute to the understanding of the ethics of care seek to integrate the moral considerations, such as justice, which other moral theories have clarified, satisfactorily with those of care, though they often see the need to reconceptualize these considerations.

Features of the Ethics of Care

Some advocates of the ethics of care resist generalizing this approach into something that can be fitted into the form of a moral theory. They see it as a mosaic of insights and value the way it is sensitive to contextual nuance and particular narratives rather than making the abstract and universal claims of more familiar moral theories.[2] Still, I think one can discern among various versions of the ethics of care a number of major features.

First, the central focus of the ethics of care is on the compelling moral salience of attending to and meeting the needs of the particular others for whom we take responsibility. Caring for one's child, for instance, may well and defensibly be at the forefront of a person's moral concerns. The ethics of care recognizes that human beings are dependent for many years of their lives, that the moral claim of those dependent on us for the care they need is pressing, and that there are highly important moral aspects in developing the relations of caring that enable human beings to live and progress. All persons need care for at least their early years. Prospects for human progress and flourishing hinge fundamentally on the care that those needing it receive, and the ethics of care stresses the moral force of the responsibility to respond to the needs of the dependent. Many persons will become ill and dependent for some periods of their later lives, including in frail old age, and some who are permanently disabled will need care the whole of their lives. Moralities built on the image of the independent, autonomous, rational individual largely overlook the reality of human dependence and the morality for which it calls. The ethics of care attends to this central concern of human life and delineates the moral values involved. It refuses to relegate care to a realm "outside morality." How caring for particular others should be reconciled with the claims of, for instance, universal justice is an issue that needs to be addressed. But the ethics of care starts with the moral claims of particular others, for instance, of one's child, whose claims can be compelling regardless of universal principles.

Second, in the epistemological process of trying to understand what morality would recommend and what it would be morally best for us to do and to be, the ethics of care values emotion rather than rejects it. Not all emotion is valued, of course, but in contrast with the dominant rationalist approaches, such emotions as sympathy, empathy, sensitivity, and responsiveness are seen as the kind of moral emotions that need to be cultivated not only to help in the implementation of the dictates of reason but to better ascertain what morality recommends.[3] Even anger may be a component of the moral indignation that should be felt when people are treated unjustly or inhumanely, and it may contribute to (rather than interfere with) an appropriate interpretation of the moral wrong. This is not to say that raw emotion can be a guide to morality; feelings need to be reflected on and educated. But from the care perspective, moral inquiries that rely entirely on reason and rationalistic deductions or calculations are seen as deficient.

The emotions that are typically considered and rejected in rationalistic moral theories are the egoistic feelings that undermine universal moral norms, the favoritism that interferes with impartiality, and the aggressive and vengeful impulses for which morality is to provide restraints. The ethics of care, in contrast, typically appreciates the emotions and relational capabilities that enable morally concerned persons in actual interpersonal contexts to understand what would be best. Since even the helpful emotions can often become misguided or worse—as when excessive empathy with others leads to a wrongful degree of self-denial or when benevolent concern crosses over into controlling domination—we need an *ethics* of care, not just care itself. The various aspects and expressions of care and caring relations need to be subjected to moral scrutiny and *evaluated*, not just observed and described.

Third, the ethics of care rejects the view of the dominant moral theories that the more abstract the reasoning about a moral problem the better because the more likely to avoid bias and arbitrariness, the more nearly to achieve impartiality. The ethics of care respects rather than removes itself from the claims of particular others with whom we share actual relationships.[4] It calls into question the universalistic and abstract rules of the dominant theories. When the latter consider such actual relations as between a parent and child, if they say anything about them at all, they may see them as permitted and cultivating them a preference that a person may have. Or they may recognize a universal obligation for all parents to care for their children. But they do not permit actual relations ever to take priority over the requirements of impartiality. As Brian Barry expresses this view, there can be universal rules permitting people to favor their friends in certain contexts, such as deciding to whom to give holiday gifts, but the latter partiality is morally acceptable only because universal rules have already so judged it.[5] The ethics of care, in contrast, is skeptical of such abstraction and reliance on universal rules and questions the priority given to them. To most advocates of the ethics of care, the compelling moral claim of the particular other may be valid even when it conflicts with the requirement usually made by moral theories that moral judgments be universalizeable, and this is of fundamental moral importance.[6] Hence the potential conflict between care and justice, friendship and impartiality, loyalty and universality. To others, however, there need be no conflict if universal judgments come to incorporate appropriately the norms of care previously disregarded.

Annette Baier considers how a feminist approach to morality differs from a Kantian one and Kant's claim that women are incapable of being fully moral because of their reliance on emotion rather than reason. She writes, "Where Kant concludes 'so much the worse for women,' we can conclude 'so much the worse for the male fixation on the special skill of drafting legislation, for the bureaucratic mentality of rule worship, and for the male exaggeration of the importance of independence over mutual interdependence.'"[7]

Margaret Walker contrasts what she sees as feminist "moral understanding" with what has traditionally been thought of as moral "knowledge." She sees the moral understanding she advocates as involving "attention, contextual and narrative appreciation, and communication in the event of moral deliberation." This alternative moral epistemology holds that "the adequacy of moral understanding decreases as its form approaches generality through abstraction."[8]

The ethics of care may seek to limit the applicability of universal rules to certain domains where they are more appropriate, like the domain of law, and resist their extension to other domains. Such rules may simply be inappropriate in, for instance, the contexts of family and friendship, yet relations in these domains should certainly be *evaluated*, not merely described, hence morality should not be limited to abstract rules. We should be able to give moral guidance concerning actual relations that are trusting, considerate, and caring and concerning those that are not.

Dominant moral theories tend to interpret moral problems as if they were conflicts between egoistic individual interests on the one hand, and universal moral principles on the other. The extremes of "selfish individual" and "humanity" are recognized, but what lies between these is often overlooked. The ethics of care, in contrast, focuses especially on the area between these extremes. Those who conscientiously care for others are not seeking primarily to further their own *individual* interests; their interests are intertwined with the persons they care for. Neither are they acting for the sake of *all others* or *humanity in general*; they seek instead to preserve or promote an actual human relation between themselves and *particular others*. Persons in caring relations are acting for self-and-other together. Their characteristic stance is neither egoistic nor altruistic; these are the options in a conflictual situation, but the well-being of a caring relation involves the cooperative well-being of those in the relation and the well-being of the relation itself.

In trying to overcome the attitudes and problems of tribalism and religious intolerance, dominant moralities have tended to assimilate the domains of family and friendship to the tribal, or to a source of the unfair favoring of one's own. Or they have seen the attachments people have in these areas as among the nonmoral private preferences people are permitted to pursue if restrained by impartial moral norms. The ethics of care recognizes the *moral* value and importance of relations of family and friendship and the need for *moral* guidance in these domains to understand how existing relations should often be changed and new ones developed. Having grasped the value of caring relations in such contexts as these more personal ones, the ethics of care then often examines social and political arrangements in the light of these values. In its more developed forms, the ethics of care as a feminist ethic offers suggestions for the radical transformation of society. It demands not just equality for women in existing structures of society but equal consideration for the experience that reveals the values, importance, and moral significance, of caring.

A fourth characteristic of the ethics of care is that like much feminist thought in many areas, it reconceptualizes traditional notions about the public and the private. The traditional view, built into the dominant moral theories, is that the household is a private sphere beyond politics into which government, based on consent, should not intrude. Feminists have shown how the greater social, political, economic, and cultural power of men has structured this "private" sphere to the disadvantage of women and children, rendering them vulnerable to domestic violence without outside interference, often leaving women economically dependent on men and subject to a highly inequitable division of labor in the family. The law has not hesitated to intervene into women's private decisions concerning reproduction but has been highly reluctant to intrude on men's exercise of coercive power within the "castles" of their homes.

Dominant moral theories have seen "public" life as relevant to morality while missing the moral significance of the "private" domains of family and friendship. Thus the dominant theories have assumed that morality should be sought for unrelated, independent, and mutually indifferent individuals assumed to be equal. They have posited an abstract, fully rational "agent as such" from which to construct morality,[9] while missing the moral issues that arise between interconnected persons in the contexts of family, friendship, and social groups. In the context of the family, it is typical for relations to be between persons with highly unequal power who did not choose the ties and obligations in which they find themselves enmeshed. For instance, no child can choose her parents yet she may well have obligations to care for them. Relations of this kind are standardly noncontractual, and conceptualizing them as contractual would often undermine or at least obscure the trust on which their worth depends. The ethics of care addresses rather than neglects moral issues arising in relations among the unequal and dependent, relations that are often laden with emotion and involuntary, and then notices how often these attributes apply not only in the household but in the wider society as well. For instance, persons do not choose which gender, racial, class, ethnic, religious, national, or cultural groups to be brought up in, yet these sorts of ties may be important aspects of who they are and how their experience can contribute to moral understanding.

A fifth characteristic of the ethics of care is the conception of persons with which it begins. This will be dealt with in the next section.

The Critique of Liberal Individualism

The ethics of care usually works with a conception of persons as relational, rather than as the self-sufficient independent individuals of the dominant moral theories. The dominant theories can be interpreted as importing into moral theory a concept of the person developed primarily for liberal political and economic theory, seeing the person as a rational, autonomous agent, or a self-interested individual. On this view, society is made up of "independent, autonomous units who cooperate only when the terms of cooperation are such as to make it further the ends of each of the parties," in Brian Barry's words.[10] Or, if they are Kantians, they refrain from actions that they could not will to be universal laws to which all fully rational and autonomous individual agents could agree. What such views hold, in Michael Sandel's critique of them, is that "what separates us is in some important sense prior to what connects us— epistemologically prior as well as morally prior. We are distinct individuals first and *then* we form relationships."[11] In Martha Nussbaum's liberal feminist morality, "the flourishing of human beings taken one by one is both analytically and normatively prior to the flourishing" of any group.[12]

The ethics of care, in contrast, characteristically sees persons as relational and interdependent, morally and epistemologically. Every person starts out as a child dependent on those providing us care, and we remain interdependent with others in thoroughly fundamental ways throughout our lives. That we can think and act as if we were independent depends on a network of social relations making it possible for us to do so. And our relations are part of what constitute our identity. This is not to say that we cannot become autonomous; feminists have done much interesting work developing an alternative conception of autonomy in place of the liberal individualist one.[13] Feminists have much experience rejecting or reconstituting relational ties that are oppressive. But it means that from the perspective of an ethics of care, to construct morality *as if* we were Robinson Crusoes, or, to use Hobbes's image, mushrooms sprung from nowhere, is misleading.[14] As Eva Kittay writes, this conception fosters the illusion that society is composed of free, equal, and independent individuals who can choose to associate with one another or not. It obscures the very real facts of dependency for everyone when they are young, for most people at various periods in their lives when they are ill or old and infirm, for some who are disabled, and for all those engaged in unpaid "dependency work."[15] And it obscures the innumerable ways persons and groups are interdependent in the modern world.

Not only does the liberal individualist conception of the person foster a false picture of society and the persons in it, it is, from the perspective of the ethics of care, impoverished also as an ideal. The ethics of care values the ties we have with particular other persons and the actual relationships that partly constitute our identity. Although persons often may and should reshape their relations with others—distancing themselves from some persons and groups and developing or strengthening ties with others—the autonomy sought within the ethics of care is a capacity to reshape and cultivate new relations, not to ever more closely resemble the unencumbered abstract rational self of liberal political and moral theories. Those motivated by the ethics of care would seek to become more admirable relational persons in better caring relations.

Even if the liberal ideal is meant only to instruct us on what would be rational in the terms of its ideal model, thinking of persons as the model presents them has effects that should not be welcomed. As Annette Baier writes, "Liberal morality, if unsupplemented, may *unfit* people to be anything other than what its justifying theories suppose them to be, ones who have no interest in each others' interests."[16] There is strong empirical evidence of how adopting a theoretical model can lead to behavior that mirrors it. Various studies show that studying economics, with its "repeated and intensive exposure to a model whose unequivocal prediction" is that people will decide what to do on the basis of self-interest, leads economics students to be less cooperative and more inclined to free ride than other students.[17]

The conception of the person adopted by the dominant moral theories provides moralities at best suitable for legal, political, and economic interactions between relative strangers, once adequate trust exists for them to form a political entity.[18] The ethics of care is, instead, hospitable to the relatedness of persons. It sees many of our responsibilities as not freely entered into but presented to us by the accidents of our embeddedness in familial and social and historical contexts. It often calls on us to *take* responsibility, while liberal individualist morality focuses on how we should leave each other alone. The view of persons as embedded and encumbered seems fundamental to much feminist thinking about morality and especially to the ethics of care (see chapter 3 for further discussion).

Justice and Care

Some conceptions of the ethics of care see it as contrasting with an ethic of justice in ways that suggest one must choose between them. Carol Gilligan's suggestion of alternative perspectives in interpreting and organizing the elements of a moral problem lent itself to this implication; she herself used the metaphor of the ambiguous figure of the vase and the faces, from psychological research on perception, to illustrate how one could see a problem as either a problem of justice or a problem of care, but not as both simultaneously.[19]

An ethic of justice focuses on questions of fairness, equality, individual rights, abstract principles, and the consistent application of them. An ethic of care focuses on attentiveness, trust, responsiveness to need, narrative nuance, and cultivating caring relations. Whereas an ethic of justice seeks a fair solution between competing individual interests and rights, an ethic of care sees the interests of carers and cared-for as importantly intertwined rather than as simply competing. Whereas justice protects equality and freedom, care fosters social bonds and cooperation.

These are very different emphases in what morality should consider. Yet both deal with what seems of great moral importance. This has led many to explore how they might be combined in a satisfactory morality. One can persuasively argue, for instance, that justice is needed in such contexts of care as the family, to protect against violence and the unfair division of labor or treatment of children. One can also persuasively argue that care is needed in such contexts of justice as the streets and the courts, where persons should be treated humanely, and in the way education and health and welfare should be dealt with as social responsibilities. The implication may be that justice and care should not be separated into different "ethics," that, in Sara Ruddick's proposed approach, "justice is always seen in tandem with care."[20]

Few would hold that considerations of justice have no place at all in care. One would not be caring well for two children, for instance, if one showed a persistent favoritism toward one of them that could not be justified on the basis of some such factor as greater need. The issues are rather what constellation of values have priority and which predominate in the practices of the ethics of care and the ethics of justice. It is quite possible to delineate significant differences between them. In the dominant moral theories of the ethics of justice, the values of equality, impartiality, fair distribution, and noninterference have priority; in practices of justice, individual rights are protected, impartial judgments are arrived at, punishments are deserved, and equal treatment is sought. In contrast, in the ethics of care, the values of trust, solidarity, mutual concern, and empathetic responsiveness have priority; in practices of care, relationships are cultivated, needs are responded to, and sensitivity is demonstrated.

An extended effort to integrate care and justice is offered by Diemut Bubeck. She makes clear that she "endorse[s] the ethic of care as a system of concepts, values, and ideas, arising from the practice of care as an organic part of this practice and responding to its material requirements, notably the meeting of needs."[21] Yet her primary interest is in understanding the exploitation of women, which she sees as tied to the way women do most of the unpaid work of caring. She argues that such principles as equality in care and the minimization of harm are tacitly, if not explicitly, embedded in the practice of care, as carers whose capacities and time for engaging in caring labor are limited must decide how to respond to various others in need of being cared for. She writes that "far from being extraneous impositions . . . considerations of justice arise from within the practice of care itself and therefore are an important part of the ethic of care, properly understood."[22] The ethics of care must thus also concern itself with the justice (or lack of it) of the ways the tasks of caring are distributed in society. Traditionally, women have been expected to do most of the caring work that needs to be done; the sexual division of labor exploits women by extracting unpaid care labor from them, making women less able than men to engage in paid work. "Femininity" constructs women as carers, contributing to the constraints by which women are pressed into accepting the sexual division of labor. An ethic of care that extols caring but that fails to be concerned with how the burdens of caring are distributed contributes to the exploitation of women, and of the minority groups whose members perform much of the paid but ill-paid work of caring in affluent households, in day care centers, hospitals, nursing homes, and the like.

The question remains, however, whether justice should be thought to be incorporated into any ethic of care that will be adequate or whether we should keep the notions of justice and care and their associated ethics conceptually distinct. There is much to be said for recognizing how the ethics of care values interrelatedness and responsiveness to the needs of particular others, how the ethics of justice values fairness and rights, and how these are different emphases.[23] Too much integration will lose sight of these valid differences. I am more inclined to say that an adequate, comprehensive moral theory will have to include the insights of both the ethics of care and the ethics of justice, among other insights, rather than that either of these can be incorporated into the other in the sense of supposing that it can provide the grounds for the judgments characteristically found in the other. Equitable caring is not necessarily better caring, it is fairer caring. And humane justice is not necessarily better justice, it is more caring justice.

Almost no advocates of the ethics of care are willing to see it as a moral outlook less valuable than the dominant ethics of justice.[24] To imagine that the concerns of care can merely be added on to the dominant theories, as, for instance, Stephen Darwall suggests, is seen as unsatisfactory.[25] Confining the ethics of care to the private sphere while holding it unsuitable for public life, as Nel Noddings did at first and as many accounts of it suggest,[26] is also to be rejected. But how care and justice are to be meshed without losing sight of their differing priorities is a task still being worked on.

My own suggestions for integrating care and justice are to keep these concepts conceptually distinct and to delineate the domains in which they should have priority.[27] In the realm of law, for instance, justice and the assurance of rights should have priority, although the humane considerations of care should not be absent. In the realm of the family and among friends, priority should be given to expansive care, though the basic requirements of justice surely should also be met. But these are the clearest cases; others will combine moral urgencies. Universal human rights (including the social and economic ones as well as the political and civil) should certainly be respected, but promoting care across continents may be a more promising way to achieve this than mere rational recognition. When needs are desperate, justice may be a lessened requirement on shared responsibility for meeting needs, although this rarely excuses violations of rights. At the level of what constitutes a society in the first place, a domain within which rights are to be assured and care provided, appeal must be made to something like the often weak but not negligible caring relations among persons that enable them to recognize each other as members of the same society. Such recognition must eventually be global; in the meantime, the civil society without which the liberal institutions of justice cannot function presume a background of some degree of caring relations rather than of merely competing individuals (see chapter 8). Furthermore, considerations of care provide a more fruitful basis than considerations of justice for deciding much about how society should be structured, for instance, how extensive or how restricted markets should be (see chapter 7). And in the course of protecting the rights that ought to be recognized, such as those to basic necessities, policies that express the caring of the community for all its members will be better policies than those that grudgingly, though fairly, issue an allotment to those deemed unfit.

Care is probably the most deeply fundamental value. There can be care without justice: There has historically been little justice in the family, but care and life have gone on without it. There can be no justice without care, however, for without care no child would survive and there would be no persons to respect.

Care may thus provide the wider and deeper ethics within which justice should be sought, as when persons in caring relations may sometimes compete and in doing so should treat each other fairly, or, at the level of society, within caring relations of the thinner kind we can agree to treat each other for limited purposes as if we were the abstract individuals of liberal theory. But although care may be the more fundamental value, it may well be that the ethics of care does not itself provide adequate theoretical resources for dealing with issues of justice. Within its appropriate sphere and for its relevant questions, the ethics of justice may be best for what we seek. What should be resisted is the traditional inclination to expand the reach of justice in such a way that it is mistakenly imagined to be able to give us a comprehensive morality suitable for all moral questions.

Implications for Society

Many advocates of the ethics of care argue for its relevance in social and political and economic life. Sara Ruddick shows its implications for efforts to achieve peace.[28] I argue that as we see the deficiencies of the contractual model of human relations within the household, we can see them also in the world beyond and begin to think about how society should be reorganized to be hospitable to care, rather than continuing to marginalize it. We can see how not only does every domain of society need transformation in light of the values of care but so would the relations between such domains if we took care seriously, as care would move to the center of our attention and become a primary concern of society. Instead of a society dominated by conflict restrained by law and preoccupied with economic gain, we might have a society that saw as its most important task the flourishing of children and the development of caring relations, not only in personal contexts but among citizens and using governmental institutions. We would see that instead of abandoning culture to the dictates of the marketplace, we should make it possible for culture to develop in ways best able to enlighten and enrich human life.[29]

Joan Tronto argues for the political implications of the ethics of care, seeing care as a political as well as moral ideal advocating the meeting of needs for care as "the highest social goal."[30] She shows how unacceptable are current arrangements for providing care: "Caring activities are devalued, underpaid, and disproportionately occupied by the relatively powerless in society."[31] Bubeck, Kittay, and many others argue forcefully that care must be seen as a public concern, not relegated to the private responsibility of women, the inadequacy and arbitrariness of private charities, or the vagaries and distortions of the market.[32] In her recent book *Starting at Home*, Noddings explores what a caring society would be like.[33]

When we concern ourselves with caring relations between more distant others, this care should not be thought to reduce to the mere "caring about" that has little to do with the face-to-face interactions of caring labor and can easily become paternalistic or patronizing. The same characteristics of attentiveness, responsiveness to needs, and understanding situations from the points of view of others should characterize caring when the participants are more distant. This also requires the work of understanding and of expending varieties of effort.[34]

Given how care is a value with the widest possible social implications, it is unfortunate that many who look at the ethics of care continue to suppose it is a "family ethics," confined to the "private" sphere. Although some of its earliest formulations suggested this, and some of its related values are to be seen most clearly in personal contexts, an adequate understanding of the ethics of care should recognize that it elaborates values as fundamental and as relevant to political institutions and to how society is organized, as those of justice. Perhaps its values are even more fundamental and more relevant to life in society than those traditionally relied on.

Instead of seeing the corporate sector, and military strength, and government and law as the most important segments of society deserving the highest levels of wealth and power, a caring society might see the tasks of bringing up children, educating its members, meeting the needs of all, achieving peace and treasuring the environment, and doing these in the best ways possible to be that to which the greatest social efforts of all should be devoted. One can recognize that something comparable to legal constraints and police enforcement, including at a global level, may always be necessary for special cases, but also that caring societies could greatly decrease the need for them. The social changes a focus on care would require would be as profound as can be imagined.

The ethics of care as it has developed is most certainly not limited to the sphere of family and personal relations. When its social and political implications are understood, it is a radical ethic calling for a profound restructuring of society. And it has the resources for dealing with power and violence (see especially chapters 8 and 9).

The Ethics of Care and Virtue Ethics

Insofar as the ethics of care wishes to cultivate in persons the characteristics of a caring person and the skills of activities of caring, might an ethic of care be assimilated to virtue theory?

To some philosophers, the ethics of care is a form of virtue ethics. Several of the contributors to the volume *Feminists Doing Ethics* adopt this view.[35] Leading virtue theorist Michael Slote argues extensively for the position that caring is the primary virtue and that a morality based on the motive of caring can offer a general account of right and wrong action and political justice.[36]

Certainly there are some similarities between the ethics of care and virtue theory. Both examine practices and the moral values they embody. Both see more hope for moral development in reforming practices than in reasoning from abstract rules. Both understand that the practices of morality must be cultivated, nurtured, shaped.

Until recently, however, virtue theory has not paid adequate attention to the practices of caring in which women have been so heavily engaged. Although this might be corrected, virtue theory has characteristically seen the virtues as incorporated in various traditions or traditional communities. In contrast, the ethics of care as a feminist ethic is wary of existing traditions and traditional communities: Virtually all are patriarchal. The ethics of care envisions caring not as practiced under male domination, but as it should be practiced in postpatriarchal society, of which we do not yet have traditions or wide experience. Individual egalitarian families are still surrounded by inegalitarian social and cultural influences.

In my view, although there are similarities between them and although to be caring is no doubt a virtue, the ethics of care is not simply a kind of virtue ethics. Virtue ethics focuses especially on the states of character of individuals, whereas the ethics of care concerns itself especially with caring *relations*. Caring relations have primary value.

If virtue ethics is interpreted, as with Slote, as primarily a matter of motives, it may neglect unduly the labor and objective results of caring, as Bubeck's emphasis on actually meeting needs highlights. Caring is not only a question of motive or attitude or virtue. On the other hand, Bubeck's account is unduly close to a utilitarian interpretation of meeting needs, neglecting that care *also* has an aspect of motive and virtue. If virtue ethics is interpreted as less restricted to motives, and if it takes adequate account of the results of the virtuous person's activities for the persons cared for, it may better include the concerns of the ethics of care. It would still, however, focus on the dispositions of individuals, whereas the ethics of care focuses on social relations and the social practices and values that sustain them. The traditional Man of Virtue may be almost as haunted by his patriarchal past as the Man of Reason. The work of care has certainly not been among the virtuous activities to which he has adequately attended.

The ethics of care, in my view, is a distinctive ethical outlook, distinct even from virtue ethics. Certainly it has precursors, and such virtue theorists as Aristotle, Hume, and the moral sentimentalists contribute importantly to it. As a feminist ethic, the ethics of care is certainly not a mere description or generalization of women's attitudes and activities as developed under patriarchal conditions. To be acceptable, it must be a *feminist* ethic, open to both women and men to adopt. But in being feminist, it is different from the ethics of its precursors and different as well from virtue ethics.

The ethics of care is sometimes thought inadequate because of its inability to provide definite answers in cases of conflicting moral demands. Virtue theory has similarly been criticized for offering no more than what detractors call a "bag of virtues," with no clear indication of how to prioritize the virtues or apply their requirements, especially when they seem to conflict. Defenders of the ethics of care respond that the adequacy of the definite answers provided by, for instance, utilitarian and Kantian moral theories is illusory. Cost-benefit analysis is a good example of a form of utilitarian calculation that purports to provide clear answers to questions about what we ought to do, but from the point of view of moral understanding, its answers are notoriously dubious. So, too, often are casuistic reasonings about deontological rules. To advocates of the ethics of care, its alternative moral epistemology seems better. It stresses sensitivity to the multiple relevant considerations in particular contexts, cultivating the traits of character and of relationship that sustain caring, and promoting the dialogue that corrects and enriches the perspective of any one individual.[37] The ethics of care is hospitable to the methods of discourse ethics, though with an emphasis on actual dialogue that empowers its participants to express themselves rather than on discourse so ideal that actual differences of viewpoint fall away.[38]

Care, Culture, and Religion

Questions that may be raised are whether the ethics of care resembles other kinds of ethical theory that are not feminist, and whether there can be nonfeminist forms of the ethics of care. Some think the ethics of care is close to Hume's ethics.[39] Others have debated whether the ethics of care resembles Confucian ethics. Chenyang Li argues that it does. He holds that the concept of care is similar to the concept of *jen* or *ren* central to Confucian ethics, and that although the Confucian tradition did maintain that women were inferior to men, this is not a necessary feature of Confucian thought.[40] Daniel Star thinks that Confucian ethics is a kind of virtue ethics, always interested in role-based categories of relationships, such as father/son and ruler/subject, and that because of this it will not be able to prioritize particular relationships, such as that between a particular parent and a particular child, as does the ethics of care.[41]

Lijun Yuan argues that Confucian ethics is so inherently patriarchal that it cannot be acceptable to feminists.[42] But other interpretations are also being developed.[43] One way in which the ethics of care does resemble Confucian ethics is in its rejection of the sharp split between public and private. The ethics of care rejects the model that became dominant in the West in the seventeenth and eighteenth centuries as democratic states replaced feudal society: a public sphere of mutually disinterested equals coexisting with a private sphere of female caring and male rule. The ethics of care advocates care as a value for society as well as household. In this there are some resemblances to the Confucian view of public morality as an extension of private morality.

It may be suggested that the ethics of care bears some resemblance to a Christian ethic of love counseling us to love our neighbors and care for those in need.[44] But when a morality depends on a given religion, it has little persuasiveness for those who do not share that faith. Moralities based on reason, in contrast, can succeed in gaining support around the world and across cultures. The growth of the human rights movement is strong evidence. One of the strengths of the dominant, rationalistic moral theories such as Kantian ethics and utilitarianism, in contrast with which the ethics of care developed, is their independence from religion. They aim to appeal only to universal reason (though in practice they may fall woefully short of doing so).

Virtue ethics is sometimes based on religion, but need not be. The universal appeal of virtue ethics, however, has been less than that of rationalistic ethics, given the enormous amount of cultural variation in what have been thought of as the virtues, in comparison to such basic moral prohibitions based on reason as those against murder, theft, and assault, thought to be able to provide the basis for any acceptable legal system.

The ethics of care, it should be noted, has potential comparable to that of rationalistic moral theories. It appeals to the universal experience of caring. Every conscious human being has been cared for as a child and can see the value in the care that shaped him or her; every thinking person can recognize the moral worth of the caring relations that gave him or her a future. The ethics of care builds on experience that all persons share, though they have often been unaware of its embedded values and implications.

Various feminist critics hold that the ethics of care can be hostile to feminist objectives. Conservatives claim to value care but often oppose women's rights and governmental social programs and resist women's progress. A traditional Confucian ethic, if seen as an ethic of care, would be a form of care ethics unacceptable to feminists; so would be communitarian views that do appreciate care but hold that women ought to do the caring while leaving "public" concerns to men. Liberal feminist critics of the ethics of care charge it with reinforcing the stereotypical image of women as selfless nurturers and with encouraging the unjust assignment of caring work to women. They think it lacks the prioritizing of equality that feminism must demand.[45] Other feminist critics find women's experience of mothering as it has occurred under patriarchal conditions suspect or fear that an ethics of care will deflect attention from the oppressive social structures in which it takes place.[46] Onora O'Neill has written that "a stress on caring and relationships . . . may endorse relegation to the nursery and the kitchen, to purdah and to poverty. In rejecting 'abstract liberalism,' such feminists converge with traditions that have excluded women from economic and public life."[47]

Still other feminists worry that the ethics of care cannot adequately handle the problem of violence against women or of violent political conflict. However, the ethics of care does not presume the peace and harmony of idealized images of family life. It knows full well that even caring relations can be fraught with conflict. It seeks to deal with violence, not merely to respond in kind (see chapter 9).

Feminist defenders of the ethics of care argue that it should be understood as a feminist ethic. It makes clear, in their view, why men as well as women should value caring relations and should share equally in cultivating them. It does not take the practices of caring as developed under patriarchal conditions as satisfactory, but it does explore the neglected values discernible through attention to and reflection on them. And it seeks to extend these values as appropriate throughout society, along with justice. If one wishes to count any view that prioritizes care as a version of the ethics of care, one must be careful to distinguish between acceptable and unacceptable versions. Fiona Robinson, arguing for the relevance of the ethics of care to international relations, writes that "it is only a narrow, 'orthodox' ethics of care,"—I would say one that has been superceded—"the view of care as essentially a morality for women, belonging to the private sphere," to which criticisms such as O'Neill's apply.[48] And I agree. The ethics of care has gone far beyond its earliest formulations, or any traditional religious or communitarian formulations it may seem to resemble, and should not be judged by them.

My own view is that to include nonfeminist versions of valuing care among the moral approaches called the ethics of care is to unduly disregard the history of how this ethics has developed and come to be a candidate for serious consideration among contemporary moral theories. The history of the development of the contemporary ethics of care is the history of recent feminist progress.

The Feminist Background

The ethics of care has grown out of the constructive turmoil of the phase of feminist thought and the rethinking of almost all fields of inquiry that began in the United States and Europe in the late 1960s. During this time, the bias against women in society and in what was taken to be knowledge became a focus of attention.

Feminism is a revolutionary movement. It aims to overturn what many consider the most entrenched hierarchy there is: the hierarchy of gender. Its fundamental commitment is to the equality of women, although that may be interpreted in various ways. A most important achievement of feminism has been to establish that the experience of women is as important, relevant, and philosophically interesting as the experience of men. The feminism of the late twentieth century was built on women's experience.

Experience is central to feminist thought, but what is meant by experience is not mere empirical observation, as so much of the history of modern philosophy and as analytic philosophy tend to construe it. Feminist experience is what art and literature as well as science deal with. It is the lived experience of feeling as well as thinking, of performing actions as well as receiving impressions, and of being aware of our connections with other persons as well as of our own sensations. And by now, for feminists, it is not the experience of what can be thought of as women as such, which would be an abstraction, but the experience of actual women in all their racial and cultural and other diversity.[49]

The feminist validation of women's experience has had important consequences in ethics. It has led to a fundamental critique of the moral theories that were (and to a large extent still are) dominant and to the development of alternative, feminist approaches to morality. For instance, in the long history of thinking about the human as Man, the public sphere from which women were excluded was seen as the source of the distinctively human, moral, and creative. The Greek conception of the polis illustrated this view, later reflected strongly in social contract theories. As the realm of economic activity was added after industrialization to that of the political, artistic, and scientific to compose what was seen as human, transformative, and progressive, the private sphere of the household continued to be thought of as natural, a realm where the species is reproduced, repetitively replenishing the biological basis of life.

The dominant moral theories when the feminism of the late twentieth century appeared on the scene were Kantian moral theory and utilitarianism. These were the theories that, along with their relevant metaethical questions, dominated the literature in moral philosophy and the courses taught to students.[50] They were also the moral outlooks that continued to have a significant influence outside philosophy in the field of law, one of the few areas that had not banished moral questions in favor of purportedly value-free psychology and social science.

These dominant moral theories can be seen to be modeled on the experience of men in public life and in the marketplace. When women's experience is thought to be as relevant to morality as men's, a position whose denial would seem to be biased, these moralities can be seen to fit very inadequately the morally relevant experience of women in the household. Women's experience has typically included cultivating special relationships with family and friends, rather than primarily dealing impartially with strangers, and providing large amounts of caring labor for children and often for ill or elderly family members. Affectionate sensitivity and responsiveness to need may seem to provide better moral guidance for what should be done in these contexts than do abstract rules or rational calculations of individual utilities.

At around the same time feminists began questioning the adequacy of the dominant moral theories, other voices were doing so also, which increased the ability of the feminist critiques to gain a hearing. With the work of Alasdair MacIntyre and others, there began to be a revival of the virtue theory that had been largely eclipsed.[51] Lawrence Blum's work on how friendship had been neglected by the dominant theories and Bernard Williams's skepticism about how such theories could handle some of the most important questions human beings face contributed to the critical discourse.[52] Arguments about how knowledge is historically situated and about the plurality of values further opened the way for feminist rethinking of moral theory.[53]

Within traditional moral philosophy, debates have been extensive and complex concerning the relative merits of deontological or Kantian moral theory as compared with the merits of the various kinds of utilitarian or consequentialist theory and of the contractualism that can take a more Kantian or a more utilitarian form. But from the newly asserted point of view of women's experience of moral issues, what may be most striking about all of these is their similarity. Both Kantian moralities of universal, abstract moral laws, and utilitarian versions of the ethics of Bentham and Mill advocating impartial calculations to determine what will produce the most happiness for the most people have been developed for interactions between relative strangers. Contractualism treats interactions between mutually disinterested individuals. All require impartiality and make no room at the foundational level for the partiality that connects us to those we care for and to those who care for us. Relations of family, friendship, and group identity have largely been missing from these theories, though recent attempts, which I find unsuccessful, have been made to handle such relations within them.

Although their conceptions of reason differ significantly, with Kantian theory rejecting the morality of instrumental reasoning and utilitarian theory embracing it, both types of theory are rationalistic. Both rely on one very simple supreme and universal moral principle: the Kantian categorical imperative, or the utilitarian principle of utility, in accordance with which everyone ought always to act. Both ask us to be entirely impartial and to reject emotion in determining what we ought to do. Though Kantian ethics enlists emotion in carrying out the dictates of reason, and utilitarianism allows each of us to count ourselves as one among all whose pain or pleasure will be affected by an action, for both kinds of theory we are to disregard our emotions in the epistemological process of figuring out what we ought to do. These characterizations also hold for contractualism.

These theories generalize from the ideal contexts of the state and the market, addressing the moral decisions of judges, legislators, policy makers, and citizens. But because they are *moral* theories rather than merely political or legal or economic theories, they extend their recommendations to what they take to be *all* moral decisions about how we ought to act in any context in which moral problems arise.

In Margaret Walker's assessment, these are idealized "theoretical-juridical" accounts of actual moral practices. They invoke the image of "a fraternity of independent peers invoking laws to deliver verdicts with authority."[54] Fiona Robinson asserts that in dominant moral theories, values such as autonomy, independence, noninterference, self-determination, fairness, and rights are given priority, and there is a "systematic devaluing of notions of interdependence, relatedness, and positive involvement" in the lives of others.[55] The theoretical-juridical accounts, Walker shows, are presented as appropriate for "the" moral agent, as recommendations for how "we" ought to act, but their canonical forms of moral judgment are the judgments of those who resemble "a judge, manager, bureaucrat, or gamesman."[56] They are abstract and idealized forms of the judgments made by persons who are dominant in an established social order. They do not represent the moral experiences of women caring for children or aged parents, or of minority service workers providing care for minimal wages. And they do not deal with the judgments of groups who must rely on communal solidarity for survival.

Feminist Alternatives

In place of the dominant moral theories found inadequate, feminists have offered a variety of alternatives. There is not any single "feminist moral theory," but a number of approaches sharing a basic commitment to eliminate gender bias in moral theorizing as well as elsewhere.[57]

Some feminists defend versions of Kantian moral theory[58] or utilitarianism,[59] or of such related theories as contractualism[60] and liberal individualist moral theory.[61] But they respond to different concerns and interpret and apply these theories in ways that none or few of their leading nonfeminist defenders do. For instance, taking a liberal contractualist approach and focusing on justice, equality, and freedom, many argue that the principles of justice should be met in the division of labor and availability of opportunities within the family and not only in public life. Of course this will require an end to the domestic violence, marital rape, patriarchal dominance, and female disadvantage in opportunities for health, education, and occupational development that still afflict many millions of women around the world, as it will require that the burdens of child care and housework not fall disproportionately on women. Achieving such aims as these would produce very radical change at the global level.

At present the most influential nonfeminist advocates of dominant moral theories have still paid little attention to feminist critiques,[62] but when these theories are extended in the ways feminists suggest, they can be significantly improved as theories.

Other feminist theorists, at the same time, have gone much further in a distinctive direction. Rather than limiting themselves to extending traditional theories in nontraditional ways, they have developed a more distinctively different ethics: the ethics of care. Although most working within this approach share the goals of justice and equality for women that can be dealt with using traditional theories, they see the potential of a very different set of values for a more adequate treatment of moral issues not only within the family but in the wider society as well. The ethics of care is a deep challenge to other moral theories. It takes the experience of women in caring activities such as mothering as central, interprets and emphasizes the values inherent in caring practices, shows the inadequacies of other theories for dealing with the moral aspects of caring activity, and then considers generalizing the insights of caring to other questions of morality.

I locate the beginnings of the ethics of care with a pioneering essay called "Maternal Thinking" by philosopher Sara Ruddick published in 1980.[63] In it, Ruddick attended to the caring practice of mothering, the characteristic and distinctive thinking to which it gives rise, and the standards and values that can be discerned in this practice. Mothering aims to preserve the life and foster the growth of particular children and to have these children develop into acceptable persons. The actual feelings of mothers are highly ambivalent and often hostile toward the children for whom they care, but a commitment to the practice and goals of mothering provides standards to be heeded. Virtues such as humility and resilient good humor emerge as values in the practice of mothering; self-effacement and destructive denial can be seen as the "degenerative forms" of these virtues and should be avoided. Her essay showed how women's experience in an activity such as mothering could yield a distinctive moral outlook, and how the values that emerged from within it could be relevant beyond the practice itself, for instance in promoting peace.

Ludicrous as it now seems in the twenty-first century, at the time this essay appeared, the practice of mothering had been virtually absent from all nonfeminist moral theorizing, there was no philosophical acknowledgment that mothers *think* or *reason*, or that one can find moral values in this practice.[64] Women were only imagined to think or face moral problems when they ventured beyond the household into the world of men. The characteristic image was one of human mothers raising their young much as animal mothers raise theirs, philosophical thinking about women or mothers having incorporated them into a natural biological or evolutionary framework. Or, if women were portrayed in a psychological or psychoanalytic framework, they might be seen as reacting emotionally, but again, they were not associated with reasoning and thinking, certainly not with the possibility that there might be distinctive and valid forms of moral thought to which they have privileged access through their extensive experience with caring.

Other caring activities, such as caring for the sick or elderly, were similarly dismissed as irrelevant for the construction of moral theory, though existing theory, for instance a Kantian respect for persons, might be applied to a problem in medical ethics, such as whether a doctor should tell a patient that he or she is dying, or a Rawlsian view of justice might be used to evaluate how health care should be distributed.

Ruddick's essay showed that attending to the experience of women in a caring practice could change how we think about morality and could change our view of the values appropriate for given activities. Though men can also engage in caring practices, if they do not, they may fail to understand the morality embedded in these practices.

In 1982, Carol Gilligan's book *In a Different Voice* provided impetus for the development of the ethics of care. Gilligan, a developmental psychologist, aimed for findings that would be empirical and descriptive of the psychological outlooks of girls as they become more mature in their thinking about morality. Gilligan was suspicious of the test results obtained by Lawrence Kohlberg, a psychologist with whom she worked, that seemed to show that girls progress more slowly than boys in acquiring moral maturity. She noted that all the children studied in the construction of the stages that were taken to indicate advancement in moral reasoning were boys; she decided to study how girls and women approach moral problems. To moral philosophers it was striking that the "highest stage" of Kohlberg's account of moral maturity closely resembled Kantian moral reasoning, presupposing such difficult questions as whether maturity in ethics really is primarily a matter of reasoning and whether a Kantian morality really is superior to all others.

Gilligan thought from her inquiries that it is possible to discern a "different voice" in the way many girls and women interpret, reflect on, and speak about moral problems: they are more concerned with context and actual relationships between persons, and less inclined to rely on abstract rules and individual conscience. Gilligan asserted that although only some of the women studied adopted this different voice, almost no men did. As she put it in a later essay, this meant that "if women were eliminated from the research sample, care focus in moral reasoning would virtually disappear."[65]

Gilligan's findings, to the extent that they were claims about men and women as such, have been questioned on empirical grounds. When education and occupation were comparable, the differences between women and men were to some researchers unclear, and African men showed some of the same tendencies in interpreting moral problems as the women she studied.[66] But the importance of Gilligan's work for moral theory has not been what it showed about how men and women brought up under patriarchy in fact think about morality, whether social position is as or more important than gender in influencing such thinking, or whether women who advance occupationally learn to think like men. It has been its suggestion of alternative perspectives through which moral problems can be interpreted: a "justice perspective" that emphasizes universal moral principles and how they can be applied to particular cases and values rational argument about these; and a "care perspective" that pays more attention to people's needs to how actual relations between people can be maintained or repaired, and that values narrative and sensitivity to context in arriving at moral judgments. Gilligan herself thought that for a person to have an adequate morality, both perspectives are needed, as men overcome their difficulties with attachment and become more caring and as women overcome their reluctance to be independent and become more concerned with justice. But she did not indicate how, within moral theory, care and justice are to be integrated.

Feminist philosophers reading Gilligan's work found that it resonated with many of their own dissatisfactions with dominant moral theories.[67] Whether or not women were in fact more likely to adopt the "care perspective," the history of philosophy had virtually excluded women's experiences. An "ethic of care" that could be contrasted with an "ethic of justice" might, many thought, better address their concerns as they understood how the contexts of mothering, family responsibilities, friendship, and caring in society were in need of moral evaluation and guidance by moral theories more appropriate to them than the dominant theories seemed capable of being. Theories developed for the polis and the marketplace were ill suited, these feminists thought, for application to the contexts of experience they were no longer willing to disregard as morally insignificant.

Soon after, Nel Noddings's book *Caring* (1984) provided a more phenomenological account of what is involved in activities of care. It examined the virtues of close attention to the feelings and needs of others, and the identification with another's reality that is central to care. The collections of papers *Women and Moral Theory* (1987), edited by Eva Kittay and Diana T. Meyers, and *Science, Morality and Feminist Theory* (1987), edited by Marsha Hanen and Kai Nielsen, contributed significantly to the further development of the ethics of care. Annette Baier's important work on trust and her appreciation of Hume's ethics as a precursor of feminist ethics added further strength to the new outlook on care.[68] Many other papers and books contributed to this discourse and during and after the 1990s the numbers expanded rapidly.[69] The ethics of care now has a central, though not exclusive, place in feminist moral theorizing, and it has drawn increasing interest from moral philosophers of all kinds.

The ethics of care builds concern and mutual responsiveness to need on both the personal and the wider social level. Within social relations in which we care enough about each other to form a social entity, we may agree for limited purposes to imagine each other as liberal individuals and to adopt liberal policies to maximize individual benefits. But we should not lose sight of the restricted and artificial aspects of such conceptions. The ethics of care offers a view of both the more immediate and the more distant human relations on which satisfactory societies can be built. It provides new theory with which to develop new practices and can perhaps offer greater potential for moral progress than is contained in the views of traditional moral theory.

2

Care as Practice and Value

What *is* care? What do we mean by the term 'care'? Can we define it in anything like a precise way? There is not yet anything close to agreement among those writing on care on what exactly we should take the meaning of this term to be, but there have been many suggestions, tacit and occasionally explicit.

For over two decades, the concept of care as it figures in the ethics of care has been assumed, explored, elaborated, and employed in the development of theory. But definitions have often been imprecise, or trying to arrive at them has simply been postponed (as in my own case), in the growing discourse. Perhaps this is entirely appropriate for new explorations, but the time may have come to seek greater clarity. Some of those writing on care have attempted to be precise, with mixed results, whereas others have proceeded with the tacit understanding that of course to a considerable extent we know what we are talking about when we speak of taking care of a child or providing care for the ill. But care has many forms, and as the ethics of care evolves, so should our understanding of what care is.

Taking Care

The last words I spoke to my older brother after a brief visit and with special feeling were: "take care." He had not been taking good care of himself, and I hoped he would do better; not many days later he died, of problems quite possibly unrelated to those to which I had been referring. "Take care" was not an expression he and I grew up with. I acquired it over the years in my life in New York City. It may be illuminating to begin thinking about the meaning of 'care' with an examination of this expression.

We often say "take care" as routinely as "goodbye" or some abbreviation and with as little emotion. But even then it does convey some sense of connectedness. More often, when said with some feeling, it means something like "take care of yourself because I care about you." Sometimes we say it, especially to children or to someone embarking on a trip or an endeavor, meaning "I care what happens to you, so please don't do anything dangerous or foolish." Or, if we know the danger is inevitable and inescapable, it may be more like a wish that the elements will let the person take care so the worst can be evaded. And sometimes we mean it as a plea: Be careful not to harm yourself or others because our connection will make us feel with and for you. We may be harmed ourselves or partly responsible, or if you do something you will regret we will share that regret.

One way or another, this expression (like many others) illustrates human relatedness and the daily reaffirmations of connection. It is the relatedness of human beings, built and rebuilt, that the ethics of care is being developed to try to understand, evaluate, and guide. The expression has more to do with the feelings and awareness of the persons expressing and the persons receiving such expressions than with the actual tasks and work of "taking care" of a person who is dependent on us, or in need of care, but such attitudes and shared awareness seem at least one important component of care.

Some Distinctions

A seemingly easy distinction to make is between care as the activity of taking care of someone and the mere "caring about" of how we feel about certain issues.[1] Actually "caring for" a small child or a person who is ill is quite different from merely "caring for" something (or not) in the sense of liking it or not, as in "I don't care for that kind of music." But these distinctions may not be as clear as they appear, since when we take care of a child, for instance, we usually also care about him or her, and although we could take care of a child we do not like, the caring will usually be better care if we care for the child in both senses. If we really do care about world hunger, we will probably be doing something about it, such as at least giving money to alleviate it or to change the conditions that bring it about, and thus establishing some connection between ourselves and the hungry we say we care about. And if we really do care about global climate change and the harm it will bring to future generations, we imagine a connection between ourselves and those future people who will judge our irresponsibility, and we change our consumption practices or political activities to decrease the likely harm.

Many of those writing about care agree that the care that is relevant to an ethics of care must at least be able to refer to an activity, as in taking care of someone. Most (though not all) of those writing on care do not lose sight of how care involves work and the expenditure of energy on the part of the person doing the caring. But it is often thought to be more than this. It is fairly clear that engaging in the work of taking care of someone is not the same as caring for them in the sense of having warm feelings for them. But whether certain feelings must accompany the labor of care is more in doubt.

There can, of course, be different emphases in how we think of care. I will be clarifying the meaning of care in contexts for which taking care of children or those who are ill and caring strongly about how those without adequate food are to be fed are in some ways paradigmatic. But the caring relations I will be thinking about go far beyond such contexts. One should be careful to not draw the boundaries of the model one has in mind narrowly, as if one were thinking only of mothering in the nuclear family. Some of us who have written on mothering have been interpreted—mistakenly, I think—as doing this. We need to make clear that caring includes also the care given by extended families, by many domestic workers and workers in hospitals, by teachers and others in their practices, and by others in many other ways. One may think hunger should be alleviated and health care assured through governmental action rather than through any "personal" connection between oneself and those cared for in these ways. But caring can still motivate the willingness to support such efforts and to see that they are carried out effectively.

In this book I will try to make clear how caring relations extend well beyond the sorts of caring that takes place in families and among friends, or even in the care institutions of the welfare state, to the social ties that bind groups together, to the bonds on which political and social institutions can be built, and even to the global concerns that citizens of the world can share.

Some Suggestions

Nel Noddings focuses especially on the attitudes of caring that typically accompany the activity of care. Close attention to the feelings, needs, desires, and thoughts of those cared for, and a skill in understanding a situation from that person's point of view, are central to caring for someone.[2] Carers act in behalf of others' interests, but they also care for themselves, since without the maintenance of their own capabilities, they will not be able to continue to engage in care. To Noddings, the cognitive aspect of the carer's attitude is receptive-intuitive rather than objective-analytic, and understanding the needs of those cared for depends more on feeling with them than on rational cognition. In the activity of care, abstract rules are of limited use. There can be a natural impulse to care for others, but to sustain this, persons need to make a moral commitment to the ideal of caring.[3] For Noddings, care is an attitude and an ideal manifest in activities of care in concrete situations. In her recent book *Starting at Home*, she explores what a caring society would be like. She seeks a broad, nearly universal description of "what we are like" when we engage in caring encounters, and she explores "what characterizes consciousness in such relations."[4]

Care is much more explicitly labor in Joan Tronto's view. She and Berenice Fisher have defined "taking care of" as activity that includes "everything that we do to maintain, continue, and repair our 'world' so that we can live in it as well as possible," and care can be for objects and for the environment as well as for other persons.[5] This definition seems almost surely too broad: Vast amounts of economic activity could be included, like retail sales, house construction, and commercial cleaning, and the distinctive features of caring labor would be lost. It does not require the sensitivity to the needs of the cared-for that others often recognize in care, nor what Noddings calls the needed "engrossment" with the other. And, Tronto explains, it excludes production, play, and creative activity, whereas a great deal of care, for instance child care, can and should be playful and is certainly creative.

If one accepts Marx's distinction between productive and reproductive labor, and then sees caring as reproductive labor, as some propose, one misses the way caring, especially for children, can be transformative rather than merely reproductive and repetitive. Although this has not been acknowledged in traditional views of the household, the potential for creative transformation in the nurturing that occurs there, and in child care and education generally, is enormous. Care has the capacity to shape new *persons* with ever more advanced understandings of culture and society and morality and ever more advanced abilities to live well and cooperatively with others.[6] Only a biased and damaging misconception holds that caring merely reproduces our material and biological realities while what is new and creative and distinctively human must occur elsewhere.

Diemut Bubeck offers one of the most precise definitions of care in the literature. She writes, "Caring for is the meeting of the needs of one person by another person, where face-to-face interaction between carer and cared-for is a crucial element of the overall activity and where the need is of such a nature that it cannot possibly be met by the person in need herself."[7] She distinguishes between caring for someone and providing them with a service; on her definition, to cook a meal for a small child is caring, but a wife who cooks for her husband when he could perfectly well cook for himself is not engaging in care but providing a service to him. Care, Bubeck asserts, is "a response to a particular subset of basic human needs, i.e. those which make us dependent on others."[8]

In Bubeck's view, care does not require any particular emotional bond between carer and cared-for, and it is important to her general view that care can and often should be publicly provided, as in public health care. She seems to think that care is almost entirely constituted by the objective fact of needs being met, rather than by the attitude or ideal with which the carer is acting. Her conception is then open to the objection that as long as the deception is successful, someone going through the motions of caring for a child while wishing the child dead is engaged in care of as much moral worth as that of a carer who intentionally and with affection seeks what is best for the child. For me, this objection is fatal. I suppose a strict utilitarian might say that if the child is fed and clothed and hugged, the intention with which these are done may be of no moral significance. But to me it is clear that in the wider moral scheme of things, though I cannot argue it here, it is significant. A world in which the motive of care is good will rather than ill will (plus any interest that may additionally be needed to motivate the care giver to do the work) is a better world. Even if the child remains unaware of the ill will (an unlikely though possible circumstance) and even if the child grows up with the admirable sensitivity to the feelings of others that would constitute a better outcome, even on a utilitarian scale, than if she does not, the motive would still matter. An important aspect of care is how it *expresses* our attitudes and relationships.

Sara Ruddick sees care as work but also as more than this. She writes: "As much as care is labor, it is also relationship . . . caring labor is intrinsically relational. The work is constituted in and through the relation of those who give and receive care. . . . More critically, some caring relationships seem to have a significance in 'excess' of the labor they enable."[9] She compares the work of a father who is bringing a small child to a day-care center and that of the day-care worker who is receiving the child. Both can perform the same work of reassuring the child, hugging him, transferring him from father to worker, and so on. But the character and meaning of the father's care may be in excess of the work itself. For the father, the work is a response to the relationship, whereas for the day-care worker, the relationship is probably a response to the work. So we may want to reject a view that equates care entirely with the labor involved.

To Bubeck, to Noddings in her early work, and to a number of others who write on care, the face-to-face aspect of care is central. This has been thought to make it difficult to think of our concern for more distant others in terms of caring. Bubeck, however, does not see her view as leading to the conclusion that care is limited to the context of the relatively personal, as Noddings's view suggested, because Bubeck includes the activities of the welfare state in the purview of the ethics of care. She thinks the care to be engaged in, as in child care centers and centers for the elderly, will indeed be face to face, but she advocates widespread and adequate public funding for such activity.

Bubeck rejects the particularistic aspects of the ethics of care. She advocates generalizing the moral principle of meeting needs, and thus the way in which an ethic of care can provide for just political and social programs becomes evident. But this comes too close, in my view, to collapsing the ethics of care into utilitarianism. In addition to being the meeting of objective needs, care seems to be at least partly an attitude and motive, as well as a value. Bubeck builds the requirements of justice into the ethics of care. But this still may not allow care to be the primary moral consideration of a person, say, in a rich country, who is engaging in empowering someone in a poor country, if there will never be in this engagement any face-to-face aspect. This is troubling to many who see care as a fundamental value with as much potential for moral elaboration as justice, but doubt that justice can itself be adequately located entirely within care, or that care should be limited to relatively personal interactive work.

Peta Bowden has a different view than Bubeck of what caring relations are like. She starts with what she calls an intuition: that caring is ethically important. Caring, she says, "expresses ethically significant ways in which we matter to each other, transforming interpersonal relatedness into something beyond ontological necessity or brute survival."[10] Adopting a Wittgensteinian approach to understanding and explicitly renouncing any attempt to provide a definition of care, she carefully examines various examples of caring practices:

mothering, friendship, nursing, and citizenship. In including citizenship she illustrates how face-to-face interaction is not a necessary feature of all caring relations, though it characterizes many.

To Selma Sevenhuijsen, the ethics of care sees moral problems first of all with "attentiveness, responsibility, responsiveness and the commitment to see issues from differing perspectives."[11] This attitude of caring will often lead to the caring work that responds to need and takes care of the vulnerable. But it may not lead to providing actual care if one does not agree with the claims with which one is presented or if one lacks the resources with which to meet them. The activity of care is seen by Sevenhuijsen as "an ability and a willingness to 'see' and to 'hear' needs, and to take responsibility for these needs being met."[12] She advocates listening to the moral deliberations about care expressed by the receivers and the providers of actual care and reflecting on the "different styles of situated moral reasoning" that can be encountered in doing so.[13]

Sevenhuijsen brings out the elements of knowledge and thoughtfulness needed to care well. Her book covers practices of care that appropriately include the labor involved in caring. But in her efforts to define *care*, her discussion leans too heavily perhaps toward motive and understanding and not enough toward the work that must be judged in terms of effectiveness as well as intention. In her eagerness to avoid a model of caring excessively built around and then mistakenly limited to mothering, she relies perhaps too much on the issues of devising policies for social workers. But she rightly keeps salient and does not lose sight of the way caring involves relatedness. "All phases of the care process," she asserts, "have relational dimensions."[14] Even when one is just beginning to understand another's needs and to decide how to respond to them, empathy and involvement are called for. And in giving and receiving the actual concrete work of care, "the direct interaction takes place in which feelings of self and other and connection between people is expressed."[15]

In his detailed discussion of caring as a virtue, Michael Slote thinks it entirely suitable that our benevolent feelings for distant others be conceptualized as caring. "An ethic of caring," in his view, "can take the well-being of all humanity into consideration."[16] Where Bubeck rejects the view of caring as motive, he embraces it. To him, caring just is a "motivational attitude," a virtue.[17] To Lawrence Blum also, care is a virtue (see chapter 3) as it is for several authors in the recent volume *Feminists Doing Ethics*.[18]

An illustration of what is missing in treating care as a virtue is provided by Lawrence Blum's discussion of what he calls "the care virtues," that is, "the virtues of care, compassion, concern, kindness, thoughtfulness, and generosity."[19] Compassion is to him an emotional attitude of an individual person, and care is put in the same category, as with traditional virtue theory.[20] He sees compassion as an altruistic attitude, a disposition to help that prompts appropriate beneficent action.[21]

As I see it, the caring promoted by the ethics of care is quite far from compassion. Even though the carer may perform tasks for the benefit of the cared-for that the cared-for cannot reciprocate, the persons in a caring relation are not competitors for benefits, hence altruism is not what is called for. Caring is a relation in which carer and cared-for share an interest in their mutual well-being.

Elsewhere than in this discussion, Blum is quite eloquent in criticizing the "radical separation between self and others" implied by the literature on egoism and altruism, noting that in community and in friendship, concern for others "is not separable from concern for self."[22] He goes on to explain this point in persuasive terms: "To be concerned for a friend, or for a community with which one closely identifies and of which one is a member, is to reach out not to someone or something wholly other than oneself but to what shares a part of one's own self and is implicated in one's sense of one's own identity."[23] Nevertheless, he sees the care virtues, in line with the virtue theory tradition, as altruistic dispositions of individuals and psychological motivations. This misses the heart of what goes on in practices of caring and misses what is of most value in them, which is that they are caring *relations*. What I am suggesting is that care, if not the traditional virtues, can extricate us from the overly personal perspective of the virtue tradition and the excessive contemporary focus on individual psychology at the expense of much else of value.

Feminists should resist seeing care as entirely or even primarily a matter of motive or of virtue, also because this runs such a risk of losing sight of it as work. Encouragement should not be given to the tendency to overlook the question of who does most of this work. But the idea that caring is not only work is also persuasive, so we might conclude that care must be able to refer to work, motive, value, and perhaps more than these.

In her influential book *Love's Labor*, Eva Kittay examines what she calls "dependency work," which overlaps with care but is not the same. She defines dependency work as "the work of caring for those who are inevitably dependent," for example, infants and the severely disabled.[24] When not done well, such work can be done without an affective dimension, though it typically includes it.[25] Kittay well understands how dependency work is relational and how the dependency relation "at its very crux, is a moral one arising out of a claim of vulnerability on the part of the dependent, on the one hand, and of the special positioning of the dependency worker to meet the need, on the other."[26] The relation is importantly a relation of trust. And because dependency work is so often unpaid, when dependency workers use their time to provide care instead of working at paid employment, they themselves become dependent on others for the means with which to do so and for their own maintenance.

Ann Ferguson and Nancy Folbre's conception of "sex-affective production" has much to recommend it in understanding the concept of care. They characterize sex-affective production as "childbearing, childrearing, and the provision of nurturance, affection, and sexual satisfaction."[27] It is not limited to the labor involved in caring for the dependent but also includes the providing of affection and the nurturing of relationships. Ferguson and Folbre are especially concerned with analyzing how providing this kind of care leads to the oppression of women. But one can imagine such care as nonoppressive, for both carers and cared-for. Bubeck and Kittay focus especially on the necessary care that the dependent cannot do without. But when we also understand how increasing levels of affection, mutual concern, and emotional satisfaction are valuable, we can aim at promoting care far beyond the levels of necessity. So understanding care as including rather than excluding the sharing of time and attention and services, even when the recipients are not dependent on these, seems appropriate.

Ruddick usefully notes that "three distinct though overlapping meanings of 'care' have emerged in recent decades. 'Care' is an ethics defined in opposition to 'justice,'; a kind of labor; a particular relationship."[28] She herself argues for a view of care as a kind of labor, but not only that, and advocates "attending steadily to the relationships of care."[29] Ruddick doubts that we ought to define an ethics of care in opposition to an ethics of justice, since we ought to see how justice is needed in caring well and in family life. But then she wonders how, if care is seen as a kind of labor rather than an already normative concept contrasted with justice, it can give rise to an ethics. Her answer follows, and these passages are worth quoting extensively,

> The "ethics" of care is provoked by the habits and challenges of the work, makes sense of its aims, and spurs and reflects upon the self-understanding of workers. The ethics also extends beyond the activities from which it arises, generating a stance (or standpoint) toward "nature," human relationships, and social institutions.... First, memories of caring and being cared for inspire a sense of obligation ... [and] a person normatively identifies with a conception of herself as someone who enters into and values caring relationships, exercising particular human capacities as well.
>
> Neither memory nor identity "gives rise" to an "ethics" that then leaves them behind. Rather there is an interplay in which each recreates the other.[30]

Care as Practice

Care is surely a form of labor, but it is also much more. The labor of care is already relational and for the most part cannot be replaced by machines in the way so much other labor can. Ruddick agrees that "caring labor is intrinsically relational,"[31] but she thinks the relationship is something assumed rather than necessarily focused on. In my view, as we clarify care, we need to see it in terms of *caring relations.*

Care is a practice involving the work of care-giving and the standards by which the practices of care can be evaluated. Care must concern itself with the effectiveness of its efforts to meet needs, but also with the motives with which care is provided. It seeks good caring relations. In normal cases, recipients of care sustain caring relations through their responsiveness—the look of satisfaction in the child, the smile of the patient. Where such responsiveness is not possible—with a severely mentally ill person, for instance—sustaining the relation may depend entirely on the caregiver, but it is still appropriate to think in terms of caring relations: The caregiver may be trying to form a relation or must imagine a relation.[32] Relations between persons can be criticized when they become dominating, exploitative, mistrustful, or hostile. Relations of care can be encouraged and maintained.

I doubt that we ought to accept the contrast between justice-as-normative and care-as-nonnormative, as the latter would be if it were simply labor, even labor done with a particular motive or emotional tone. I find it better to think of contrasting practices and the values they embody and should be guided by. An activity must be purposive to count as work or labor, but it need not incorporate any values, even efficiency, in the doing of it. Chopping at a tree, however clumsily, to fell it, could be work. But when it does incorporate such values as doing so effectively, it becomes the practice of woodcutting. So we do better to focus on practices of care rather than merely on the work involved.

Practices of justice such as primitive revenge and an eye for an eye have from the earliest times been engaged in and gradually reformed and refined. By now we have legal, judicial, and penal practices that only dimly resemble their ancient forerunners, and we have very developed theories of justice and of different kinds of justice with which to evaluate such practices. Practices of care—from mothering to caring for the ill to teaching children to cultivating social relations—have also changed a great deal from their earliest forms, but to a significant extent without the appropriate moral theorizing. That, I suggest, is part of what the ethics of care should be trying to fill in. The practices themselves already incorporate various values, often unrecognized, especially until recently by the philosophers engaged in moral theorizing who ought to be attending to them. And the practices themselves as they exist are often riddled with the gender injustices that pervade societies in most ways but that especially characterize most practices of care. So, moral theorizing is needed to understand the practices and to reform them.

Consider, for instance, mothering, in the sense of caring for children. It had long been imagined in the modern era after the establishment of the public/private distinction to be "outside morality" because it was based on instinct. Feminist critique has been needed to show how profoundly mistaken such a view is. Moral issues are confronted constantly in the practice of mothering and other caring work. There is constant need for the cultivation of the virtues appropriate to these practices, and of moral evaluation of how the practices are being carried out. To get a hint of how profoundly injustice has been embedded in the practice of mothering, one can compare the meaning of "mothering" with that of "fathering," which standardly has meant no more than impregnating a woman and being the genetic father of a child. "Mothering" suggests that this activity must or should be done by women, whereas, except for lactation, there is no part of it that cannot be done by men as well. Many feminists argue that for actual practices of child care to be morally acceptable, they will have to be radically transformed to accord with principles of equality, though existing conceptions of equality should probably not be the primary moral focus of practices of care. This is only the beginning of the moral scrutiny to which they should be subject.

This holds also for other practices that can be thought of as practices of care. We need, then, not only to examine the practices and discern with new sensitivities the values already embedded or missing within them but also to construct the appropriate normative theory with which to evaluate them, reform them, and shape them anew. This, I think, involves understanding care as a value worthy of the kind of theoretical elaboration justice has received. Understanding the value of care involves understanding how it should not be limited to the household or family; care should be recognized as a political and social value also.

Care as Value

We all agree that justice is a value. There are also practices of justice: law enforcement, court proceedings, and so on. Practices incorporate values but also need to be evaluated by the normative standards values provide. A given actual practice of justice may only very inadequately incorporate within it the value of justice, and we need justice as a value to evaluate such a practice. The value of justice picks out certain aspects of the overall moral spectrum, those having to do with fairness, equality, and so on, and it would not be satisfactory to have only the most general value terms, such as 'good' and 'right,' 'bad' and 'wrong,' with which to do the evaluating of a practice of justice. Analogously, for actual practices of care we need care as a value to pick out the appropriate cluster of moral considerations, such as sensitivity, trust, and mutual concern, with which to evaluate such practices. It is not enough to think of care as simply work, describable empirically, with 'good' and 'right' providing all the normative evaluation of actual practices of care. Such practices are often morally deficient in ways specific to care as well as to justice.

If we say of someone that "he is a caring person," this includes an evaluation that he has a characteristic that, other things being equal, is morally admirable. Attributing a virtue to someone, as when we say that she is generous or trustworthy, describes a disposition but also makes a normative judgment. It is highly useful to be able to characterize people (and societies) in specific and subtle ways, recognizing the elements of our claims that are empirically descriptive and those that are normative. The subtlety needs to be available not only at the level of the descriptive but also within our moral evaluations. "Caring" thus picks out a more specific value to be found in persons' and societies' characteristics than merely finding them to be good or bad, or morally admirable or not, on the whole. But we may resist reducing care to a virtue if by that we refer only to the dispositions of individual persons, since caring is so much a matter of the relations between them. We value caring persons in caring relations.

Diana Meyers examines the entrenched cultural imagery that can help explain the hostility often encountered by advocates of the ethics of care who seek to expand its applicability beyond the household and to increase care in public life.

Oscillating sentimentality and contempt with regard to motherhood and childhood fuel this problem.... If motherhood and childhood are conditions of imperfect personhood, as they are traditionally thought to be, no one would want to be figured as a mother or as a child in relations with other persons. This perverse constellation of attitudes is enshrined in and transmitted through a cultural stock of familiar figures of speech, stories, and pictorial imagery.[33]

As she explores various illustrative tropes, she shows how the myth of the "independent man" as model, with mothers and children seen as deficient though lovable, is part of what needs to be overcome in understanding the value of care.

The concept of care should not, in my view, be a naturalized concept and the ethics of care should not be a naturalized ethics.[34] Care is not reducible to the behavior that has evolved and that can be adequately captured in empirical descriptions, as when an account may be given of the child care that could have been practiced by our hunter-gatherer ancestors, and its contemporary analogues may be considered. Care as relevant to an ethics of care incorporates the values we decide as feminists to find acceptable in it. And the ethics of care does not accept and describe the practices of care as they have evolved under actual historical conditions of patriarchal and other domination; it evaluates such practices and recommends what they morally ought to be like.

I think, then, of care as practice and value. The practices of care are of course multiple, and some seem very different from others. Taking care of a toddler so that he does not hurt himself yet is not unduly fearful is not much like patching up mistrust between colleagues and enabling them to work together. Dressing a wound so that it will not become infected is not much like putting up curtains to make a room attractive and private. Neither are much like arranging for food aid to be delivered to families who need it half a world away. Yet all care involves attentiveness, sensitivity, and responding to needs. Needs are of innumerable subtle emotional and psychological and cultural kinds, as well as of completely basic and simple kinds, such as for sufficient calories to stay alive. It is helpful to clarify what different forms of care have in common, as it is to clarify how justice in all its forms requires impartiality, treating persons as equals, and recognizing their rights. This is not at all to say that a given practice should involve a single value only. On the contrary, as we clarify the values of care we can better advocate their relevance for many practices from which they have been largely excluded.

Consider police work. Organizationally a part of the "justice system," it must have the enforcement of the requirements of justice high among its priorities. But as it better understands the relevance of care to its practices, as it becomes more caring, it can often accomplish more through educating and responding to needs, building trust between police and policed, and thus preventing violations of law than it can through traditional "law enforcement" after prevention has failed. Sometimes the exclusion of the values of care is more in theory than in practice. An ideal market that treats all exchanges as impersonal and all participants as replaceable has no room for caring. But actual markets often include significant kinds of care and concern, of employers for employees, of employees for customers, and so on. As care is better understood, the appropriate places for caring relations in economic activity may be better appreciated (see chapter 7).

At the same time, practices of care are not devoted solely to the values of care. They often need justice as well. Consider mothering or fathering in the sense of caring for a child, or "parenting," if one prefers this term. This is probably the most caring of the caring practices since the emotional tie between carer and cared-for is characteristically so strong. This practice has caring well for the child as its primary value. But as understanding of what this involves becomes more adequate, it should include normative guidance on how to avoid such tendencies as parents may have to unduly interfere and control, and it can include the aspect well delineated by Ruddick: "respect for 'embodied willfulness.'"[35] Moreover, practices of parenting must include justice in requiring the fair treatment of multiple children in a family and in fairly distributing the burdens of parenting.

Ruddick worries that if we think of justice and care as separate ethics, this will lead to the problem that, for instance, responding to needs, as economic and social rights do, cannot be part of the concerns of justice. To hold this would be especially unfortunate just as the economic and social rights of meeting basic needs are gaining acceptance as human rights at the global level (even if not in the United States, where having such needs met is not recognized as a right). I believe Ruddick's concern is not a problem and that the difference here is one of motive. The motive for including economic and social rights among the human rights on the grounds of justice is that it would be unfair and a failure of equality, especially of rights to equal freedom, not to do so.[36] When meeting needs is motivated by care, on the other hand, the needs themselves are responded to and the persons themselves with these needs are cared for.

This contrast is especially helpful in evaluating social policies, for instance, welfare policies. Even if the requirements of justice and equality would be met by a certain program, of payments, let's say, we could still find the program callous and uncaring if it did not concern itself with the actual well-being (or lack of it) brought about by the program. One can imagine such payments being provided very grudgingly and the recipients of them largely disdained by the taxpayers called on to fund them. One can imagine the shame and undermining of self-respect that would be felt by the recipients of these payments. Except that the amounts of the payments and the range of recipients of them never came close to what justice would require, the rest of this description is not far from what welfare programs in the United States have often been like. One can compare this with what a caring program would be like. In addition to meeting the bare requirements of justice, it would foster concern for the actual needs of recipients, offer the needed services or jobs to meet them, and express the morally recommended care and concern of the society for its less fortunate and more dependent members.

It seems to me that justice and care as values each invoke associated clusters of moral considerations, and these considerations are different. Actual practices should usually incorporate both care and justice but with appropriately different priorities. For instance, the practice of child care by employees in a child care center should have as its highest priority the safeguarding and appropriate development of children, including meeting their emotional as well as physical and educational needs. Justice should not be absent: The children should be treated fairly and with respect, and violations of justice such as would be constituted by racial or ethnic discrimination against some of the children should not be tolerated. But providing care rather than exemplifying justice would be the primary aim of the activity. In contrast, a practice of legislative decision on the funding to be supplied to localities to underwrite their efforts to improve law enforcement should have justice as its primary aim. Localities where crime is a greater threat should receive more of such funding, so that equality of personal security is more nearly achieved. Care should not be absent: Concern for victims of crime, and for victims of police brutality, should be part of what is considered in such efforts. But providing greater justice and equality rather than caring for victims would be the primary aim of such legislative decision.

If we say of persons that they should be "brought to justice," we mean that the law should be applied, and if they are found guilty they should be punished. We do not say of children that they should be brought to justice, though we may well think they should be punished and that the punishment should be fair. But the meaning of justice is tied to rules and laws, as well as to fairness in ways that the meaning of care is not.

We sometimes use "take care of" in a way that is close to "deal with" and far away from what care ordinarily implies. A mob boss might say to an underling, for example, that he should "take care of" someone in the sense of eliminating him as a threat. Or a manager might tell an employee to take care of a certain business problem. But the meanings of care in these cases would not be close to those of justice either, any more than when care is spoken of in the contexts and practices of care such as child care or education or health care.

Ruddick does not consider justice inherently tied to a devaluation of relationships. But justice and its associated values may be more committed to individualism than she seems to think. It seems to me that it is on grounds of care rather than justice that we can identify with others enough to form a political entity, and develop civil society (see chapter 8). Relations of care seem to me wider and deeper than relations of justice. Within relations of care, we can treat people justly, as if we were liberal individuals agreeing on mutual respect. This can be done in more personal contexts, as when friends compete fairly in a game they seek to win or when parents treat their children equally. Or it can be done in public, political, and social contexts, as when people recognize each other as fellow members of a group that is forming a political entity that accepts a legal system. When justice is the guiding value, it requires that individual rights be respected. But when we are concerned with the relatedness that constitutes a social group and is needed to hold it together, we should look, I argue, to care.

Caring Relations

My own view, then, is that care is both a practice and a value. As a practice, it shows us how to respond to needs and why we should. It builds trust and mutual concern and connectedness between persons. It is not a series of individual actions, but a practice that develops, along with its appropriate attitudes. It has attributes and standards that can be described, but more important that can be recommended and that should be continually improved as adequate care comes closer to being good care. Practices of care should express the caring relations that bring persons together, and they should do so in ways that are progressively more morally satisfactory. Caring practices should gradually transform children and others into human beings who are increasingly morally admirable.

Consider how trust is built, bit by bit, largely by practices of caring. Trust is fragile and can be shattered in a single event; to rebuild it may take long stretches of time and many expressions of care, or the rebuilding may be impossible. Relations of trust are among the most important of personal and social assets. To develop well and flourish, children need to trust those who care for them, and the providers of such care need to trust the fellow members of their communities that the trust of their children will not be misplaced. For peace to be possible, antagonistic groups need to learn to be able to trust each other enough so that misplaced trust is not even more costly than mistrust. To work well, societies need to cultivate trust between citizens and between citizens and governments; to achieve whatever improvements of which societies are capable, the cooperation that trust makes possible is needed. Care is not the same thing as trust, but caring relations should be characterized by trust, and caring and trust sustain each other.

In addition to being a practice, care is also a value. Caring persons and caring attitudes should be valued, and we can organize many evaluations of how persons are interrelated around a constellation of moral considerations associated with care or its absence. For instance, we can ask of a relation whether it is trusting and mutually considerate or hostile and vindictive. We can ask if persons are attentive and responsive to each other's needs or indifferent and self-absorbed. Care is not the same as benevolence, in my view, since it is more the characterization of a social relation than the description of an individual disposition, and social relations are not reducible to individual states. Caring relations ought to be cultivated, between persons in their personal lives and between the members of caring societies. Such relations are often reciprocal over time if not at given times. The values of caring are especially exemplified in caring relations, rather than in persons as individuals.

To advocates of the ethics of care, care involves moral considerations at least as important as those of justice. And when adequately understood, the ethics of care is as appropriate for men as for women. Both men and women should acknowledge the enormous value of the caring activities on which society relies and should share these activities fairly. They should recognize the values of care, as of justice.

Caring relations form the small societies of family and friendship on which larger societies depend. Caring relations of a weaker but still evident kind between more distant persons allow them to trust one another enough to live in peace and respect each others' rights. For progress to be made, persons need to care together for the well-being of their members and their environment.

Lawrence Blum explores the way communities can shape the moral reality of and sustain (or not) the virtues of individual persons. For instance, depending on the community, a given level of concern for others will be interpreted as an "undue burden."[37] We can understand how a caring community will sustain and validate the efforts of caring persons, and how much more difficult it is for persons to cultivate caring relations when the messages from the "community" promote, instead, the values of egoism, competition, and the victory of the fittest. In one response to the latter, there is blatant inconsistency between how persons regard "their own," such as the members of their own families or small groups, and how they regard those beyond, as in the traditional image of the family as a "haven in a heartless world." In another response, there is, even within families and among friends, consistent self-interested striving tempered only by contractual restraints. Neither response is morally satisfactory.

The ethics of care builds relations of care and concern and mutual responsiveness to need on both the personal and wider social levels. Within social relations in which we care enough about one another to form a social entity, we may agree on various ways to deal with one another. For instance, for limited purposes we may imagine each other as liberal individuals in the marketplace, independent, autonomous, and rational, and we may adopt liberal schemes of law and governance, and policies to maximize individual benefits. But we should not lose sight of the deeper reality of human interdependency and of the need for caring relations to undergird or surround such constructions. The artificial abstraction of the model of the liberal individual is at best suitable for a restricted and limited part of human life, rather than for the whole of it. The ethics of care provides a way of thinking about and evaluating both the more immediate and the more distant human relations with which to develop morally acceptable societies.

3

The Caring Person

Being caring is not one of the virtues we immediately think of when we try to recall the lists of virtues we have encountered. But most of us think that it is admirable to be caring, and we want our children to become caring persons.

Edmund Pincoffs, in his book *Quandaries and Virtues*, lists 221 qualities or properties of persons from which to select some to consider virtuous or vicious, qualities such as being benevolent, charitable, courageous, fair-minded, and honest, and alternatively, cruel, selfish, and vindictive.[1] Being caring is not included, even in this lengthy list of qualities that includes friendly, gentle, cold, and lazy. Other qualities, such as being compassionate, considerate, cowardly, deceitful, obsequious, and trustworthy, are also missing, and this reminds us of how long the list could be. But the absence of caring is still indicative, now that so many of us think of care as a highly important value—on a par with justice—and many think it an important virtue.

Care and caring are also not mentioned in the indexes of Alasdair MacIntyre's *After Virtue*,[2] or James Wallace's *Virtues and Vices*,[3] or the volume called *Virtues and Reasons*,[4] devoted to leading virtue theorist Philippa Foot. Care and caring are not even mentioned in the index of MacIntyre's more recent book, *Dependent Rational Animals: Why Human Beings Need the Virtues*, in which he acknowledges the enormous dependency of human beings on one another.[5] Some people suggest that caring is close to the Christian virtue of *caritas*, but caritas is equivalent to charity. Care, however, is not the same as charity—when we take care of our children we are not being charitable—and being caring is not the same as being charitable. Valuing care is entirely independent of any religious foundation, and is the stronger for this, since those not sharing a given religious tradition have few reasons to attend to arguments that appeal to that tradition. Understanding the value of care can be based on a universal experience of having been cared for and being able to engage in caring.

I argue that to be a caring person is not the same as to be a person with a virtue we call caring. But what else could it be?

Let's begin with the question of persons: Who and what are they? I start with a normative framework, asking how we should think of persons capable of wondering how they should live. Then I'll ask whether they should be caring and what that should mean.

I thus resist the current tendency, in talking about persons, of taking the concepts and presuppositions and frameworks of science and thinking that what we say about persons must fit within that third-person perspective. That is one perspective, certainly useful for some purposes, but not, I think, for normative questions. Instead, I will see persons as moral subjects, capable of action and of shaping their lives and institutions and societies over time, at least to some extent, through cultivating in themselves and others certain characteristics and practices and values.

What is a person who is a moral subject? A great deal has been written in recent years about neo-Humean views, according to which there is no unity of the person, but rather a collection of psychological events. Sydney Shoemaker notes of Derek Parfit: "He does not think of experiences . . . as entities that of their very nature require subjects." The existence of Parfit's experiences, as of Humean perceptions "is independent of, and in some sense more fundamental than, that of the subjects that have them."[6]

I cannot argue for it here, but I begin with the position that from the point of view of a moral subject trying to take responsibility for living a life she can find acceptable, such a view is self-defeating and shows that we should not begin with its assumptions. I begin instead with the self-awareness I think we have of being saddled with moral responsibility. The experience of parenthood is one of the best to bring the point home. When a helpless infant is in one's care and will die if one fails to feed and safeguard it, one must not dissolve into helpless moments, however tempting that might be. One is morally compelled to congeal into an entity capable of agency. One may fail to do so, but then one is probably no longer a morally responsible person.

So, we experience ourselves, I take it, as moral subjects and as persons. From the normative perspective of considering how we should live, we must assume there is an I capable of responding to proposed recommendations with acceptance or rejection (even children partially grasp this) and capable of being responsible for many of our choices.

Moral personhood is also a status conferred on human biological entities by morality, law, and a variety of human practices. There are no persons in nature as conceptualized independently of the human beings experiencing it. But within human history and the social worlds that create it, many practices recognize us as moral persons.

Children are potentially (if not actually) moral subjects. When they fail to do what they ought, we disapprove with the intention of gradually steering them to take moral responsibility for themselves. At given stages, we may not expect them to understand the moral significance of their behavior, but we can try to cultivate in them from early ages the appropriate characteristics and bring about their participation in moral practices.

Hilde Nelson, along with various others, shows how "identities are narratively constructed," although this may not be all they are.[7] She also shows how we can change our identities through "counterstories." Diana Meyers says that "narrativity clarifies how people can be profoundly influenced by their social context and yet retain their capacity to shape self-determined moral lives—to transvalue values, reroute their own pathways, and reconfigure their social ideals."[8] This may be a helpful way of thinking about how we shape our selves and even how we are able to go in new directions. It leaves open our questions about how we *should* continue our stories: Should we become more caring, more concerned with injustice, less assertive in pursuing our interests, more demanding of respect? And why?

I start, then, with a normative perspective. But instead of the Kantian normative perspective some things I have said might suggest, I will start with that of the ethics of care. Unlike some of those who write about the ethics of care, I do not think it should be thought of as a naturalized ethic.[9] Yes, care takes place and we should examine it empirically and clarify the values embedded in it. We should consider the epistemological means that have been used to discount it and that can now be used to realize its importance and value. But I see the ethics of care from as fully a normative point of view as any other ethic. It addresses questions about whether and how and why we ought to engage in activities of care, questions about how such activities should be conducted and structured, and questions about the meanings of care and caring. It especially evaluates relations of care.

The Person in the Ethics of Care

It is characteristic of the ethics of care to view persons as relational and as interdependent. Deontological and consequentialist moral theories of which Kantian moral theory and utilitarianism are the leading examples concentrate their attention on the rational decisions of agents assumed to be independent, autonomous individuals. Virtue theory also focuses on individual persons and their dispositions. The ethics of care, in contrast, conceptualizes persons as deeply affected by, and involved in, relations with others; to many care theorists persons are at least partly constituted by their social ties. The ethics of care attends especially to relations between persons, evaluating such relations and valuing relations of care. It does not assume that relations relevant for morality have been entered into voluntarily by free and equal individuals, as do dominant moral theories. It appreciates as well the values of care between persons of unequal power in unchosen relations such as those between parents and children and between members of social groups of various kinds. To the ethics of care, our embeddedness in familial, social, and historical contexts is basic.

Jean Keller argues that this conception of the person is central to feminist ethics. She writes that "whatever shape feminist ethics ends up taking, it will incorporate a relational model of moral agency. That is, the insight that the moral agent is an 'encumbered self,' who is always already embedded in relations with flesh-and-blood others and is partly constituted by these relations, is here to stay."[10] I would slightly modify this position because I see feminist ethics as wider than care ethics, but it is largely true, I think, of the ethics of care.

Here is Marilyn Friedman's characterization of relational persons as developed by contemporary feminists:

> According to the relational approach, persons are fundamentally social beings who develop the competency of autonomy... in a context of values, meanings, and modes of self-reflection that cannot exist except as constituted by social practices.... It is now well recognized that our reflective capacities and our very identities are always partly constituted by communal traditions and norms that we cannot put entirely into question without at the same time voiding our very capacities to reflect.
>
> We are each reared in a social context of some sort, typically although not always that of a family, itself located in wider social networks such as community and nation. Nearly all of us remain, throughout our lives, involved in social relationships and communities, at least some of which partly define our identities and ground our highest values.[11]

Some criticize Friedman's more developed conception of the person for the way it interprets social relations as merely causal rather than constitutive elements.[12] What we can say, however, is that in the view of most feminists, the individual is seen as *at least* more causally affected by social relations than in the traditional liberal myth of the "self-made man," and is often seen as partly but importantly constituted by social relations.

Diana Meyers describes what she sees as various currently influential conceptions of the self. "The feminist relational self," she writes,

> is the interpersonally bonded self.... As relational selves... people share in one another's joys and sorrows, give and receive care, and generally profit from the many rewards and cope with the many aggravations of friendship, family membership, religious or ethnic affiliation, and the like. These relationships are sources of moral identity, for people become committed to their intimates and to others whom they care about, and these commitments become central moral concerns.[13]

The concept of the relational person might solve some of the current puzzles of how it is that we feel empathy for others.[14] In examples of small children trying to alleviate the distress of other children, we see something that appears to be direct and spontaneous sympathetic feeling with others and wanting to help them overcome their unhappiness.[15] The idea that "human nature" is displayed in the image of toddler Hobbesian egoistically fighting all obstacles to get what he wants is seen to have another side. If small children do not yet have a sense of themselves as separate persons, perhaps they are simply feeling the pain of the other child as their own. But if they do understand themselves as individuals, what is going on? Lawrence Blum shows how the "inference" model and the "projection" model fail to apply to many observed cases.[16]

If we see the person as an embodied nexus of relations, the relations constituting one child are different from those constituting another, and even a small child can be aware that he is different from others. But when the other child is in distress, the relation between them may be upset, and he may wish it would be better. This would not be inconsistent with his feeling glee on another occasion at the pain of the other child if he felt that the other child was a threat, say, to his own possession of a toy. This sort of explanation might be explored along with others.

A conception of the self as relational allows for the moral salience of ties to other persons and groups, but such a self becomes, as it develops, also a moral subject shaping her identity and life and actions. How to theorize this interplay of outer and inner aspects has been a topic of much feminist discussion.

Caring and Autonomy

Can caring persons be autonomous? The edited collection *Relational Autonomy* is full of essays reconceptualizing autonomy for relational persons. Autonomy is still to be sought, but it will be a quite different kind of autonomy than that of the self-sufficient, atomistic self that can be distilled, uncharitably, from traditional liberal theory. The editors see relational autonomy as a range of perspectives premised on "the conviction that persons are socially embedded and that agents' identities are formed within the context of social relationships." Persons are shaped by a complex of intersecting social factors, including race, class, gender, ethnicity, and ties of family and community. "The focus of relational approaches," the editors continue, "is to analyze the implications of the intersubjective and social dimensions of selfhood and identity."[17]

Diana Meyers's description of autonomy as a set of competencies is persuasive: The autonomous person, she says, will have developed a "repertory of skills through which self-discovery, self-definition, and self-direction are achieved." Relational persons can develop these skills, though for some it will be harder than for others. "As with other competencies," she notes, "one learns through practice and practice augments proficiency."[18]

Often, we learn to be autonomous through our interactions with others, though we are not prisoners of our upbringings and circumstances. Our personal, familial, social, political, and economic relations with others enable or inhibit our access to significant options.[19] And we are both enmeshed in and capable of shaping such relations.

We should be careful about attributing fewer options to those in other societies than we recognize in our own. Uma Narayan helpfully contests the way Western feminists sometimes see the women of other cultures as either prisoners of patriarchy with no capacities to resist, or willing dupes having no desires to do so. Using the example of veiling in Muslim societies, she argues that many women who wear veils realistically and autonomously choose this course of action within societies that exert pressure to do so. She compares these pressures to those on women in Western societies to conform to certain standards of grooming and appearance that are aggressively promoted through advertising, cultural ideals, and corporate expectations. If Western women do not conform, they may fail to get or may lose jobs; they will be subjected to disdain or ridicule. In all cases, there are social constraints, but autonomy is possible within them. As Meyers writes, "A social and economic environment that makes a wide range of attractive options available to all individuals is conducive to, not necessary for, autonomy."[20]

The point, for relational persons, is that as we modify and often distance ourselves from existing relations, it is for the sake of better and often more caring relations, rather than for the splendid independence, self-sufficiency, and easy isolation of the traditional liberal ideal of the autonomous rational agent.

Are some persons just caused by their upbringings and friends, perhaps with the help of their genes, to be caring and considerate, sensitive to and respectful of the feelings of others, and adept at engaging in the practices of care, whereas others are brought up in such a way that they simply lack and can never attain these competencies? The goal of being a caring person can certainly and should be a matter of autonomous choice. A person who has merely unthinkingly and uncritically followed the caring practices into which she has been brought up can seem in outward appearance to be caring but will lack the appropriate motive of consciously and reflectively recognizing the value of care. Learning and cultivating the relevant abilities to be a caring person will depend on many efforts by a moral agent and by others in relations with that person. Given practices should be subjected to critical scrutiny and improved. Some persons at any given time will fail to be caring persons; I doubt that any person has a permanent incapacity to become caring.

Relational Persons and Overcommitment

To some critics of the ethics of care, the conception of the person as relational with which it works is thought to be dangerously submerged in unchosen social relations. Daryl Koehn, for instance, castigates the ethics of care for seeing the self as "nothing but" relational and for exalting caring above any other value. She goes on to say that we should not give ourselves over to batterers, or empathize too strongly with murderers, or be so concerned about oppressed groups that we never find time to play with our pets.[21] She does provide some useful insights into how to avoid the self-righteousness and tendency to be manipulative she worries about in caregivers. But her criticisms result largely from focusing on a few of the earliest formulations of the ethics of care and of the relational person. Many of those engaged in developing the ethics of care have been providing the further interpretations, elaborations, and evaluations that avoid the overstatements she claims to discern. Many have been emphasizing how the ethics of care must take account of the experience of recipients of care as well as providers, how care must not be overbearing; they have also been exploring the many ways caring can go wrong as well as the many ways it should be promoted. Care has been seriously undervalued in the past by dominant moral theories. Those now clarifying its value aim to correct this but do not suggest that it is the only value to which we need to attend.

Meyers has been an important participant in recent discussions of care and its values. But she, too, has concerns about the feminist conception of the relational person. Having summarized a number of conceptions of the self, she says that the conception of the self as relational might be seen as insufficiently separated from others, "too entangled in its relational web to achieve a distinctive moral identity." Valued relationships, she writes, can "morph into" what Margaret Walker calls a "plague of commitments."[22]

This concern can be addressed. It misses a point made by many feminists—that it is deficient social assistance that makes so many of the commitments of the relational person so burdensome and hard to fulfill. For instance, what puts so much of the burden of caring for aged parents on their daughters is society's failure to take responsibility for the care of the elderly. And that mothers have such trouble with entanglement in their relational webs is highly related to the paucity of adequate child care arrangements.[23] An adequately cared for and caring elderly parent can be content with an occasional phone call from a busy daughter, affirming a bond of relational closeness that includes a mutual understanding that the parent does not want her to and the adult child does not need to expend large amounts of time or energy to reaffirm the relation. Children well cared for and happy in publicly provided daycare do not need to interact constantly with their parents to understand that they are loved and valued and that their relation with their parents is strong and close.

Sometimes, certainly, the actual demands made by other persons on the relational person will seem overwhelming, and the demands may not be of the kind for which society could take responsibility, even if it included mental health services along with other health care provisions. But when relationships are so entangling that they impede free agency, they are often the kind of relationship that is in need of revision.

The difference here may often be like that between persons who feel they must constantly talk with a partner for the relationship to be close, which is not a problem if the partner feels the same way. But there can be close relationships in which mutual understanding allows both to be absent or silent for long periods and certainly to be fully independent moral agents. Many of the relationships in which we are entangled are ones we did not choose but simply found ourselves in, as with our parents and siblings. But even these relationships can be ones we strive to revise. Among the relations we choose, we can steer our lives toward those that will be harmonious with respect to the degree of entanglement they require and in terms of their level of demandingness. Friends can recognize each other as highly caring without constant demonstrations of care.

Care as a Virtue of Persons

It is easy to suppose that caring is a virtue that persons can have and to interpret the virtues, as virtue theory standardly does, as *dispositions of individuals*. Some think of caring as another name for benevolence, a familiar virtue. I will show why I do not agree.

Michael Slote sees the person who is caring as close to the person who is benevolent, except that benevolence characteristically aims at the well-being of all of humanity, whereas caring, though it can be extended to include a "substantial concern for all human beings," can allow for preferring those who are near and dear.[24] He has offered one of the most comprehensive accounts available of an ethics built on a conception of the caring person. He argues for an agent-based virtue ethics of caring. He thinks that justice, right action, and the rest of what ethics should be concerned with can be based on the motives of the caring person. To deal with the problem of good intentions but bad results, he argues that the caring person will care about how his efforts are working and about whether they are achieving the goals of, say, keeping a child healthy. If one intends to be a good parent, one will inform oneself on what children need, and so forth. So he thinks that all that is needed for the whole of morality are the virtues, properly understood and elaborated, of caring, benevolent persons.

I welcome his decided appreciation of the value of care and his effort to unify ethics. But I think Slote misses the centrality of caring *relations* for an ethic of care. A caring person, in my view, will not only have the intention to care and the disposition to care effectively but will participate in caring relations. If persons lack the capacity to do so, they can be persons who are trying to be caring, but they are not yet caring persons. To be a caring person requires more than the right motives or dispositions. It requires the ability to engage in the practice of care, and the *exercise* of this ability. Care, as we saw, is *work* as well as en emotion or motive or intention. The caring person participates in this work in ways that roughly meet its standards. Care is not *only* work, however. So it is not enough that the work get done and the child get fed if done without an appropriately caring motive. But, in my view, having caring motives is not enough to make one a caring person.

In an interesting article, Howard Curzer argues that the ethics of justice and care are just the descriptions of the virtues of justice and care.[25] Both apply to almost the full range of situations in human life, and they are actual rather than ideal virtues, in his view. Sometimes the virtues of justice and care conflict; such conflicts can lead to admirable immorality or to problems of dirty hands, but this, he thinks, is not threatening to morality. It merely shows that moral virtue is not a complete guide to moral action, but must be supplemented by practical wisdom.

There is much that is appealing in this account. Curzer explicitly rejects—rightly I think—views that try to privilege the ethics of justice and see care as a value but not a moral value or see it as a less developed form of moral reasoning, or as a nice additional consideration to tack on to or incorporate into a more important ethics of justice or an ethic of justice that always retains priority over care. Curzer appropriately acknowledges the differences between care and justice, and the relatively great importance of each.

But in seeing care as simply a virtue, I think he misses a central feature of care: its evaluations of and recommendations concerning relations *between* persons. He says "a person is caring if he or she is disposed to make and maintain the right sort of relationships, with the right people, in the right way, at the right times, for the right motives, etc. The caring person must also feel the right level and sort of fondness and responsibility for people standing in various different relationships to him or her."[26] He acknowledges the affinities between this definition and Aristotle's of friendship.

This goes a considerable way toward describing a caring person, but it is limited to evaluating an individual's dispositions and behavior, including interactions with others, but not relations themselves between persons. Descriptions of the virtues concentrate on the characteristics of persons as individuals. These individuals should "make and maintain," as Curzer puts it, various relations. But this misses the enormous reality of the relations we are already enmeshed in from the moment we are born. For many years we are *in* relations, we gradually *find* and become aware of them, we do not "make" them. Many of these relations will be highly unsatisfactory, certainly not chosen by us, and we may have to struggle to unmake them. But often where they are unsatisfactory, we can try to modify, improve, and transform them. In all these cases we need moral evaluations of *relations*, not just dispositions. And we need moral recommendations for whether to maintain or change or try to break them, though the extent to which the latter is even possible is a serious question, since they will often remain part of who we are. We will never, for instance, cease to be the child of given parents, or the person brought up with a certain group identity, even if we repudiate these. The ethics of care and our conceptions of caring persons should be able to offer these evaluations and recommendations, I think.

Some feminists find an Aristotelian approach to moral problems far more hospitable to their concerns than Kantian or utilitarian ones. Some have felt close to Hume in their moral orientations. Virtue theory, however, including that of Aristotle and Hume, has characteristically seen the virtues as attaching to individual persons. The ethics of care, in contrast, is more concerned with relations between persons. A *relation* of caring is seen as valuable or faulty, more than the dispositions of persons apart from this. Of course valuable relations between persons depend to a considerable extent on the characteristics of the persons in them, but persons with individually valuable characteristics may still fail to have good relations between them.

For all these reasons, care should not in my view be seen as just another component—hitherto neglected—in the longer lists or shorter compendiums of virtues. The ethics of care is an alternative moral approach of its own.

I am trying to see the caring person from the point of view of the ethics of care. The ethics of care values caring relations rather than merely caring persons in Slote's sense of persons with caring or benevolent dispositions. Judgments about relations often need to be rather different from judgments about individuals. Two individuals can be personally virtuous in the sense of having virtuous dispositions and yet have a relationship that is hostile, conflictual, and unhelpful to either. A caring relationship requires *mutuality* and the cultivation of ways of achieving this in the various contexts of interdependence in human life. Noticing interdependencies, rather than thinking only or largely in terms of independent individuals and their individual circumstances is one of the central aspects of an ethics of care. A caring person will cultivate mutuality in the interdependencies of personal, political, economic, and global contexts. A caring person will appropriately value caring relations and will seek to modify existing relations to make them more caring. And yes, caring persons will do this in the right ways, with the right motives, and all that. But the focus will remain, for the caring person, on his or her *relations* rather than on his or her own dispositions, and on the *practice* of care (see chapter 2 for further discussion).

Sensitivity and Knowledge

Caring relations seem to require substantial capacities on the part of those in them for being sensitive to the feelings of others. Parents need to understand when their children are hurt or afraid or merely pretending, and children seem to have quite acute abilities to discern parental disapproval or encouragement. Mistaken interpretations are usually frequent on both sides, but in a good relationship there is steady progress in mutual sensitivity and awareness, so that the members learn how to avoid unintentionally provoking anger or hurt feelings.

Can a person who has grown up and continued into adulthood with a gross lack of sensitivity to the feelings of others but with much goodwill or benevolence be a caring person? I am inclined to think not. We don't call a person a biker or a swimmer if they are thoroughly unable to bicycle or to swim. We might out of generosity extend the term to a child with high aspirations but still just learning to ride a bicycle or swim, but we would realize that this is not an accurate description. We might refrain from *blaming* thoroughly insensitive persons, if their shell or their numbness has resulted from deprivations in their childhood that they had not yet succeeded in overcoming. And if they are trying to learn to be sensitive, we could say that they are trying to become caring persons. If they are not even trying to overcome their insensitivity, we could criticize them for this, since care is a value and being a caring person morally valuable. But if persons are thoroughly unaware of what others are feeling and thinking, and grossly unable to read the moods and intentions of others, they would not be very capable of sustaining caring relations or engaging in practices of care. They would not, I think, really be caring persons.

Can sensitivity be learned? Yes, although some people probably have more talent for it than others. But it is not simply a trait we are born with or without, like being left-handed. It is important for being a caring person.

Whether it is necessary or can be compensated for by other abilities is unclear. I suspect that whatever is considered as a possible compensatory ability is just contributing to sensitivity in another way than how a sensitive person would usually understand the feelings of another. One person might intuitively know when another person is in distress, say, whereas another might have to elicit verbal responses to figure it out. But both would be trying to exercise sensitivity.

Sensitivity is of course not always an admirable capacity: It can be used to inflict pain more effectively. But for the caring person it is close to necessary. One can imagine a person who understands and accepts another's lack of sensitivity and maintains a caring relation in spite of this, but this would be going around the deficiency in the caring of the first person, not denying that it is a deficiency.

To engage in a caring practice, one need not know precisely the requirements of a given practice, for instance, how much formula to feed an infant or to what temperature to heat it. But a mere intention to be benevolent would not be enough to make one a caring person. On the other hand, merely going through the motions of a caring activity and doing the work—for instance feeding the infant, but without any of the appropriate feelings or intentions of seeking her well-being—would not be caring either.

If a caring person is a participant in a practice of care, and the practice can be continually improved through greater knowledge and understanding, as in knowing better how to help children become responsible and cooperative, can persons become more caring simply by increasing their knowledge? There seems to be something problematic about such a claim. If the knowledge is part of a practice, however, it should not be thought problematic, if the person has the requisite motives, as discussed earlier. One becomes a better participant in a better practice of caring, the more the practice employs the most knowledgeable insights available and the better the participant understands these.

Problems with Care as a Disposition

If we think of a caring person as having a virtuous disposition instead of (as I am advocating) as engaging in a caring relational practice, consider the many ways that care as a disposition can go wrong. To continue to have strong feelings of affection for someone who does not want those feelings but wants rather to be left alone, can be a failure of care in the sense of failing to constitute a caring relation. Of course one cannot simply shut off one's affectionate feelings at will, but one can cultivate distance, stop bestowing gifts or unwanted praise, and so forth. On the other hand, someone who seems to want to be left alone, such as a young person trying to distance himself from an overly concerned parent, may actually welcome continuing affection despite the appearance of disdaining it. Both parent and child may acknowledge that the caring relation is important and solid and needs only reinterpretation to allow for greater mutual autonomy.

Mutual autonomy is very different from what traditional autonomy would be, if there were such a thing. Traditionally, autonomy has been understood in terms of self-sufficiency, noninterference, self-direction, rational control, and the like. Feminist and other critics have pointed out the artificial and misleading aspects of ideals of these kinds of autonomy. We are all in fact thoroughly dependent as children and for periods of illness and deeply interdependent as inhabitants of modern societies. Holding up liberal ideals of self-sufficiency masks these facts of dependency and interdependence, and distorts the realities of, among other things, caring labor. There can certainly be lives of greater or lesser capacity to make choices in life without undue outside constraints. Choices can be interfered with by educational inadequacies, economic pressures, political and legal compulsions, and coercive persons. They can also be constrained by the psychological pressures that those to whose affections we are vulnerable can exert. To live and act as we choose requires the resources and capacities to do so.[27] So there can be more, or less, self-direction within the interdependencies that surround us, and caring relations often contribute to such autonomy. But more self-sufficiency is not always better: Cooperative activity involves mutual dependence. The critique of domination basic to the ethics of care can contribute to fostering appropriate kinds of autonomy.

The ideal of rational control asks us to exclude emotional influence in achieving autonomy. But the emotions thus excluded would include the moral emotions of empathy, sensitivity, and mutual consideration, as well as the emotions that threaten morality. We may thus do well to question the ideal of autonomy as rational control. Through appropriate relations with caretakers and through education and practice, we can learn the competencies of thinking for ourselves and resisting undue pressure from others. Such autonomy is fully consistent with the ethics of care and should be cultivated, but does not require the suppression of emotion.

Mutual autonomy is different from individual autonomy. It includes mutual understandings and acceptances of how much sharing of time, space, daily decisions, and so on there will be, and how much independently arrived at activity. Caring relations can well include much mutual autonomy. The tendency to equate caring with a kind of overbearing attention, benevolent but smothering, is a distorted but widespread view of care. Care as a disposition often misleads people into thinking they are caring when they only have the good motives of wanting to care, to help others, to be benevolent, and so on, however much the intention misinterprets the recipient's wishes and perceptions and however much such good intentions may fail to contribute to a caring relation. Seeing care as an admirable caring relation rather than merely as a disposition better equips us to see how care can go wrong, as it often does with respect to mutual autonomy.

Another limitation in seeing care as a virtue becomes apparent when we ask how caring we should be. The person who tries to be caring but is instead selfless to the point of lacking self-respect, can be criticized as failing to have the requisite virtue. The servile housewife, the martyr mother, aspire to virtue but miss it. We can discern the deficiencies in their dispositions, but we can discern them even more clearly when we examine the relations in which they display them. The servile housewife contributes to the macho husband and martinet father who disdain her. The martyr mother produces children who either flee from indebtedness to her or face the world presuming they are owed deference. The person who participates in an admirable practice of care will not only respect himself but will foster mutual respect and mutual sensitivity.

Consider also how easily care or benevolence can go wrong as a public virtue when seen as a matter of motive rather than of relationship. Charity is often not what those in need want, need, or deserve. Rather, when the issues concern distribution, persons should receive a fair share of the resources and rewards the efforts of interdependent members of communities make possible. Often, the issues concern (or should do so) shared public goods, rather than distributable shares. A shared public park expresses mutual respect far better than multiple privately owned lawns. Those with benevolent motives in a position to offer charity should instead express through appropriate social programs and policies the mutual concern members of communities should have for one another. Something like a comprehensive public education system or health care system for all would do this far more satisfactorily than comparable expenditures by the rich for charity to be bestowed on needy individuals.

In political and economic contexts, care as benevolence and as motive fails to understand the relations of power that can so easily undermine the value of care. Differences of actual power are inevitable in public as well as in personal contexts, and we do well to recognize them rather than mask them behind liberal fictions of equality. But when we focus on relations, we can come to see how to shape good caring relations so that differences in power will not be pernicious and so that the vulnerable are empowered. Good caring relations can involve not only mutual recognition of moral equality but practices that avoid subtle as well as blatant coercion where it is disrespectful and inconsiderate. We can foster trust and mutuality in place of benevolent domination. Caring persons may often need to exercise power, but they will also understand how best to do so and especially how to avoid doing so in ways that become violent and damaging.

Caring Relations and Trust

Annette Baier has argued that trust should be seen as a central concept of morality, and has explored it in some detail.[28] Trust is a good example of a value inherent in an ethic of care, since good caring relations require and are characterized by it. Trust is a relation between persons, not a value achievable by persons in isolation. The value of trust cannot be divided into the value of the dispositions of the persons in the relation, or to the value of the relation *to* the individuals involved.

Baier examines the virtues of persons and finds them to be "mental attitudes [toward] our mutual vulnerability."[29] The value of these attitudes, she argues, lies in their "contribution to the climate of trust within which the person lives."[30] She points out the ways "respect for the lives and property of others, as virtues, makes a vital contribution to a climate of trust" as do all the virtues, in her view. And since "until they trust their human environment, [persons] cannot be expected to be themselves trustworthy," the virtues in turn depend on a climate of trust.[31] Should a trusting society, then, be the ultimate aim of morality?

Trust is highly important for care, and to a caring society. But I think it is not enough. Trust is a matter of mutual understanding of intention. To trust is not simply to predict what someone will do; it is most needed when what others will do is uncertain. It is an understanding that another person or persons will have trustworthy intentions, rather than intentions to take advantage of one. For there to be trust between persons, such understanding must be mutual.[32]

Trust is not an individual virtue, since it can so easily be misplaced. To be trusting of someone who is untrustworthy may be worse than foolish: It may encourage persons to take advantage of the naive and gullible. Trust requires cooperation, not the individual dispositions of altruism. Two altruists will be at loggerheads, as will two egoists. I have argued for a normative position that persons ought to take a chance on trust if they lack reasons to mistrust, in contrast with the Hobbesian position that unless one has reason to trust, one should not do so. A trusting society and a caring society require us, I think, to overcome the Hobbesian stance.[33]

Trust, however, is not enough for a flourishing society. Trust implies little about actually doing the work of care that needs to be done or doing it well. Baier has argued that trust is always trust in some particular respect, as when we trust someone to safeguard our possessions or repair our vehicles.[34] To have a flourishing society, we would need to specify the ways in which persons should trust one another and what they should trust one another to do. To say "I trust him to take care of me when I am ill," or "we trust our neighbors to support an increase in funding for education when it is badly needed," are in no way redundant. Trust does not itself imply that the care on which flourishing depends will be forthcoming. To have a caring community, persons would need to trust one another to respond to their needs and to create and maintain admirable caring relations.

Caring relations actually sustain persons, getting done the work that responds to their vulnerabilities. A climate of trust assures that persons will have the right trustworthy intentions, but it does not assure that they will do what is needed. It does not provide that persons are proficient at meeting the needs of the vulnerable. Caring persons, in contrast, are participants in practices of care. Although each cannot participate in all the different caring practices that incorporate the values of care, caring persons express these values through their activities. And they strive to continually improve the practices.

Good caring relations should prevail in both personal and public contexts. Caring persons will participate adeptly in the practices of care that sustain them.

4

Justice, Utility, and Care

A student studying ethics or a concerned citizen consulting a moral philosopher in the last third of the twentieth century would probably have encountered, among normative theories purporting to be able to address moral problems, one or both of the few theories dominant in that period. They would become acquainted with deontological, especially Kantian theories, and consequentialist, especially utilitarian theories. Both these kinds of theory are theories of right action. Both rely on universal norms and recommend simple, abstract principles assumed to be applicable to all cases in which decisions are to be made about what we morally ought to do. The moral epistemology of both Kantian and utilitarian theories is rationalist. To the Kantian we are to rely on reason to understand the implications of the categorical imperative and we are to act in accordance with the rational will, not our feelings. What matters morally is the motive with which we act, not the consequences that happen to result. To the utilitarian, we are to bring about the greatest happiness or utility or satisfaction of preferences for all concerned. The morality of the act depends entirely on its consequences, on whether it does or does not in fact alleviate human suffering or increase well-being. In deciding what morality requires us to do, we are to employ rational calculation and rely on reason to make rational choices.

Arguments have been pursued at length about which of these theories is superior or which has the least severe unacceptable implications. Arguments within both Kantian and utilitarian theories have been explored extensively. Within a Kantian approach, for instance, arguments about universalizability and formalism, about the connections between reasons and motives, about the responsibilities of agents, and about ideal contracts have become ever more sophisticated—some would say scholastic. And within a utilitarian approach, arguments about interpersonal comparisons of utility, about rational choices and contracts in situations of uncertainty or conflict, about social choices and individual utilities and free riders, have also become ever more sophisticated— some would say removed from reality.

In the last quarter of the twentieth century, renewed interest in virtue theory arose. To some, virtue theory is an alternative to deontological and consequentialist theories and should replace them. If we cultivate good character in persons and achieve a society of virtuous persons, it is thought, we will not need additional theory: Virtuous persons will do what is best or what is morally required. Virtue theory recognizes the subtleties of human character and the complexities of moral situations.

Also in the last quarter of the century, feminist theory developed, and it led to feminist philosophy and feminist views in ethics. Feminist moral theory is increasingly recognized as a distinct and interesting alternative approach to moral issues. It is seen by many philosophers (not all of them women) as making an important contribution to normative ethics and to metaethics. There are by now a large number of books in the area of feminist morality,[1] and a number of general texts now include segments on feminist ethics among their theories and topics covered.[2]

Feminist Moral Inquiry

Before there was feminist philosophy, there was philosophical thinking about women. Much of it was appalling.

Aristotle held that women are defective men, human beings lacking in what is essential to the nature of man: the ability to reason. Though he thought women somewhat able to reason, he thought that whereas the nature or function of man is to reason in ways that are distinctively human, the nature and function of woman is to reproduce, like other animals.[3]

In the thirteenth century, Aquinas shared these conceptions of the natures of women and men. In the eighteenth century, Rousseau thought that society would crumble unless women were inculcated from childhood to be subservient to men. Kant, because he based morality entirely on reason and shared the view that women were deficient in reason, concluded that women are incapable of being full moral persons. In the twentieth century Freud extended comparable views into the domains studied by the new and growing fields concerned with human behavior, conceptualizing women as psychologically inferior through their anatomical deficiency: their lack of a penis.

In the long history of philosophy and in thought influenced by philosophy as almost all thought is, it had been thought that reason, to establish its honored place in human development and history, had to overcome and leave behind what were seen as the female and dark forces of unreason, passion, emotion, and bodily need. Although the conception of these dark forces changed at different times in history and in different places, the identification of them as female was almost constant. A long line of thinking about women had thus seen them as defective, deficient, and dangerous.[4]

Such ideas about women were both reflections within philosophy of dominant misconceptions of their times and in turn significant contributions to the continuation of male dominance. Philosophical ideas about women lent strong support to the failure to include women among those gaining political rights with the advent of democratic forms of government, the failure to extend to women the possibilities of economic advancement brought about by industrialization and the more widespread ownership of the property it produced, and the exclusion of women from most of the professions that burgeoned in the twentieth century.

Philosophical thought about women's inferiority was thus both an effect and a cause of women's subordination generally. Similarly, feminist philosophy in our time is both an effect and a cause of the growing equality of women in the wider society. It offers a very distinct and, for philosophy, almost entirely new contribution of women's voices concerning not only women but everything else in philosophy. And since philosophy concerns the most fundamental questions about all of our thinking about everything, feminist philosophy is rethinking life, society, and knowledge across the board. To challenge male dominance in our thinking is to challenge how we live and organize our worlds and pursue what we take to be knowledge and understanding and progress and value.

Instead of seeing the human as Man, with woman as the Other or the one lacking some essential capacity of Man, feminist thought sees human beings as women, men, and children. Feminist thought notes that although women *can* reason as well as men, it is doubtful that reason *should* leave behind all that belongs to emotion and the body. Feminist moral theorists, for instance, have emphasized the important and useful role of emotions such as caring and empathy in the moral life and moral understanding of human beings.

With respect to the body, instead of seeing women as, for instance, lacking a penis, feminist thought notices that women possess, among other abilities, a capacity men lack: the capacity to give birth to new human beings. When psychologists look for it, they can indeed find evidence of womb envy in little boys. One often fails to find what one is not looking for, and scientific research that has been looking for female weaknesses and passivities has often failed to pay attention to women's strengths. Feminist thinking is changing what is looked for and what is found. It is making visible a vast amount of bias in what has been taken to be "knowledge," especially in the social sciences, psychology, history, and of course philosophy.[5] It is reconceptualizing such basic concepts as that of the "public," seen as the sphere of the human and the creative, and of the "private," seen as the locus of mere reproduction (see also chapters 1 and 2). It is reshaping concepts of women, in all their diversity of race, sexual orientation, and economic, ethnic, and historical location, demanding that women's experiences be seen as of equal importance with those of privileged men's.[6] It leads us to reformulate our ideas of personhood, identity, self, and society. The most important change feminist thinking is bringing about in the area of moral theory is that it is making women's experience—including experience in the household and in bringing up children and in caring for the

dependent—and the experience of children and of others who are not independent relevant to moral theory and moral inquiry in ways that had not been
seen before. Dominant moral theories seem to have been modeled on the
experience of men in the public life of state and market. Feminist perspectives
illuminate the bias in such moralities.

Feminist moral theory of all varieties is united by certain core commitments: Men's domination of women should end; women are entitled to equal
rights; the moral experience of women is as important as that of men. Of course
the meanings and implications of all of these positions require much interpretation.

Feminist inquiry exploring the moral experience of women has led to a
recognition of how this domain has been neglected by other moral theories and
of how clumsy the dominant theories often are in dealing with the moral issues
in it. Of course "women's experience" is potentially much more like men's
experience than it has been, but historically women have had a vast amount of
experience labeled "private" and "irrelevant." When it is recognized that it is
anything but irrelevant, moral theory needs to be rethought accordingly.

As women care for children and others who need care, moral issues are ever
present, yet this kind of experience has hardly entered into the thinking of
moral theorists developing the dominant outlooks. Traditionally, women's
caring activities have been assimilated to what is natural and instinctual, rather
than to what has moral significance and involves moral choice. As recently as
1982, David Heyd, in a way that was entirely typical, dismissed a mother's
sacrificing for her child as an example of the supererogatory because it belongs, as he put it, to "the sphere of natural relationships and instinctive feelings
(which lie outside morality)."[7]

Among the clearest positions feminist moral theorists take is that such a
dismissal of women's moral experience is unacceptable. In taking such experience seriously, much feminist moral inquiry has developed what has come to
be best described as the ethics of care. Starting with Sara Ruddick's examination of the thinking involved in mothering, Carol Gilligan's empirical studies
of the ways girls and women seem to interpret moral problems, and Nel
Noddings's phenomenological inquiry into what caring involves and how we
evaluate it, feminist moral inquiry has illuminated the importance of caring
activities and relationships in human life, and has established the moral significance of care (see chapter 1 for further discussion). Caring well should be a
moral goal, and basic caring relations are a moral necessity. The values involved
in the practices of caring need to be understood and cultivated, and the failures
of many practices to reflect these values also need to be understood. Caring as an
actual practice should be continually evaluated and improved. To bring about
such improvement, radical transformations may be needed in the social and
political contexts in which caring takes place.

Many cautions have been raised about the ethics of care. To the extent that
women have been confined to the work of caretaking, an ethic that reflects this
may have the effect of prolonging inequality. It may mistake a merely historical
fact—that women have done most of this labor—for a claim about women's

outlooks on moral issues. To the extent that caring is for particular others with whom we have actual relationships, some critics fear it may draw attention away from the oppressive social structures in which such caring occurs. To elevate the activities of caring (which should be shared by men and not assigned automatically to women) into an ethic of care associated with women's experience, can thus be thought problematic.

How the ethics of care should be formulated continues to be a central subject of feminist moral inquiry, which includes far more than care ethics. I think the objections to it can be answered and result largely from an undue focus on a few early formulations only. How it should be understood and defended as a distinct moral theory or approach have been considered in chapter 1 and are the major themes of this book.

Care versus Justice

As thinking about care developed, care and justice were often seen as alternative values. "Care" and "justice" were taken to name different approaches to moral problems and characteristically different recommendations concerning them. Care valued relationships between persons and empathetic understanding; justice valued rational action in accord with abstract principles. Carol Gilligan saw these as alternative interpretations that could be applied to given moral problems, yielding different ways of construing what the moral problem was and how it should be handled. For instance, should a contemplated abortion be interpreted as a way of avoiding or constituting a threat to the well-being of existing children and their relationships with their mother, or should it be interpreted as a conflict of rights between a fetus and a pregnant woman? Gilligan saw both approaches as valid, but because interpretation from the perspective of care had been grossly neglected in the construction and study of dominant moral theories, it should now be seen as valid, and the deficiency corrected. Gilligan argued that if one sees a moral problem as an issue to be dealt with in terms of care, one cannot at the same time see is as an issue to be dealt with in terms of justice because the two perspectives organize the problem differently. A given person can recognize both interpretations and examine them one at a time. Morality, she argued, should include the concerns of both care and justice. But with respect to a given problem, this suggestion leaves us with alternative interpretations but no advice on choosing between them. *Why* should we see an issue as one of justice primarily or as one primarily of care?

If women are discriminated against in their chances for professional education, let's say, as they still are in many parts of the world, should we see this as an issue of justice or of care? If a parent hurts his child through his insensitivity, is this an issue of care or of justice? One can see how both points of view will illuminate different aspects of the problems. But which should we favor when their recommendations conflict? Seeing justice and care as alternative approaches did not help us decide.

Other theorists, Nel Noddings, for instance, thought care should replace justice as the central concept of morality. On this view, care could provide the guidance needed for whatever moral problems we face, and justice should be displaced to the sidelines. An ethic of care would be sufficient. But this view was open to many objections. How could care alone deal with the structural inequalities and discriminations of gender, race, class, and sexual orientation. How could sensitivity, responsiveness to the needs of the dependent, and cultivation of caring relations be adequate to preventing domestic violence, criminal coercion, and violent conflict between states? Moral decisions and outcomes seemed to require justice.

In these debates, the dominant ethic of justice was taken to include both Kantian and utilitarian approaches. John Rawls's *A Theory of Justice* was seen as emblematic of a Kantian approach.[8] Such theory requires abstract, universal principles to which all (taken as free, equal, and autonomous individual persons choosing impartially) could agree. It sees justice as the most important basis on which to judge the acceptability of political and social arrangements. It insists on respecting persons through recognition of their rights and provides moral constraints within which individuals may pursue their interests. It seeks fair distributions of positions of differential power and of the benefits of economic activity.

Utilitarianism is less obviously a morality of justice. It recommends maximizing the utility, or the preference satisfaction, of all, taken as individuals pursuing their own interests. It is better than Kantian and other deontological approaches in recognizing the importance of satisfying needs, because it can weigh them heavily in the calculus of preference satisfaction. But it still relies on an abstract universal principle appealing to rational individuals. In its requirement that the utility of each individual is to be seen as of equal importance to that of any other, it tries to build justice into its foundations. It justifies the political recognition of individual rights, the focus of justice, as highly conducive to general utility. Like Kantian moral theory's categorical imperative, utilitarianism has one very general universal principle, the principle of utility, on which it relies.

To those whose focus is on the differences between Kantian and utilitarian theories, it may seem unwarranted to classify them together as theories of justice, and defenders of both Kantian and utilitarian approaches have denied that they cannot well handle issues of care. Both have tried to assimilate care into their own favored frameworks.

Those developing the ethics of care, however, focus on persons responding with sensitivity to the needs of particular others with whom they share interests. From this perspective, the similarities between Kantian and utilitarian theories are of more significance than the differences: Both are rationalist in their moral epistemologies; both rely on simple, abstract, universal rules; both assume a concept of person that is individualistic and independent; both are theories of right action aimed at recommending rational choices; both can be interpreted as far more suitable for guiding the decisions of persons in "public" life than for dealing with moral issues of family life or of friendship or of group solidarity.

Finally, both are concerned with issues such as justice—through rights and through public policy—though a Kantian foundation may be better and stronger for rights, and a utilitarian one for many issues of public policy.[9] In these ways the ethics of care contrasts with both. And to those focused on the values of care, it is apparent that if women, in their justifiable quest for equality, pursue justice at the expense of care, morality will suffer. For those previously engaged in care to become more and more like the free and equal, rational and unencumbered individuals of theories of justice will leave no one to nurture the relations of family and friendship, and to cultivate the ties of caring. To treat friends and family members as if relations between them were contractual bargains based on self-interest undermines mutuality and undercuts trust.[10]

For some time debates concerning an ethic of care became formulated as care versus justice. Participants were asked to consider which was more suitable for the concerns of feminists and their allies. Those concerned especially with oppressive social structures and unjust economic and political institutions were dubious about focusing on the family and personal relationships. They continued to see demands for equality as primary, although notions of liberal equality were often reconceptualized, and they saw such concerns as best handled through an ethic of justice. Some argued that justice required socialist institutions and economic democracy.[11] Many argued for the extension of justice to women in the household as well as in the workplace.[12] And others argued that an ethic of justice is superior to an ethic of care to protect women against violence and abuse.[13]

Others defended an ethic of care against charges that it is tied to women's traditional roles and complicit in them, making clear that the practices of care to be recommended were not those conducted under patriarchal oppression but those to be sought in postpatriarchal society. They showed how care could be extended beyond the contexts of family and friendship to call for deep restructurings of society; of economic, political, and legal institutions; of professional practices; and of international relations.[14] A caring society would reorder its social roles and transform its practices. Care could be seen as a public and not only a private value, if one uses those unsatisfactory concepts. As Monique Deveaux, introducing a symposium on care and justice wrote, "A care perspective relies centrally on a conception of human good and entails a deep commitment to a transformative politics." Not only have care thinkers asked "what difference contextual moral reasoning might make to politics, but more radically, they've asked what it would mean to fundamentally reorder our social and political priorities to reflect the central role of care in all of our lives."[15]

Instead of seeing law and government or the economy as the central and appropriate determinants of society, an ethic of care might see bringing up children and fostering trust between members of the society as the most important concerns of all. Other arrangements might then be evaluated in terms of how well or badly they contribute to the flourishing of children and the health of social relations. That would certainly require a radical restructuring of society! Just imagine reversing the salaries of business executives and those of child care workers.

Many questions become open in feminist theorizing rather than closed by what have become entrenched ways of thinking. Not only are arrangements *within* different spheres of society rethought from a feminist point of view—for instance, who does the housework and why, or why do laws against rape protect men from false accusations better than they protect minority women from forced sex? The relations *between* the spheres of society need also to be rethought from a feminist point of view. Practices to ensure bringing up children in the best possible ways should perhaps have the highest priority of all, along with education. What a change from recent years that might be, where in the United States most parents are left to scrounge as best they can for the few expensive places available for adequate child care, and many children grow up deeply deprived while social programs of all kinds are sacrificed in the race for global economic and military dominance.

Instead of leaving to the greed and vagaries of the market the creation and distribution of cultural images and influences, a feminist view of society would suggest that we take responsibility as a society for providing the best culture possible. The current media culture strongly shapes the aspirations and behavior of children, young people, and adults. To concede that the basis on which cultural arrangements will be structured is no more than that of commercial gain is morally irresponsible from many moral points of view, especially so from that of the ethics of care. This is not to say that commercial production should be forbidden or censored any more than private schools are. But modern states have made available for their members vast systems of public education, including higher education based on merit rather than wealth. They ought to support comparable public alternatives to commercial culture, protected by standards of artistic freedom matching those of academic freedom now recognized as at least an ideal for universities. Such alternatives would make it possible for the best artists and writers to offer the best cultural products, both popular and more selective, and thus to help societies improve morally and aesthetically through their culture. They would liberate culture from domination by commercial interests.

Of course a feminist concern for embodied persons will make the meeting of genuine economic needs a high priority. But an ethic of care would recommend that economic activity be organized to actually do so, rather than satisfy primarily the lust for wealth of the self-interested who manipulate society and its arrangements through culture, advertising, and influence on governments. The ethics of care would suggest that a great many activities should be outside the market rather than in it (see chapter 7).

These are some examples of the kinds of social transformations that the ethics of care might demand. The charge that a feminist ethic of care is particularistic, limited to the contexts of family and friends, or merely descriptive of the kinds of restricted lives of caring for others to which women have traditionally been confined, is based, I believe, on a misunderstanding of this ethic. When one thinks about the restructurings that would be required by taking the ethics of care seriously, the idea that care ethics is a conservative ethic tied to women's traditional roles seems very implausible.

Feminism is a revolutionary program, since it is committed to overthrowing the deepest and most entrenched hierarchy of all—the hierarchy of gender. It does not seek to substitute women for men in the hierarchy of domination but to overcome domination itself. The care that is valued by the ethics of care can—and to be justifiable must—include caring for distant others in an interdependent world, and caring that the rights of all are respected and their needs met. It must include caring that the environment in which embodied human beings reside is well cared for. The ethics of care will strive to achieve these transformations in society and the world nonviolently and democratically but with persistence. A feminist ethic of care— and I have argued that no ethic of care that is not feminist is entitled to call itself that—is an ethic for all who start out, as we all do, as human children.

At the same time, the concerns of justice must not be overlooked, though they may be more limited than had been thought. How to integrate the values of both justice and care have remained central concerns of feminist moral inquiry.

Feminism and the Discourse of Rights

The ethics of care is not the same as feminist morality. As we have seen, some feminist moral theorists reject it. In my view, feminist moral theory will in time certainly include the ethics of care. Views that an ethic of justice alone, even revised in the light of feminist concerns, can be adequate are, I believe, coming to be seen as mistaken. But so is the view that an ethic of care alone is sufficient. Views that virtue ethics alone can substitute for justice or can incorporate care adequately are also unpersuasive.

Recent debates among feminist moral theorists have generally moved beyond the justice versus care formulations. The questions now being posed are often about how these core values should be thought to be related or combined. How should the framework that structures justice, equality, rights, and liberty, mesh with the network that delineates care, relatedness, and trust?

Feminist morality is surely concerned with the equality of women and with women's rights. If we look at the work of feminist legal theorists, we can see both criticisms of the justice approach, and a determination not to lose what it can provide. Catherine MacKinnon has argued, for example, that "in the liberal state, the rule of law—neutral, abstract, elevated, pervasive—both institutionalizes the power of men over women and institutionalizes power in its male form. . . . Male forms of power over women are affirmatively embodied as individual rights in law. . . . Abstract rights authorize the male experience of the world."[16] Many Critical Legal Studies and feminist legal scholars have been critical of focusing even legal argumentation (much less moral argument generally) on rights. They see rights claims as promoting individualistic, self versus other conflicts, and have argued that conceptualizations of issues in terms of rights claims "limit legal thinking and inhibit necessary social change."[17] Carol Smart shows how one can see a "congruence" between law and "masculine culture," and she examines the way law "disqualifies women's experience" and women's knowledge.[18] She urges feminists not to focus on law and rights in working to bring about the changes they seek. Feminist legal theorists have also shown, however, how rights cannot be replaced by what an ethic of care alone would provide. When rights are viewed in the context of social practices rather than in the abstract, they can effectively express the aspirations of a social movement and "articulate new values and political vision."[19] Patricia Williams, for instance, argues that "although rights may not be ends in themselves, rights rhetoric has been and continues to be an effective form of discourse for blacks," whereas describing needs has not been politically effective.[20] And Frances Olsen, well aware of the deficiencies in relying on law to reduce the subordination of women, nevertheless shows in detail how with respect to statutory rape, rights analyses can lead to reforms taking place and people's lives being changed in ways that empower women.[21]

The area of sexual harassment illustrates the potential of legal rights to bring about social change that decreases the subordination of women. Feminist jurisprudence turned the harms that women have long experienced in sexual harassment into a form of discrimination from which they could seek to be protected by the law. MacKinnon notes that the victims of sexual harassment "have been given a forum, legitimacy to speak, authority to make claims, and an avenue for possible relief. . . . The legal claim for sexual harassment made the events of sexual harassment illegitimate socially, as well as legally for the first time."[22] Women now have a name for the harm that occurs when sexual pressure is imposed on subordinates in the workplace or institution. This may well provide a strong argument for the potential of law to bring about social change for women.

The importance to women of reproductive rights has become ever clearer as such rights are threatened and constantly challenged and continue to be denied to vast numbers of women around the world. Reproductive freedom is thought by most feminists to be a precondition for other freedoms and for equality for women. Patricia Smith argues that "it is inconceivable that any issue that comparably affected the basic individual freedom of any man would not be under his control in a free society."[23] As women strive to overcome their subordination in other areas of society, their rights to control their own sexuality and reproduction and to avoid being commodified are especially crucial.[24]

Among feminist moral theorists (as distinct from legal theorists), there has also been much appreciation of the discourse of justice and rights along with the development of the ethics of care. Not all theorists have combined an interest in both, but there has been continued and mutually enlightening dialogue between those whose primary interests have been in one or the other approaches. I interpret many critiques of justice and rights as critiques of the dominance of this approach. That rights arguments serve well for some domains should not be taken to indicate that they serve well for the entire spectrum of moral or political concerns, or that legal discourse should be the privileged or paradigmatic discourse of morality or social interpretation. The framework of justice and rights should be one among others rather than dominant.

Moralities of rights and justice can well be interpreted as generalizations to the whole of morality and social evaluation of ways of thinking developed in the contexts of law and public policy. Such expansions of legalistic approaches are and should be resisted by feminists. These ways of thinking are *unsuitable* for many contexts, and many of the contexts now thought best handled through justice and rights should be transformed so that a care approach could be employed and would be seen to be more suitable.

Even within the law, where justice and rights should generally have priority, various issues in family law can illustrate their limits, and how other moral considerations should play a larger role. Selma Sevenhuijsen has shown, for instance, how in decisions concerning the custody of children, an approach in terms of conflicting rights is a poor guide.[25] The ethics of care would do better at offering recommendations (see chapter 9).

To argue that justice and rights should not dominate our moral thinking, however, does not mean that they are dispensable. Though the law does treat persons as conceptually self-contained individuals—a conception the ethics of care can recognize as an artificial and misleading abstraction—we can also assert that for some legal and political purposes, it may be a useful abstraction as long as it is not imagined to be the appropriate concept of the person for the whole of morality.

Feminist theorists are also well aware that women must have sufficient autonomy and individual subjectivity to resist and reformulate the ties of traditional communities and families. Rights may be needed to assure this. The feminist self is not absorbed into its social relationships.[26] Feminist critiques of communitarianism make this clear.

The Meshing of Care and Justice

Feminist understandings of justice and care have enabled us to see that these are different values, reflecting different ways of interpreting moral problems and expressing moral concern. Feminist discussion has also shown, I think, that neither justice nor care can be dispensed with: Both are extremely important for morality. Not all feminists agree, by any means, but this is how I see the debates of the last few decades on these issues.

What remains to be worked out is how justice and care and their related concerns fit together. How does the framework that structures justice, equality, rights, and liberty mesh with the network that delineates care, relatedness, and trust? Or are they incompatible views we must (at least at a given time and in a given context) choose between?

One clearly unsatisfactory possibility is to think that justice is a value appropriate to the public sphere of the political, whereas care belongs to the private domains of family and friends and charitable organizations. Feminist analyses have shown how faulty are traditional divisions between public and private, the political and the personal, but even if we use cleaned-up versions of these concepts, we can see how unsatisfactory it is to assign justice to public life and care to private, although in earlier work I may have failed to say enough along these lines.[27] I have argued that we need different moral approaches for different domains, and I have mapped out which are suitable for which domains. There is an initial plausibility, certainly, in thinking of justice as a primary value in the domain of law and care as a primary value in the domain of the family. But more needs to be said.

Justice is badly needed in the family as well as in the state: in a more equitable division of labor between women and men in the household, in the protection of vulnerable family members from domestic violence and abuse, in recognizing the rights of family members to respect for their individuality. In the practice of caring for children or the elderly, justice requires us to avoid paternalistic and maternalistic domination.

At the same time, we can see that care is badly needed in the public domain. Welfare programs are an intrinsic part of what contemporary states with the resources to do so provide, and no feminist should fail to acknowledge the social responsibilities they reflect, however poorly. The nightwatchman state is not a feminist goal. Almost all feminists recognize that there should be much more social and public concern for providing care than there now is in the United States, although it should be provided in appropriate and empowering ways very different from those in place. There should be greatly increased public concern for child care, education, and health care, infused with the values of care.

Care is needed by everyone when they are children, ill, or very old, and it is needed by some most of their lives. Assuring that care is available to those who need it should be a central political concern, not one imagined to be a solely private responsibility of families and charities. Providing care has always fallen disproportionately to women and minorities, who do the bulk of unpaid or badly paid actual work of caring for those needing it. But in addition to a fairer division of responsibilities for care, the care made available through the institutions of the welfare state needs to be strengthened as well as reformed. Care and justice, then, cannot be allocated to the separate spheres of the private and the public. But they are different, and they are not always compatible.

Consider the well-being of citizens that states seek to safeguard. One way of thinking about the issues surrounding it and recommending action would be from a perspective of justice, equality, and rights. We could then recognize basic well-being, or welfare, as something to which each person is entitled by right under conditions of need and ability of the society to provide. Welfare rights would be recognized as basic rights guaranteeing persons the resources needed to live.[28] Against the traditional liberal view that freedom is negative only, we would recognize the positive rights of persons to what they need to act freely. And persons in need would be seen as entitled to the means to live, not as undeserving supplicants for private or public charity. An interpretation of such rights within the framework of justice would then be likely to yield monetary payments, such as social security checks and unemployment insurance supplemented by other such payments for those in need. For many competent persons whose only major problem is a lack of money or a temporary lack of employment, such arrangements would seem recommended and would be preferable to an array of social workers who are expected to practice care but who, whether because of paternalistic tendencies or bureaucratic constraints, often threaten the autonomy of persons in need.

Many persons, however, are not competent, autonomous, and only temporarily unemployed. Often, due to deficiencies of care at earlier stages or in various areas of their lives, their needs are complex and persistent. Inadequately cared for as children at home, in school, and elsewhere or inadequately provided with work and earning experience, they have grown up with more serious problems than lack of money, or they suffer from illness or disability. In such cases, care itself is needed. It should be addressed to specific persons and their specific needs. Dealing with these needs requires other specific persons to provide actual care and caring labor, not a machine turning out equal payments to all in a given category. The care should be sensitive and flexible, allowing for the interaction of care provider and care receiver in such a way that the receiver is gradually empowered to develop toward needing less care when such a decrease is part of a process of growth or training or recovery. When the care needed will be lasting, practices should evolve that preclude the provision of care from becoming dominating and the receiving of care from becoming humiliating. Much recent work on disability has illuminated the values in practices of care, not only of the disabled but also of others.[29]

Whether we employ the perspective of justice or care will affect how we interpret the moral problems involved and what we recommend as institutional policies or individual actions. We might try to combine care and justice into a recommendation concerning welfare that each person is entitled to the care needed for appropriate development, but such a recommendation will remain an abstract and empty formulation until we deal with just the kinds of very different policies and practices I have tried to outline.

If we try to see justice and care as alternative interpretations that we can apply to the same moral problem, as Carol Gilligan recommends, we can try to think of care and justice as different but equally valid. But we are still left with the question of which interpretation to apply when we act, or which to appeal to when we draw up our recommendations. If we are merely describing the problem and possible interpretations of it, as in alternative literary accounts, we could maintain both of these alternative moral frameworks and not have to reject either one. But if decisions must be made about the problem, we will sometimes have to choose between these interpretations. Moral theory should provide guidance for choice about actions and policies, as well as educate our sensibilities about possible attitudes. If a child must live with either one parent or the other because the parents are divorcing and live far apart, should the determination be made on grounds of the rights of the genetic parent or the parent with the higher income who can best "provide" for the child, or on grounds of who has been actually taking care of the child and with which parent does the child have the most trusting and solid relationship? The problems of choosing between the interpretive frameworks of justice and care often persist after we have clarified both frameworks and what they would suggest.

When the concerns of justice and care conflict, how should we try to reconcile these values? Does either have priority as a general rule? Many philosophers have supposed that justice is the primary value of political institutions to which other values could be assimilated, but the examples concerning welfare and child custody are from important functions of the modern state, and they do not yield the clear ability of justice to handle the moral problems even in the political or legal realm, and certainly not as deeper moral issues. To suppose that the "justice system" of courts and law enforcement is the only really important function of the contemporary state is surely unhelpful; to what extent it should or should not be would be among the very questions to be addressed by an adequately integrated ethic.

One possibility I have considered in the past is that justice deals with moral minimums, a floor of moral requirements beneath which we should not sink as we avoid the injustices of assault and disrespect. In contrast, care deals with what is above and beyond the floor of duty. Caring well for children, for instance, involves much more than honoring their rights to not be abused or deprived of adequate food; good care brings joy and laughter. But as a solution to our problem, I have come to think that this is not clear. Perhaps one can have ever more justice in the sense of more understanding of rights, equality, and respect. Certainly there are minimums of care, even of the kind that cannot be handled by a right to them, such as by rights to adequate nourishment or medical care, that must be provided for persons to develop normally, though excellent care will far exceed them.

Another possible metaphor is that justice and rights set more or less absolute bounds or moral constraints within which we pursue our various visions of the good life, which would for almost everyone include the development of caring relationships. But this metaphor collapses for many of the same reasons as does that of justice as a floor of moral minimums. For instance, if there is anything that sets near absolute constraints on our pursuit of anything, including justice, it is responding to the needs of our children for basic, including emotional, care.

I now think that caring relations should form the wider moral framework into which justice should be fitted. Care seems the most basic moral value. As a practice, we know that without care we cannot have anything else, since life requires it. All human beings require a great deal of care in their early years, and most of us need and want caring relationships throughout our lives. As a value, care indicates what many practices ought to involve. When, for instance, necessities are provided without the relational human caring children need, children do not develop well, if at all. When in society individuals treat each other with only the respect that justice requires but no further consideration, the social fabric of trust and concern can be missing or disappearing.

Though justice is surely among the most important moral values, much life has gone on without it, and much of that life has had moderately good aspects. There has, for instance, been little justice within the family in almost all societies but much care; so we know we can have care without justice. Without care, however, there would be no persons to respect and no families to improve. Without care, there would be no public system of rights—even if it could be just. But care is not simply causally primary, it is more inclusive as a value. Within a network of caring, we can and should demand justice, but justice should not then push care to the margins, imagining justice's political embodiment as the model of morality, which is what has been done.

From a perspective of care, persons are relational and interdependent, not the individualistic autonomous rational agents of the perspective of justice and rights. This relational view is the better view of human beings, of persons engaged in developing human morality. We can decide to treat such persons *as* individuals, to be the bearers of individual rights, for the sake of constructing just political and legal and other institutions. But we should not forget the reality and the morality this view obscures. Persons *are* relational and interdependent. We can and should value autonomy, but it must be developed and sustained within a framework of relations of trust.

At the levels of global society and our own communities, we should develop frameworks of caring about and for one another as human beings who are members of families and groups. We should care for one another as persons in need of a habitable environment with a sufficient absence of violence and with sufficient provision of care for human life to flourish. We need to acknowledge the moral values of the practices and family ties underlying the caring labor on which human life has always depended, and we need to consider how the best of these values can be better realized. Within a recognized framework of care we should see persons as having rights and as deserving of justice, most assuredly. And we might even give priority to justice in certain limited domains. But we should embed this picture, I think, in the wider tapestry of human care.

Feminist Morality and Reductionism

My own view, then, is that care and its related concerns should be seen as the wider network within which justice and utility and the virtues should be fit. This does not mean that the latter can all be essentially reduced to aspects of care, or that the ethics of care can substitute for ethics of justice. The model of reductionism seems to be the wrong model.

In her discussion of various influential conceptions of the self, Diana Meyers concludes that none is in itself satisfactory. She suggests that we should "drop the synthetic imperative" and think of the five conceptions as "five dimensions of subjective experience, five foci of value, five schemas for understanding oneself and others, and five foci of moral concern."[30] Admittedly, this may be confusing, but "parsimony and completeness may not be jointly attainable."[31] She finds promise in narrativity, since "in self-narratives, people effortlessly weave together the disparate themes that the unitary self, the social self, the divided self, the relational self, and the embodied self highlight."[32] She goes on to find deficiencies in narrativity also. But let's consider the metaphors with which we can try to conceptualize the relations between different theories. We can see them as different "dimensions" of the matter in question, different "foci" of what is important about them, and so on. We can resist the pressure to synthesize them and especially to reduce them to just one way of thinking about the issues.

Care seems to me to be the most basic of moral values. Without care as an empirically describable practice, we cannot have life at all since human beings cannot survive without it. Without some level of caring concern for other human beings, we cannot have any morality. These requirements are not just empirical givens. In every context of care, moral evaluations are needed. Then, without some level of caring moral concern for all other human beings, we cannot have a satisfactory moral theory.

Within a network of caring relations, we can demand ever better and more morally admirable care. We can demand justice, fairness, rights. Out of caring concern we can determine that it is sometimes best for the sake of justice to imagine persons as abstract individuals. But these ways of thinking, we need to remember, are suitable *only* for limited domains, such as those of public law, taxation policy, commercial transactions, assuring basic human rights and basic levels of equal treatment—including in the household. Although assuring basic rights is an enormously important task, it is not all that morality should concern itself with. Caring well for our children requires vastly more than simply treating them fairly and not violating their basic rights. And the discourse of justice and rights should not overwhelm other discourse, as has happened, as if the concerns of justice would suffice for morality in general.

We need new images for the relations between justice and care, rejecting the impulse toward reductionism. The idea that one kind of value can be reduced to another or one kind of moral recommendation to another, may be a legacy of imagining that deductive or scientific approaches are most suitable for moral understanding. They are not. The aims of science are to describe or explain and predict what is the case in the natural world as seen from a third-person perspective. The aims of morality are fundamentally different: with it we seek to recommend how we ought to live and what we ought to do as seen from the first-person perspective of the conscious moral agent choosing how to live and to act.[33]

Although we can acknowledge that our moral conceptions *could* be arranged along neat and clean lines if only the messy concerns of morality could be reduced to the categorical imperative or the principle of utility, actual experience with most moral problems and especially with those in the contexts of care—understood narrowly rather than as including all the rest—show that this is a mistaken goal. A generally Kantian approach does seem suitable for various legal contexts, but many other contexts such as those of friendship and family are not best handled with such approaches. Whereas utilitarian ways of thinking may be those that can often best guide the policy choices of governments, they are not well suited to upholding rights and assuring fairness, and they are not suited for contexts such as those of family relations and friends, where it is the particularity of persons (not their universal features) that matters most.

If moral concerns about right action could be reduced to the cultivation of the virtues, it would simplify our efforts at moral education and at structuring society in justifiable ways. But I think they clearly cannot.[34] Although virtue theory is not (in my view) reducible to theories of right action—merely equating virtue with acting in accordance with principles of right action—neither are justice or utility reducible to whatever attitudes or dispositions virtuous persons will have. We need objective standards for the care of children, the safety and health of citizens, and so forth. Virtuous dispositions fail to tell us what they are, let alone ensure that we meet them.

The ethics of care, I have argued, cannot be reduced to an aspect of either kind of ethic of justice or to virtue ethics. But if I argue for care as the wider moral network within which moral concerns are to be placed, is this not to argue for a reduction of justice, utility, and virtue to the ethics of care?

The answer is no. We need new analogies, metaphors, and images to deal with these questions. We can appreciate the freedom with which some writers devise new metaphors with which to convey their ideas.[35] In the case of the ethics of care, instead of the metaphor of reduction through logical relation or conceptual analysis, perhaps we should think of a painting or a tapestry or a glass sculpture. There is an overall design within which are salient and less salient components. The overall moral design of feminist moral theory, I believe, will be one of caring relations. But within that overall design there will be a number of salient components organized around the values of justice and utility. And there will be many interesting and detailed elements concerning the virtues. The whole should be harmonious, but that does not mean that the components cannot differ significantly. I think less in terms of narrativity and more in terms of visual metaphors. But if we do think of narratives, the point might be that we should not try to reduce one genre to another or all genres to an underlying ur-genre.

Such a morality of care might lack the appeal of what various reductionist programs aim at but fail to achieve. It might, however, offer a design we could live with. To the objection that without clear and fairly simple principles we will not be able to teach morality to children, we should remember that children have never been taught the principle of utility or the categorical imperative. Children have been and should be taught aspects of the overall design of morality such as that we should care about the well-being of others, we should treat them fairly, and we should not harm them. We should imagine or try to gain experience of how we would feel if treated as we treat others and be sensitive to how others actually feel in various situations. We should be the sorts of persons others can trust, and we should value the caring relations that connect us with those close to us and those far away with whom we share the global environment.

But how can a theory be like a work of art? A scientific theory is part of the practice of scientific inquiry, but a theory in philosophy of science is a theory about this practice. It may hold that biological theories are in some sense reducible to those in physics or that they are not.

The practice of morality, I think, should contain many recommendations that could be thought of as moral theories for particular areas of life: economic activity, medical practice, bringing up children, and so on. But the philosophy of morality should consider whether there is or is not some one underlying theory to which the others can be reduced. At this level the various theories embedded in various practices might more appropriately be thought to be features of an overall design for living good lives in caring relationships with others, rather than as abstract formulations logically reducible to simpler ones. Moral practice can certainly be thought of as an art. Perhaps it is possible to outline some general recommendations for the development of what we usually think of as art: seek to create what is beautiful and "true" independently of such pressures as those from tyrannical governments or commercial interests, strive for artistic integrity, and so on. But we do not imagine that the practice of painting can be reduced to that of needlework or glassblowing. Perhaps morality in all its different forms is more like the practices of art than it is like the sciences.

5

Liberalism and the Ethics of Care

Although some feminists are liberal feminists, the basic presuppositions of liberal political theory are often seen as conflicting with much feminist theorizing. This is especially apparent in the theorizing devoted to developing the ethics of care, thinking of persons as relational, and conceptualizing society and its institutions in the light of the values of care and caring activities. I argue in this chapter against various liberal critiques of these feminist projects and for the further development of the feminist thinking they involve.

Care and Citizens

Those of us who defend a feminist ethics of care and feminist views of persons as relational and societies as potentially caring, frequently encounter the criticism that such views cannot or should not apply at levels beyond the personal. The ethics of care, it is said, fails to treat people as adult individuals. Adult citizens, our critics claim, usually don't care about strangers, don't want to be expected to care for them, and don't want to be cared for by them. Liberal theories are designed to address standard adult situations, it is said. Such theories demand respect for individuals and assurances of autonomy, and they specify what justice requires between independent individuals. Adult individuals, the critics hold, don't want to be seen for moral purposes as enmeshed in relationships they did not choose, such as being the child of certain parents or a person brought up with a certain religious heritage; rather, they see themselves as individual, rational moral agents, and they expect to be so regarded for moral purposes. The persons of liberal theory recognize obligations to respect others' rights. But caring is something they see as limited to particular relations of family, lovers, or friends and as largely irrelevant to political institutions and even to moral theory. They fear that if we conceptualize citizens in terms of their personal connections, we threaten their autonomy and risk treating them paternalistically. Thus Ann Cudd writes, "Care is not what most normal adults need or want from most others in society."[1]

These criticisms of care ethics fail to note that the feminist views in question are often presented as a corrective, to question the expansion of liberal individualism from the political domain to the whole of morality, rather than to deny that political liberalism has any value. In developing a view of morality different from an expanded liberal individualism, feminists interested in the ethics of care consider whether there may be value in thinking also about the political realm from a care perspective rather than solely from the familiar perspective of liberalism. This is only the beginning, not the end, of the care ethics exploration.

For instance, when I have suggested that in trying to understand social relations between persons we should think about how they would look if we used as a model the relation between a mothering person and child instead of using the more usual model of contracts between self-interested strangers, my point has been to suggest the alternative model as an exercise of the imagination. Missing this point, critics have found it offensive to think of citizens as either children or parents rather than as autonomous adults with no special obligations to care for other citizens.[2]

I have not claimed that there is no room for standard liberal individualism, but that liberal ideology has been increasingly leaving no room for anything else. My argument is that there must be room for much more than liberal individualism for either persons or societies to flourish.

Ann Cudd rejects being thought of as a child because, she says, "I am not a child."[3] This misses the point. When we think of ourselves as very young or very old, highly dependent on others, seriously ill or under heavy medication, or ignorant of the relevant factors on which policy is decided, it might sometimes be more suitable to imagine how we would wish to be treated by those who would care about us *if we were children,* rather than to imagine what we and others would choose from the even more remote and inappropriate position of the fully independent, self-sufficient, and equal rational agent.[4] How would we have wanted our parents to treat us? How could they have avoided inflicting some of the humiliations and harms we experienced even though we could not then be equally autonomous rational agents? Are some of the values appropriate in such contexts values we could also foster in relations between the bureaucracies of the welfare state and its "beneficiaries"?

A comparable thought experiment applies to those of us who are adult and for the moment relatively capable of independence, as we consider how to treat fellow members of society or humanity. What can we learn from being engaged in practices of care that might be relevant *if* we cared about others in a way that was less encompassing than parental care but not so different as to approach the emotional indifference assumed by liberal theories? Sara Ruddick emphasizes how the experience of mothering, or "fathering" (if we understand it not in its traditional sense but as similar to mothering), is highly relevant to fostering peace in the world. Others may show how those thoughtfully involved in the work of bringing up children or caring for the dependent may design better public institutions for child care, education, health care, welfare, and the like—not just better in terms of efficiency but in embodying the relevant values. Political institutions that have the task of governing activities in which the value of care is more obviously relevant may also be greatly improved by considering their design from the perspective of mother/child relations rather than only from the perspective of the liberal rational contractor.

Critiques of the Ethics of Care

Through the 1980s, the most influential liberal theorists and their leading communitarian critics paid virtually no attention to feminist arguments, as Susan Okin demonstrated.[5] A well-known liberal theorist who has taken the ethics of care sufficiently seriously to criticize it is Brian Barry. Devoting much of chapter 10 of his book *Justice as Impartiality* to the feminist critique of impartiality, he attributes the feminist critique to misunderstandings. Unfortunately, he fails himself to understand much of what characterizes feminist ethics and the ethics of care.

Thoroughly disparaging Lawrence Kohlberg, the psychologist of moral development criticized by Carol Gilligan, Barry faults Kohlberg's abilities as a philosopher and blames him for the confusions he believes are responsible for the feminist critique of impartiality. Barry, however, misinterprets Kohlberg: Contrary to Barry's account, Kohlberg did not specify the "right answers" to the dilemmas with which he presented his experimental subjects and then score them as moral reasoners according to such answers. The scoring depended on the kinds of reasons supplied by the moral reasoners under study in reaching their answers—whether their reasons were general, universal principles, for instance, or whether they were particular loyalties. More important, much of what feminist moral philosophers have written about feminist morality and the ethics of care has little to do with Kohlberg, but does have much to do with the kind of justice as impartiality that Barry defends.

Barry advocates what he calls second-order impartiality, which requires of the moral and legal rules of a society that they be "capable of attaining the . . . assent of all" taken as free and equal individuals.[6] This does not require, he maintains, universal first-order impartiality, according to which we cannot be partial to our own children and spouses. As long as we can all accept a set of impartial rules, he notes, these rules can permit us to give special consideration to our families and friends.

Barry admits that most second-order impartialist theories, such as John Rawls's theory of justice, are designed for judging institutions in a nearly just society and are of little use for prescribing actions under currently existing conditions, especially when such actions would be performed in the context of seriously unjust institutions. He neglects to recognize that a merit of the ethics of care is that it carries no such limitation. Barry allows that there can be second-order impartiality theories that endorse the morality of breaking some bad laws instead of waiting for them to be changed. His arguments for impartiality are in many ways an improvement over what others have offered. But he sides with impartialists generally in holding that justice, in his case justice as second-order impartiality, always has priority over considerations of care. For Barry, care should be the basis of choice only where the requirements of justice have already been fulfilled. He argues that there can be no genuine conflicts between this kind of justice and care: They deal with different matters.

This interpretation does not address the arguments of defenders of the ethics of care who question rather than accept the priority of justice as impartiality (even second-order), yet do not reject impartiality altogether. These advocates of care deny that we are simply talking about different matters: We are both talking about morality, and we disagree about it. The issue is often which would be better in a given case, the approach of justice or the approach of care? This question can arise in public as well as in personal contexts, and we may wonder whether we should treat persons as if the liberal assumptions of impartial justice apply to them. I disagree with Barry that we should always prioritize justice as impartiality and relegate care to the status of an optional extra for personal contexts.[7] Sometimes the points of view of care and of justice provide different moral evaluations and recommendations on the same issues. When they do, we must choose between them. At any rate, we may not be able to follow both.

Marcia Baron, a Kantian moral philosopher, also relies on the idea of " 'levels' at which impartiality might be deemed requisite."[8] She notes how "a utilitarian may thus hold that the principle of utility is to be applied not at the level of individual actions but a step up: at the level of principles or rules to guide our conduct. The same approach can be taken by an impartialist," including a Kantian one, who can argue that from an impartial perspective there are, for instance, good reasons to "honor thy mother and father."[9] Baron, like Barry, thinks that anyone who fails to accept this notion of different levels is making an "error." But this way of handling issues in the way rule utilitarianism tries to has been fairly conclusively undermined by arguments that rule utilitarianism reduces to act utilitarianism.

In the end we have to deal with moral dilemmas one at a time, as we act one action at a time. We are always faced with the question of whether to obey a lower level rule or to break it if it yields an answer inconsistent with a higher level principle like the principle of utility. Only when the lower level rules are consistent with the higher level principles can they be recommended as useful shorthand calculations. These arguments apply also to Kantian rules and principles, where lower level rules may be shorthand derivations, but if they are inconsistent with the categorical imperative, it is unlikely that, to the Kantian, we should ever follow them. Hence, to the impartialist, impartiality always trumps partiality after all, rather than genuinely allowing it, as Baron suggests. The issue might be put in terms of questions about *why* one should honor one's father. To the impartialist the answer would be some form of: because all persons ought always to honor their fathers, ceteris paribus. For the partialist it might be something like: you probably ought to honor this particular person who is your father because over many years he helped bring you up. It would be the particular persons involved and the relation between them, rather than the general principle, that would be the source of the honoring. Of course the ethics of care does not deny that we can make some generalizations about the value of care, just as we can use the general terms of language. The issues concern what constitutes and gives rise to value.

Some feminists, of course, have defended liberal contractualism. Among their arguments are that contractual views ought to be extended beyond the political sphere to assure women's equality in the family.[10] These liberal feminists are critical of and often reject the ethics of care. Feminists defending the ethics of care agree that, of course, women are to be treated as equals but deny that justice and equality are the only or even the primary moral considerations by which we ought to be guided in the family and not only in the family but often elsewhere as well. They deny that a morality built on liberal individualism can be adequate to all these contexts.

Some other feminists reject the contrast between care and justice and dispute their conceptualizations as distinct points of view.[11] But the liberal critique of the ethics of care does assume that there is a contrast and that justice always has priority. This chapter is primarily addressed to this position, the priority of justice.

The Critique of Liberalism

Criticism of the liberal, contractual model of social relations takes at least two forms: a charge of inaccuracy and an evaluative criticism. The charge of inaccuracy claims that the contractual model distorts reality by leaving out vast areas of human experience that it claims to apply to but in reality cannot cover. Contractualists may respond by saying that they intend to cover only interactions between strangers and not relations of love and affection. This response, however, does not take account of the ways such dominant moral theories as utilitarianism and Kantian ethics are built on the liberal model of social relations between strangers, and yet are moral theories that standardly claim to cover all situations.

Rational choice theory and moralities built on it are even more explicit in accepting liberal, contractualist assumptions about social relations,[12] while making claims about rationality in general and what the rational decision would be in any situation. Even if the conclusions of liberal individualism are confined to the political domain, the response fails to deal with assumptions made in conceptualizing the relevant assemblage of strangers. It fails to address, for instance, the appropriateness, implications, and effects of treating just any social relations as if they were between independent, autonomous, self-interested individuals.

The second kind of criticism of the contractual model is evaluative. It suggests that even if, in advanced capitalist societies, relations between persons have indeed become more and more like contractual relations between self-interested strangers, this is not a morally good model for relations between persons to aim to be. Moreover, applying a contractual model to more and more situations, the way rational choice theory does, promotes the wrong kind of social development—anomie and walled enclaves for the affluent, for instance. To encourage morally better social relations, this critique holds, we should limit rather than expand the use of the liberal, contractual model, both in our institutions and practices and in the ways we think about social issues.

Turning first to the charge in inaccuracy, consider the liberal image of the individual citizen. Liberals suggest that we should choose principles for the design of our political institutions that would be acceptable to us as free, equal, rational, and fully impartial persons. The principles and institutions thus recommended will be those to which we could contractually agree for furthering the rational pursuit of our individual interests. Within these principles and institutions we will pursue our economic interests. Doing so will produce industries in which we can choose to be employed, and it will yield products we can choose to consume. Within the constraints of the laws recommended by our political principles and made and enforced through our political institutions, we can develop whatever ties of sociality and affection we wish. How plausible is it to conceptualize citizens and thus persons in this familiar way?

A glaring deficiency of the liberal image of the individual citizen is that it abstracts from an interconnected social reality, taking the ideal circumstances of an adult, independent head of a household as paradigmatic and ignoring all the rest. It overlooks the social relations of an economy that makes its members (including heads of household) highly interdependent. Members of any national economy are deeply dependent on each other, and they are increasingly dependent on others around the globe. The liberal view overlooks the facts that citizens have all been helpless infants, totally dependent on others for years of affectionate care, and that those who have cared for them have often been dependent on still others for support while their labor was expended in such care. It overlooks that at any given time a large percentage of any society's population are children and an increasingly large percentage are the frail elderly. Nearly all persons have periods of their lives in which they are seriously ill. Much of the time, what persons need and want are thus not the services that autonomous, self-interested individuals can buy or insure themselves for; they need and want the relational care that escapes the model of the aggregate of free and equal individuals agreeing to the terms of a social contract.

To the extent that we are economically interdependent, we need and want public policies and arrangements that will enable us to provide care to those we care about (who need not be limited to our immediate "loved ones") and that will enable us to receive care when we need it. These are just as important aims as having policies and arrangements that will advance our independently determined economic self-interest. If a contractual model is applied directly to situations of economic interdependence, it treats the economically powerless and the economically powerful as if they were equally autonomous, obscuring the conditions conducive to exploitation and deprivation.

The contractual model is demeaning when applied to domains of experience where care is the primary value. If parents care for children now only so that their children will care for them when they are aged, and both children and parents understand the terms of this bargain, the relation of parent and child is deprived of the valuing of both for their own sakes and for the sake of the relation of caring between them. If apparent friends maintain their practices of meeting, conversing, exchanging gifts, or visits or intimacies only because each believes it will serve his or her own interests to do so, we would judge such "friendships" to be superficial at best. Although some aspects of their friendship may be beneficial to each individually, if self-interest is all that motivates them, trust between them will be absent and they will not long be friends. And if a person who is ill or otherwise dependent is cared for by people who are only going through the motions of doing what they are paid to do, we know that this care is not the best.

Many liberals contend that the contractual model is intended to apply only to the political rather than to the personal sphere.[13] But then, where do the health care and the child care industries belong? They are certainly not within the domain of the private or familial as conceptualized by the forefathers of contemporary liberalism. Industrial economies have never fit satisfactorily into the traditional liberal framework of public and private, structured as they are by public decisions and capable as they are, in turn, of shaping political outcomes. Robert Dahl, for instance, wrote already in 1970 that to think of the contemporary corporation as private is "an absurdity," and this statement is even more compelling at the beginning of the twenty-first century.[14]

Still, to see human relations in the marketplace as contractual and based on rational self-interest does not clash grossly with our experience of them. Health care and child care, however, are more problematic. Should they be regarded as among the arrangements and services for which free, equal, rational, and autonomous persons contract? To do so seems questionable, for before any of us can actually become the kind of person liberalism imagines, we have already received many years of child care that has been more than what merely contracted services can provide. Children do not become autonomous rational agents without having been cared for and valued for their own sakes. People born disabled or ill may never become the rational contractors of liberal theory. When people become ill or dependent on others' care, they may be too far removed from the assumptions of the contractual model for it to apply to them. Moreover, all who provide care for others without earning wages for their services forgo what they could otherwise use that labor capacity to earn and hence are often deprived of resources they need and want. Yet it would clearly be a mistake to think of children, the disabled, the ill, and all those who care for them as beyond the reach of moral guidelines and the practices ordering public life. An implication is that the terms of liberal discourse are less suitable for thinking about the whole of society and large parts of it than they are thought to be by liberals who dismiss the political significance of the ethics of care. If the terms of liberal discourse are too limited, it may be fruitful to try the experiment of thinking in terms of values discernible most clearly in the domains of family and friends and to consider extending those values to other domains.

When, for instance, managed health care becomes increasingly driven by market considerations, questions certainly can be and are being raised about the appropriateness of the liberal contractual model for this domain. The value of care, understood best in a context of family and friends, can be sought for this domain of social activity, which ought to provide what members of a political community need when they are medically vulnerable. Whether we are providers or recipients of care in the household, the care that has the most value for us is largely overlooked by the liberal contractual model. Perhaps we should seek values comparable to this care in the services provided by public arrangements and institutions as well as in the household.

The Effects of Liberal Assumptions

Let's consider further the effects of treating persons and their relations as if they could be adequately captured by the liberal assumptions in question, while we recognize their distance from actual reality. Liberals believe this approach will promote the justice required by principles that would be agreed to by hypothetical rational agents in contractual relations. But critics of liberal individualism draw different conclusions. Because the liberal model assumes indifference to the welfare of others, employing this model leads to a narrowing of the gap between model and reality and to the wider acceptance of the assumption of indifference as standard and appropriate—not only as assumption but as description and guide. It promotes only calculated self-interest and moral indifference in place of the caring and concern that citizens often have for fellow citizens (albeit less intense than for family and friends), that members of smaller communities still more often have for each other, and that most persons could have for other persons, even in foreign places and distant lands.

The liberal critic of the ethics of care may prefer such indifference to paternalistic interference, but a discussion of the issues involved here will show that the liberal is wrong to suppose that these are the only alternatives. The defender of care ethics can show that paternalism is of course not the only alternative to calculated self-interest. Mothering and other care can and usually should include promoting the competent but not disconnected autonomy of the child or other person being cared for. It should be sensitive to the importance of avoiding paternalistic domination, and moral evaluations of care will include subtle understandings of how caring relations that do not involve domination should be developed. Examining such issues from the point of view of children and recipients of care are projects for ongoing inquiries in the ethics of care.

Adopting the assumptions of liberalism contributes to making actual indifference to others more pervasive. This does not mean that we must choose between the ethics of care and due regard for autonomy. Many feminist moral theorists interested in the ethics of care have been showing how autonomy as self-governance is compatible with (not antagonistic to) the ethics of care (see chapter 3 for further discussion).

Thinking of persons as relational does not mean that we cannot make autonomous choices to resist various of the social ties we grew up with or find ourselves in and to reshape any relations we maintain. On the contrary, it often requires that we do so. The ethics of care suggests that we can conceptualize these choices as taking place within social relations that partially constitute us as what we are. We maintain some relations, revise others, and create new ones, but we do not see these as the choices of independent individuals acting in the world as though social ties did not exist prior to our creating them, as does the contractual model.[15] Moral agents guided by the ethics of care are "encumbered" and "embedded" in relations with actual other persons, but they can still be free moral agents.

An aim of the ethics of care is to promote the responsible autonomy of the cared-for where this is appropriate. Conceptions of autonomy within care can then be much more satisfactory for thinking about large domains of activity, including public activity, than are liberal contractualist conceptions of individual autonomy. The ethics of care requires us to pay attention to, rather than ignore, the material, psychological, and social prerequisites for autonomy. Persons without adequate resources cannot adequately exercise autonomous choices. Autonomy is exercised within social relations, not by abstractly independent, free, and equal individuals.

David Gauthier provides a good example of a theorist who wishes to base morality on the assumptions of traditional liberalism. Morality, he argues, can be based entirely on rational agreement between persons who seek some advantage for themselves and have no concern for others' interests. A choice is rational for a person if it will maximize the satisfaction of his or her interests. Because agents will be affected by what others do, it is rational for them to agree on certain bargained constraints applying to all. Morality, then, provides impartial rational constraints on the pursuit by individuals of their interests. "Morality," Gauthier argues, "can be generated as a rational constraint from the non-moral premises of rational choice."[16] This, then, is a claim about morality, not just about the social contract of traditional liberalism, presumed to underlie our political institutions. It employs the assumptions of liberalism about the conceptual and normative priority of individuals over social relations, about the basic characteristics of individuals, and about their choices.

Writing about Gauthier's book, Peter Vallentyne says that "Gauthier's project is to ground morality in rational agreement, and rational agreement, he maintains, requires mutual advantage."[17] A result is that children, the members of future generations, the severely disabled, and animals, because they cannot be parties to the agreement, are "included in the scope of morality only to the extent that those party to the agreement care about them."[18] This means that *if* we care about them, their well-being will be counted among our preferences, but that whether we do or do not is a contingent empirical fact about which morality will be silent. Gauthier's morality cannot advise us that we ought to care about such nonparties to the agreement or show us how to improve our relations with them.

Vallentyne observes that "like Rawls, Gauthier assumes that the parties [to the agreement] are mutually unconcerned (do not care how others fare)."[19] Vallentyne admits this may be a limitation of the theory, because it is counterfactual. Actual people do care about others, so showing that an agreement is rational for persons who are mutually unconcerned does not show that it would be rational for those who are not, given Gauthier's instrumental conception of rationality and his effort to ground his argument on rationality for actual persons rather than, as for Rawls, persons ignorant of their actual preferences.

We can go even further with such a critique. To Gauthier it is an advantage of his theory that it doesn't require that anyone be concerned for anyone else. His is a morality that theoretically can do without care. But this is absurd in its way. Without care there is no society, there are no people. Why should we even look for a basis for morality that disregards care, whether or not Gauthier's version of such a theory succeeds in its aim?

Gauthier claims to have solved the problem of compliance (it may be rational to enter into an agreement, but is it rational to actually comply with it?) without the machinery of enforcement which others think limits contractualism to the political domain. But even if what some think of as morality *could* be based on a bargain between rational, mutually unconcerned individuals, would this be the morality we should seek?

Jean Hampton, a liberal feminist, observes uncontroversially that "most . . . of Western political philosophy has been highly individualistic in character."[20] In a book called *The Second Bill of Rights,* legal theorist Cass Sunstein argues, as have many before him, for guarantees of the food, housing, education, employment, and medical care without which citizenship in a democracy means little.[21] Sunstein blames "a pernicious form of individualism" that has been influential in the United States for the U.S. failure to recognize the guarantees of social welfare common in most other Western societies. Historian David Kennedy, reviewing Sunstein's book, observes that such individualism "runs deep in American culture" and shows few signs of receding.[22]

These are among the effects of liberal individualist assumptions. They have turned out to provide weak defenses against the conservative and libertarian onslaughts against governmental social programs in recent Republican presidencies. In contrast with most other Western societies, the socialist tradition has had little success in tempering such assumptions in the United States. Possibly the ethics of care might provide a new and stronger basis than previous moralities on which to recognize the responsibilities of society to respond to the needs of the vulnerable.

The Dilemma of Liberal Morality

Thinking of society's members, then, as if they were fully independent, free, and equal rational agents obscures and distorts the condition of vast numbers of them at the very least and has the effect of making it more difficult to address the social and political issues that would be seen as relevant and appropriate if these conditions were more accurately portrayed and kept in view. The liberal portrayal of the self-sufficient individual enables the privileged to falsely imagine that dependencies hardly exist, and when they are obvious, to suppose they can be dealt with as private preferences, as when parents provide for their infants. The illusion that society is composed of free, equal, independent individuals who can choose to be associated with one another or not obscures the reality that social cooperation is required as a precondition of autonomy.

There is a considerable body of literature on whether the social contract at the level of either theory or practice can even get started (let alone sustain itself) without assuming a social cohesion or trust or civic friendship on which it is parasitic.[23] If the view is correct that contractual relations require some deeper level of social cohesion or trust or concern, the ethics of care may be an excellent source of insight for understanding the relevant factors in such cohesion or trust. Looking at the closest ties, how they are developed, and how trust is cultivated within them may be instructive. A thin version of such social cohesion may provide a framework within which fellow citizens can trust each other for certain purposes, perhaps agreeing that for political purposes they will regard one another as independent rational contractors committed to a limited set of political principles and institutions. Or, for organizing their interactions in the marketplace, they may see each other as self-interested economic agents who can contractually agree to various rules. But they and we should not lose sight of how society is vastly more than its political system and its economy. We need moral practices and evaluations to guide us in this wider or deeper domain as well as in the more limited areas of market and politics.

Instead, over several centuries of traditional ethics, the assumptions and conceptions of political liberalism have been pushed outward to other domains, with the result that even morality intended to apply at the most inclusive levels of whole societies and the most affectional levels of family and friends has been constructed on assumptions and conceptions originated for political liberalism. The image of the rational contractor then becomes ubiquitous, and recommendations based on it are thought of as suitable guidance for moral decisions in any context.

This morality, however, runs into obvious difficulties in many domains. To conceptualize relations between mothers and children as based on a rational contract is bizarre. To suppose that a Kantian morality can serve well for the context of the family is highly problematic when we move beyond questions of the minimal respect owed to each person: We don't, for instance, play with our children out of respect for the moral law, and yet giving our children a morally good upbringing involves a great deal of playing with them. Or consider a very different context, the international one: It makes little sense to try to account, on the individualistic grounds of liberal theory, for "national identity," or whatever it is that enables a political entity to be an entity within which liberal norms can be accepted. Social ties that enable persons to identify themselves as members and to recognize others as fellow members of a community or state are presupposed by the norms of any political entity, though we should not assume that these ties are necessarily national ones.[24] To move beyond merely local or national norms to something more like global ones, some sense of care and concern for or solidarity with other inhabitants of the globe is needed.

Because of the deficiencies of liberal individualist morality in contexts such as those of families and groups, one of two directions tends to be pursued by theorists defending it. Either liberal individualist morality is pressed onto informal, personal, and collective domains regardless of its difficulties in them. Or the human bonds of families, friends, groups, and nations are relegated to the status of the "merely sentimental" or the "instinctual," "natural," "emotional," and "irrational," as opposed to the rational and the moral.[25] They are then regarded as lying "outside morality" and are left unexamined from the moral point of view in a region to be empirically described but about which morality is thought to have nothing to say.

Thus, either liberal morality is pressed onto domains other than that of the already existing state, in which case it is an unsatisfactory morality, or it is not applied at all to such domains, and morality—which has been equated with liberal morality—is imagined to have nothing to contribute in thinking about or acting in such domains. This result is clearly also unsatisfactory. The problems parents confront in bringing up children are *moral* problems much of the time, and we can understand that we ought to deal with the *moral* aspects of how nations draw their boundaries and decide on their membership as well as act toward one another.

We need better moralities than the traditional ones. If, in constructing them, the ethics of care seems adequate for various regions of experience, we might usefully think about applying it to other regions.

The Acceptance of Limited Liberalism and Wider Care

Those who argue for the importance of the ethics of care usually share a commitment to many of the achievements of liberalism in their appropriate domains: political institutions democratically constituted and systems of fundamental rights upheld by an independent judiciary. They are not conservatives fond of traditional communities.

An example of this can be seen in feminist treatments of rights. At first, many feminists in thinking about rights were struck by how fully rights reflect masculine interests and how much the very concept of a "right" seemed to clash with the approach of caring. Nel Noddings, speaking from the perspective of the ethics of care, to the development of which she greatly contributed, warned of "the destructive role of rules and principles" of which rights are reflections. If we "come to rely almost completely on external rules," she said, we "become detached from the very heart of morality: the sensibility that calls forth caring."[26] And Annette Baier wrote that "rights have usually been for the 'privileged,' and the 'justice perspective' and the legal sense that goes with it are shadowed by their patriarchal past."[27]

However, despite these apparent rejections of the liberal focus on the centrality of rights, most feminists—even when influenced by the ethics of care—have also come to accept the necessity of rights for feminist aims. The potential of rights claims to bring about social change is clear. Reformulating conceptions of equal rights, women have argued successfully for pregnancy leave, child care provisions, and more equitable pension arrangements. Rights to freedom from sexual harassment have made the climate of many workplaces less hostile to women. Rights have been of the utmost importance for decreasing racial discrimination and attaining the most basic protections for women globally. Women's human rights urgently need to be advanced. Even Martha Minow, deploring the ways rights have ignored relationships, has moved toward "a conception of rights in relationships" that can counter oppressive forms of public and private power. She wants to "rescue" rights rather than abandon them.[28]

When liberal conceptions are confined to their appropriate domain of the legal-political institutions of society and the contested issues within them, feminists are generally willing to employ these conceptions. But those developing the ethics of care have argued that the assumptions and conceptions of liberal individualism do not serve us well in many of our other experiences as human persons in a large variety of relationships and that these other perspectives should also inform our views of the legal and the political.

Much of the interest feminists have had in the ethics of care has been to establish care as having at least as much importance for morality as liberal justice.[29] For those who are convinced that justice and care are comparably important and that neither can be reduced to the other, the debate can then concern the relations between care and justice. Is justice primary and care an essential supplement? Are they alternative frameworks of interpretation within which any moral problem can be considered? Is care the more fundamental value within which domains of justice should be developed? How should either or both be reconceptualized in the light of feminist understandings?

I am suggesting in this book that care and its related considerations are the wider framework, or network, within which room should be made for the liberal individualism that has contributed so much to our understanding of justice and well-being. This perspective does not mean that all other values, points of view, or the practices or institutions they recommend can be reduced to aspects of care, because reduction does not seem the right approach (see chapter 4 for further discussion).

Within a network of caring relations we can require the justice and equality, fairness and rights highlighted by liberal political theory. To understand their implications it may be appropriate, within political and legal domains, to imagine persons as abstract, independent rational agents contracting with each other as equals, to see what rights they would then have. We should keep in mind, however, that these ways of thinking are suitable only for limited domains and not for the whole of morality.

It is sometimes claimed that liberal political principles are needed exactly when relations of affection or of special ties are absent. But unless we have sufficiently strong motives to care about our fellow human beings and value this caring, we will not care whether their rights are respected or not, especially in the case of people who are too weak to make serious trouble for us, as the history of domination, exploitation, and indifference makes evident.

Some who argue for the ethics of care, especially its earliest advocates, want clearly to distinguish *caring* from a vague *caring about*, fearing that if the distinction is not maintained the essential features of what an activity such as taking care of a small child is like will be lost. Thus Noddings wrote that the caring about that is involved in our giving money for famine relief is not genuine caring, because caring is an interactive relation in which each party recognizes the other as a particular person; it involves personal engagement.[30]

Others, however, as I have argued in this book, think the value of caring that can be seen most clearly in such activities as mothering is just what must be extended, in less intense but not entirely different forms, to fellow members of societies and the world. To many feminists, thinking about the social world in terms of caring is entirely appropriate, though it is an entirely different way of thinking about it than the way of liberal individualism.

6

Caring Relations and Principles of Justice

The question of whether impartial, universal, rational moral principles must always be given priority over other possible grounds for moral motivation continues to provoke extensive debate. David Velleman has added to the defenses of Kantian ethics offered by various others against recent challenges to the priority of impartial rules. The challenges have come from Bernard Williams and others, and especially from certain feminist advocates of the ethics of care.

An example of the controversy was a session of the American Philosophical Association in Philadelphia in December 1997 where Velleman presented a paper called "Love and Duty" and defended Kantian ethics against the kind of challenge presented by Bernard Williams.[1] Like most such defenses of the priority of universal moral rules, Velleman's did not address the challenge presented by the ethics of care, but other defenders of Kant and of the priority of universalistic principles have begun to do so. They have offered a variety of answers to the feminist critiques of claims about the adequacy of moralities build on universal principles of rational impartiality. In this chapter I will discuss the feminist challenge and defend it against these responses.

Velleman's paper has subsequently been published as an article entitled "Love as a Moral Emotion."[2] He discusses the case that Bernard Williams addresses, originally put forward by Charles Fried and much discussed since, of whether a man may justifiably save his wife rather than a stranger, if he can save only one in a disaster. Williams suggests that if the man stops to think about whether universal principles could permit him to give special consideration to his wife rather than treating both persons impartially, the man is having "one thought too many."[3] Velleman disagrees, arguing that "once we distinguish love from the likings and longings that usually go with it . . . we will give up the assumption that the emotion is partial in a sense that puts it in conflict with the spirit of morality."[4]

The issue, Velleman says, is not simply whether it would be permissible to act before or without constantly performing the rational deductions required to see if the maxim of our action can be universalized, a view Velleman attributes to Henry Allison, Barbara Herman, and Marcia Baron. On this view, one would be deterred if one did do the deduction and found a conflict. To Velleman, this concedes too much to the critic of Kant, because on Velleman's view *there just is no conflict.*

What Kantian respect for persons requires is that we value every person as of *incomparable* value. "The incomparable value of a person is a value that he possesses solely by virtue of his being a person—by virtue . . . of what Kant calls his rational nature."[5] Much more controversially, Velleman maintains that love is similar. "The value to which we respond in loving a person," he claims, "is the same as that to which we respond in respecting him—namely, the value of his rational nature, or personhood."[6] As Velleman sees them, "respect and love [are] the required minimum and optional maximum responses to one and the same value."[7] To Velleman, this does not undermine regarding the person we love as special: Being treasured as special entails "being seen to have a value that forbids comparisons."[8] And love, which Velleman sees as disarming our emotional defenses and making us "vulnerable to the other,"[9] is in his view entirely consistent with Kantian requirements.

To Velleman, the man in Williams's example should save his wife not because her value outweighs that of the stranger but because their values are incomparable and he and his wife have mutual commitments. The critic may argue, however, against Velleman, that finding the alternatives of saving his wife or saving a stranger incomparable merely evades the issue of what we ought to do if our love recommends one course of action and universal principles another inconsistent with it. Velleman says he is not dealing in his article with the question of whether there can be practical conflicts between love and duty, but rather with the supposed psychological conflict.[10] But if the motives of caring for a beloved, and obeying a universal law *do* conflict, we can ask by which we ought to be guided. The answer offered by the ethics of care may well be different from that offered by Kantian ethics.

Velleman's interpretation of love has much to recommend it, arguing as it does against a raft of philosophers overly committed to belief-desire analyses. He asserts that love is "an attitude toward the beloved himself but not toward any result at all."[11] My disagreement concerns his interpretation of the "attitude toward the beloved himself." He sees it as an attitude toward something universal—a rational nature or the status of being incomparable possessed by every person—in the beloved. The ethics of care, in contrast, would see the beloved herself as a unique, particular person to be valued for herself, rather than for her exemplification of something universal, and it would value the particular relation between the person and the beloved.

A note of Velleman's is indicative. Speaking of a passage in Kant on reverence, Velleman says it "is meant, I think, to rule out persons as proper objects of reverence *insofar as they are inhabitants of the empirical world.*"[12] The ethics of care, in contrast, would have no trouble, I think, describing the feelings of parents toward a newborn child, in all her empirical embodiment, as reverence. The feeling a parent of a newborn may have, that this child is the center of the universe and that there is nothing more important in all the world, is not only a temporary emotional distortion that will soon be modified. It also expresses a deeply moral sense of responsibility for a vulnerable being in need of one's care. And if the responsibility to care for this person would conflict with what the universal norms of Kantian morality required, it would for the ethics of care be an open question whether the person *ought* to obey the moral law.

At the American Philosophical Association session, one commentator, Thomas Hill, changed Williams's example to avoid any sexist stereotypes, but agreed with the defense of Kantian impartiality against the kind of attack Velleman considered.[13] Harry Frankfurt, another commentator, gave more support to Williams's critique.[14] None of the three speakers addressed the versions of the challenge to Kantian principles offered by the feminist ethics of care. These resemble Williams's in some respects, but differ from it in others.

Williams's arguments are presented from the point of view of a man with a set of projects, the sorts of projects that make life worth living for this man. The image, like its Kantian alternative, is still that of an individual deliberator. Williams pits the individual's particular goals—to live life with his wife or, in another case, to be a painter—against the individual's rational and impartial moral principles, and he doubts that the latter should always have priority. Williams disputes the view that our particular projects must always be constrained by universal principles, so that we should only pursue what universal principles permit.[15] If a man's life would only be worth living if he put, say, his art ahead of his universalizable moral obligations to his family, Williams is not willing to give priority to his moral obligations. In the example of the man and the drowning others, the man's wife may be his project, but the dilemma is posed in terms of an individual's own particular goals versus his universal moral obligations. At a formal level it remains within the traditional paradigm of egoism versus universalism. Williams is unwilling to yield the claims of the ego, especially those that enable it to continue to be the person it is, to the requirements of universalization. But he does not reject the traditional way of conceptualizing the alternatives. Like Thomas Nagel in *The Possibility of Altruism,*[16] and most other philosophers before him, the problem is seen by Williams as pitting the claims of an individual ego against those of impartial rules.

The challenge to Kantian moralities offered by the ethics of care does require a change in this paradigm. It does not pit an individual ego against universal principles, but considers a particular relationship between persons, a caring relationship, and questions whether it should always yield to universal principles of justice. It sees the relationship as not reducible to the individual projects of its members. When universal principles endanger relationships, the feminist challenge disputes that the principles should always have priority. The feminist critique of liberalism as moral theory and of Kantian morality gives us reason to doubt that in terms of how the debate has been framed, justice should always have priority over care.

Stephen Darwall is a philosopher who has tried to address the challenge presented by feminist ethics. He finds that the ethics of care usefully calls attention to the actual relationships that are such an important part of our lives. But he denies that the ethics of care really presents an alternative opposed to the moralities of impartial universal principles, the moralities of Kant and utilitarianism. He argues that we arrive at the basic idea of utilitarianism, "that everyone's welfare matters and matters equally,"[17] by thinking about why we value an actual particular child who engages our attention. We realize that it is because the particular child we care about is "someone with a conscious life that can be affected for good or ill" and that the sympathy we feel for a particular child is something we can feel for any other. Similarly, according to Darwall, Kantian respect for persons "involves recognizing an individual's dignity or value in himself, but it is grounded in features that a person shares with any other moral agent."[18] Hence we extend to all persons the kind of respect we can recognize that an individual we know deserves. To Darwall, then, the ethics of care is a "supplement" to "morality as conceived by the moderns,"[19] but both aim at the same ideas of equal concern and respect.

This interpretation, like Brian Barry's before it (see chapter 5) and Velleman's since, fails to recognize the challenge to moralities of universal, impartial principles that the ethics of care, or Bernard Williams, present. To an advocate of the ethics of care, Darwall's interpretation of what it is in our child that leads us to value or respect him is rather questionable in terms of descriptive persuasiveness. What a parent may value in her child may well not be what makes this child like every other, but the very particularity of the child and of the relationship that exists between them, such that she is the mother of this child and this particular person is her child. If we think of how we would respond to the question "why do you care about this child?" asked perhaps by an official of a hypothetical regime threatening to take the child for adoption by more favored parents, or for a scientific experiment authorized by the regime, we are probably more likely to imagine our response being "because she is my child" than "because she has a conscious life, like all children."

This does not mean that we associate our child with our property, thinking of her as belonging to us, or thinking of ourselves as individuals who own our children as well as our things. Nor does it mean we think the reasons the government should or should not take our child are like the reasons it should or should not appropriate our property: The relationship we have with our child is very different from the relationship we have to our property. We might favor policies that would allow governments to appropriate significant amounts and kinds of property in ways that would be fair, yet strongly oppose policies that would sever bonds with our children, even if they would be fair.

In elaborating the reasons the two kinds of cases are different, we might refer to the conscious life of our child and all other children or to Kantian principles against treating persons as means. But the relationship between a particular child and a particular parent is a more plausible source of the valuing of each by the other than are the features they share with all other children and parents. So if the moral recommendations grounded on this relationship ever conflict with the moral recommendations derived from universal moral principles, the problem of which has priority remains, despite Darwall's efforts to dissolve it.

Differences among Feminists

Martha Nussbaum is another philosopher who argues for liberal universalism against the ethics of care; she believes that the kind of liberalism for which she argues will be better for women than care ethics and should be embraced by feminists. She acknowledges that some of the feminist critique of liberalism can conflict with what she sees as the "norms of reflective caring that are preferred by liberalism."[20] The latter norms would demand that love or attachment be based on uncoerced choice from a position of equality, whereas the ethics of care recognizes that many of our attachments cannot or need not be based on such choice; a most obvious example is that no child can choose his parents, who are for many years more powerful than he. Though Nussbaum does not acknowledge it, many defenders of the ethics of care favor reflective care over blind care, but they part company with Nussbaum in not seeing care primarily in terms of individual interest or choice. Nussbaum cites Nel Noddings's description of the maternal paradigm of care and writes: "Liberalism says, let them give themselves away to others—provided that they so choose in all freedom. Noddings says that this is one thought too many— that love based on reflection lacks some of the spontaneity and moral value of true maternal love."[21] To Nussbaum, such a view does present a challenge to the Kantian liberalism she defends. But she thinks the position of the ethics of care should be rejected; she thinks it bad for women. Her reasons, in my view, are based on too limited a view of the ethics of care, a view that identifies it unduly with its earliest formulations.

Many feminists who criticize the liberal individualist view of persons do not deny, as Nussbaum implies, the importance of implementing women's rights (see chapters 4 and 9). When women are denied, as they are in many parts of the world, an equal share of the food or education available to a family, when women are subject to marital rape and domestic violence, extending liberal rights to women is of course enormous progress. So is it appropriate also when, as in the United States, women receive equal shares of basic necessities but are still expected and pressured to make greater sacrifices for their children than are men. The point that feminists often make, however, is that the progress should not stop with equal rights and that the liberal individualist way of formulating the goals of morality is one-sided and incomplete. Nussbaum claims that "what is wrong with the views of the family endorsed by [many liberals] is not that they are too individualist, but that they are not individualist enough"[22] because they do not extend liberal individualism to gender relations within the family as she thinks they should.

Contrary to Nussbaum's characterization of them, however, most feminists, including those who defend the ethics of care, agree with her that various individual rights should be extended to gender relations in the family: Rights not to be assaulted, for instance, should protect women and children in the family, and women should assert rights to a more equitable division of labor in the household. But those who advocate the ethics of care have a very different view from liberal individualists on what gender relations, relations between children and parents, relations of friendship, and human relations generally should be like even when these rights are extended to those previously left out from the protections they provide.

The feminist critique of liberalism that a view such as Nussbaum's misses is the more fundamental one that turning everyone into a liberal individual leaves no one adequately attentive to relationships between persons, whether they be caring relations within the family or social relations holding communities together. It is possible for two strangers to have a so-called relation of equality between them, with nothing at all to bind them together into a friendship or a community. Liberal equality doesn't itself provide or concern itself with the more substantial components of relationship. It is in evaluating and making recommendations for the latter that the ethics of care is most appropriate. As many feminists argue, the issues for moral theory are less a matter of justice versus care than of how to appropriately integrate justice and care, or care and justice if we are wary of the traditional downgrading and marginalizing of care. And it is not satisfactory to think of care, as it is conceptualized by liberal individualism, as a mere personal preference an individual may choose or not. Neither is it satisfactory to think of caring relationships as merely what rational individuals may choose to care about as long as they give priority to universal, impartial, moral principles.

Marilyn Friedman calls attention to when partiality is or is not morally valuable. "Personal relationships," she writes, "vary widely in their moral value. The quality of a particular relationship is profoundly important in determining the moral worth of any partiality which is necessary for sustaining that relationship."[23] Partiality toward other white supremacists on the part of a white supremacist, for instance, does not have moral worth. When relationships cause harm or are based on such wrongful relations as that of master and slave, we should not be partial toward them. But when a relationship has moral worth, as a caring relationship between parents and children, or a relation of trust between friends and lovers clearly may have, the question of the priority or not of impartiality can arise. And as moralities of impartial rules so easily forget, and as Friedman makes clear, "close relationships call . . . for personal concern, loyalty, interest, passion, and responsiveness to the uniqueness of loved ones, to their specific needs, interests, history, and so on. In a word, personal relationships call for attitudes of partiality rather than impartiality."[24]

Evaluating the worth of relationships does not mean that universal norms have priority after all. It means that from the perspective of justice, some relationships are to be judged unjustifiable, often to the point that they should be ended to the extent possible, although this is often a limited extent. (For instance, we will never stop being the sibling of our siblings, or the ex-friend or ex-spouse of the friends or spouse with whom we have broken a relation.) But once a relationship can be deemed to have value, moral issues can arise as to whether the claims of the relationship should be subordinated to the perspective of justice. That is the issue I am examining. Moreover, the aspects of a relationship that make it a bad relationship can often be interpreted as failures in appropriate caring for particular others, rather than only as violations of impartial moral rules. Certainly, avoiding serious moral wrongs should take priority over avoiding trivial ones, and pursuing highly important moral goods should take priority over pursuing insignificant ones. But this settles nothing about caring relations versus impartial moral rules, now that we know enough to reject the traditional view that what men do in public life is morally important whereas what women do in the household is morally trivial. Some caring relations are of the utmost importance, morally as well as causally— human beings cannot flourish or even survive without them—and some of the requirements of impartial moral rules are relatively insignificant. And sometimes it is the reverse.

The practice of partiality, as Friedman argues, cannot be unqualified. "When many families are substantially impoverished, then [various] practices of partiality further diminish the number of people who can achieve well-being, integrity, and fulfillment through close relationships. . . . Partiality, if practiced by all, untempered by any redistribution of wealth or resources, would appear to lead to the integrity and fulfillment of only some persons."[25] But this only shows, as defenders of the ethics of care usually agree, that partiality and the values of caring relationships are not the only values of concern to morality. The social conventions through which partiality is practiced need to be evaluated and justified, and impartial moral principles can be relevant in doing so. But a morality of impartial principles will be incomplete and unsatisfactory if it stops with impartial evaluations of what individuals are forbidden or permitted to do. Morality needs to evaluate relationships of care themselves, showing for instance, how shared consideration and sensitivity and trustworthiness enhance them and increase their value, and showing also how they can degenerate into mere occasions for individuals to pursue their own interests or to reluctantly fulfill the duties imposed on individuals by impartial rules. When relationships are valuable, moral recommendations based on them may conflict with moral recommendations that would be made from the point of view of impartiality.

Lawrence Blum focuses on the qualities of persons needed for caring relations, and shows how some "standard features of many dominant moral theories are inhospitable to—or may even be incapable of expressing—those virtues of mature persons of which responsiveness is a developmental precursor. These are the virtues of care, compassion, concern, kindness, thoughtfulness, and generosity."[26] I have argued for the centrality in the ethics of care of caring relations rather than simply of caring persons, but of course for such relations caring persons are needed. Impartialist moral theories fail to address their development. As Blum observes, caring involves a "coherent and intelligible form of moral motivation and moral understanding not founded on moral principle or impartiality."[27] The ethics of care is concerned with this kind of moral understanding on the part of persons, along with its interpretations and evaluations of social relations.

A Look at Some Cases

Let me now try to examine in greater detail what can be thought to be at issue between the ethics of care and morality built on impartiality and why a satisfactory feminist morality should not accept the view that universal, impartial, liberal moral principles of justice and right should always be accorded priority over the concerns of caring relationships, which include considerations of trust, friendship, and loyalty. The argument needs to be examined both at the level of "personal" relationships and at the level of societies. Advocates of the ethics of care have argued successfully against the view that care—within the bounds of what is permitted by universal principles—is admirable in personal relations, but that the core value of care is inappropriate for the impersonal relations of strangers and citizens. I will explore cases of both kinds.

Consider, first, the story of Abraham. It has been discussed by a number of defenders of the ethics of care who do not agree with the religious and moral teaching that Abraham made the right decision when be chose to obey the command of God and kill his infant son.[28] (That God intervened later to prevent the killing is not relevant to an evaluation of Abraham's decision for anyone but a religious consequentialist, if such a position can be thought coherent.) From the perspective of the ethics of care, the relationship between child and parent should not always be subordinated to the command of God or of universal moral rules. But let's consider a secular case in which there is a genuine conflict between impartialist rules and the parent/child relation. Attempts such as those of Barry, Darwall, and Velleman to reshape the Williams and feminist problems so that there is no conflict merely deal with a different kind of case and fail to address the question of what has priority when there is a conflict.

Suppose the father of a young child is by profession a teacher with a special skill in helping troubled young children succeed academically. Suppose now that on a utilitarian calculation of how much overall good will be achieved, he determines that from the point of view of universal utilitarian rules he ought to devote more time to his work, staying at his school after hours and so on, and letting his wife and others care for his own young child. But he also thinks that from the perspective of care, he should build the relationship he has with his child, developing the trust and mutual consideration of which it is capable. Even if the universal rules allow him some time for family life, and even if he places appropriate utilitarian value on developing his relationship with his child—the good it will do the child, the pleasure it will give him, the good it will enable the child to do in the future, and so on—the calculation still comes out, let's say, as before: He should devote more time to his students. But the moral demands of care suggest to him that he should spend more time with his child.

I am constructing the case in such a way that it is not a case of the kind Barry suggests where impartial moral rules that all can accept permit us to favor our own children within bounds set by impartial rules. Rather, I am taking a case in which the impartial rules that all could accept direct the father to spend more time practicing his profession, but considerations of care urge him to spend more time with his child. It is a case for which the perspective of impartiality and the perspective of care are in conflict.

No doubt there could be ways of interpreting the problem that would avoid a conflict between impartial moral rules and the pull of the relationship between parent and child, but then the problem would not be the one I am considering. The case I examine is one where the moral agent must choose whether impartiality or care should have priority. And moral philosophers must consider whether the decision such an agent might make in such a case can be normatively justified.

If it would be objected that this is not the way such calculations would in fact come out, my response is that in evaluating alternative moral theories, we can be interested in imagined situations where it would be the case that the calculations came out a certain way. The force of the deontologists' objections to utilitarianism can appropriately rest on such arguments as that if, on a utilitarian calculation, a torture show would produce more pleasure for those who enjoyed it than pain for its victims and critics, then it would be morally recommended. That is enough of an argument against utilitarianism; we don't also need to show that the example is empirically likely.

Suppose the argument the father considers is presented in Kantian rather than utilitarian forms. Then we could say he considers increasing his work at the school an imperfect duty, he considers his duty to spend more time with his child an imperfect duty also, and he thinks the former outweighs the latter. Even if he interprets such duties only negatively, as Velleman advocates, in terms of what we must avoid, the father concludes in this example that with respect to the time he spends fulfilling both duties, his duty to avoid neglecting his students outweighs his duty to avoid neglecting his child.

Kantians can of course, like utilitarians, try to reinterpret the problem so that the conflict dissolves, but defenders of the ethics of care can try to formulate hypothetical problems less easy to reinterpret in ways that refuse to acknowledge the conflict. Whether we can come up with cases that will convince committed universalists is unclear. But many persons are convinced there *is* a conflict between their commitments to the particular persons for whom they care and what morality might ask from an impartial point of view.

Returning to our example, the argument for impartiality might go something like this: Reasoning as an abstract agent as such,[29] I should act on moral rules that all could accept from a perspective of impartiality. Those rules recommend that we treat all persons equally, including our children, with respect to exercising our professional skills, and that when we have special skills we should use them for the benefit of all persons equally. For example, a teacher should not favor his own child if his child happens to be one of his students. If one has the abilities and has had the social advantages to become a teacher, one should exercise those skills when they are needed, especially when they are seriously needed.

But the father in my example also considers the perspective of care. From this perspective, his relationship with his child is of enormous and irreplaceable value. He thinks that out of concern for this particular relationship he should spend more time with his child. He experiences the relationship as one of love, trust, and loyalty and thinks that in the case being considered he should subordinate such other considerations as exercising his professional skills to this relationship. He thinks he should free himself from extra work to help his child feel the trust and encouragement from which his development will benefit, even if this conflicts with impartial morality.

He reflects on what the motives would be in choosing between the alternatives. For one alternative, the motive would be: because universal moral rules recommend it. For the other the motive would be: because this is my child and I am the father of this child and the relationship between us is no less important than universal rules. He reflects on whether the latter can be a moral motive and concludes that it can in the sense that he can believe it is the motive he ought to act on. And he can do this without holding that every father ought to act similarly toward his child. He can further conclude that if Kantian and utilitarian moralities deny that such a motive can be moral then they have mistakenly defined the moral to suit their purposes and, by arbitrary fiat, excluded whatever might challenge their universalizing requirements. He may have read Annette Baier's discussion of women's possible tendency to resist subordinating their moral sensitivities to autonomously chosen Kantian rules and found the arguments persuasive.

Baier writes: "What did Kant, the great prophet of autonomy, say in his moral theory about women? He said they were incapable of legislation, not fit to vote, that they needed the guidance of more 'rational' males. Autonomy was not for them; it was only for first-class, really rational persons."[30] But rather than simply protesting that women can indeed be as rational as men, women who value their capabilities on the basis of their own experience may instead reject the assumptions about morality that have been used to exclude them.

The father in my example may think fathers should join mothers in paying more attention to relationships of care and in resisting the demands of impartial rules when they are excessive. From the perspective of all, or everyone, perhaps particular relationships should be subordinated to universal rules. But from the perspective of particular persons in relationships, it is certainly meaningful to ask: Why must we adopt the perspective of all and everyone when it is a particular relationship that we care about at least as much as "being moral" in the sense required by universal rules? This relationship, we may think, is central to the identities of the persons in it. It is relationships between persons, such as in families, that allow persons to develop and to become aware of themselves as individuals with rights. And relationships between persons sustain communities within which moral and political rights can be articulated and protected. Perhaps the perspective of universal rules should be limited to the domain of law, rather than expected to serve for the whole of morality. Then, in my example, the law should require gender fairness in parental leaves. Beyond this, it might allow persons with professional skills to work more or fewer hours as they choose; but the case as I developed it was to consider the moral decision that would still face the father in question after the law had spoken. Even if the law permitted him to work less, would it be what he morally ought to do? From the perspective of universal impartial utilitarian rules: no. But from the perspective of care: yes. This is the moral issue I am trying to explore. What I argue is that the ethics of care considers the moral claims of caring as no less valid than the moral claims of impartial rules. This is not to say that considerations of impartiality are unimportant; it does deny that they morally ought always to have priority. This makes care ethics a challenge to liberalism as a moral theory, not a mere supplement.

The Reach of Justice

The concern expressed by liberals such as Nussbaum that every person is a separate entity with interests that should not be unduly subordinated to the "good of the community" can be matched by a defender of care who maintains that relationships of care should not be unduly subordinated to universal rules conferring equal moral rights and obligations and designed for contexts of conflict. The law and legalistic approaches should be limited to an appropriate domain, not totalized to the whole of human life and morality (see chapter 9).

Susan Mendus, in a discussion of Brian Barry's *Justice as Impartiality*, notes that the issues are often about the scope of justice: How widely should impartiality be expected to apply?[31] Barry himself thinks it would be absurd to apply it in one's choice of friends: We choose our friends because we enjoy their company, and discretion is permissible. But he holds this is only because impartial rules have already been given priority, and some of them permit us to be partial to our friends up to a point.

Where to put justice first and where to consider it secondary or out of place is often the issue between those who argue for moralities of impartial rules and their critics. The critics often want to shrink the reach of justice, recognizing that the values of caring relationships have been greatly neglected by traditional moralities. They resist the priority of impartiality in personal relationships, and then, having explored the moral priorities in these domains, they consider extending the values of caring, trust, and solidarity, beyond personal relationships. Political and social life need also to be rethought in the light of the ethics of care. Here those arguing for the ethics of care may meet up with communitarians, but since the latter have so seldom dealt with the ethics of care, and care ethics has serious disagreements with most forms of communitarianism, there is by no means a match between an extended ethics of care and communitarianism as so far developed.[32]

For liberalism, as we have seen, individuals are conceptually and normatively prior to social relations or groups. It is assumed that we should start in our thinking with independent individuals who can form social relations and arrangements as they choose and that the latter only have value instrumentally to the extent that they serve the interests of individuals. Many arguments we have touched on concerning human beings as social beings show how artificial such assumptions are, as we see how the material and experiential realities of any individual's life are fundamentally tied to those of others and how the social relations in which persons are enmeshed are importantly constitutive of their "personhood." Feminist arguments that take into account the realities of caretaker/child relations show how misleading is this liberal individualist assumption, ignoring as it does that for any child to become a liberal individual she must have been for many years enmeshed in the caring social relations of caretakers and children.[33] The adult liberal individual regarding himself as "separate" is formed as well by innumerable social bonds of family, friendship, professional association, citizenship, and the like.

Certainly we can decide that for certain contexts, such as a legal one, we will make the assumption that persons are liberal individuals. But we should never lose sight of the limits of the context for which we think this may be an appropriate assumption, nor of how unsatisfactory an assumption it is for more complete conceptions of persons and their relations. Nussbaum's revealing note on her experience of motherhood and of the essential separateness of herself and her daughter sidesteps many of the issues and is in no way conclusive. She writes,

> Perhaps I am handicapped by the fact that I simply do not recognize my own experience of motherhood in Noddings's descriptions of fusing and bonding. My first sharp impression of Rachel Nussbaum was as a pair of feet drumming on my diaphragm with a certain distinct separateness, a pair of arms flexing their muscles against my bladder. Before even her hair got into the world a separate voice could be heard inside, proclaiming its individuality or even individualism, and it has not stopped arguing yet, 24 years later. I am sure RN would be quite outraged by the suggestion that her own well being was *at any time* merged with that of her mother, and her mother would never dare to make such an overweening suggestion. This liberal experience of maternity as the give and take of argument has equipped me ill to understand the larger mysteries of Noddings's text.[34]

Such thoughts could well mark the beginnings of a debate rather than its conclusion. A statement such as "My child and I are separate individuals" overlooks the tie between us, the ways the well-being of a fetus and its mother, a child and his parents, are intimately connected. In the absence of a debate about how it is or is not true, the liberal assumption of individual independence remains an ideological and unexamined starting point with no more support than its familiarity.

Children do not develop adequately when others merely go through the motions of meeting their basic needs, although even this requires enormous amounts of care and relatedness. Children need to experience social relations of trust and caring. Arguably, then, caring relations are in some sense normatively prior to individual well-being in families. But the priority is not just developmental or causal. Without the social relations within which persons constitute themselves as individuals, they do not have the individuality the liberal seeks. At the level of larger groups, persons do not constitute themselves into political or social entities unless social relations of trust and loyalty tie members together into a collectivity of some kind. As Neil MacCormick observes in a discussion of *Justice as Impartiality* and of Adam Smith, "justice matters to people who are already in community with each other."[35] Arguably, then, social relations of persons caring enough about one another to respect them as fellow members of a community are normatively prior to individuals being valued as holders of individual rights, or to citizenship in a liberal state, and the like. Gradually, the community within which such ties need to be developed so that members can be respected as having human rights is the global, human community.

We might conclude, then, that what have priority are relationships of care or fellow-feeling within which we seek rules that all can agree on for treating each other with equal concern and respect in those ways and for those kinds of issues where impartial rules will be appropriate, recognizing that much that has moral value in both personal and political life is "beyond justice." Such a view denies that the rules of impartial morality always have priority and that we ought only to pursue what other values these rules permit. The view that moral rules of impartiality always take priority over considerations of care expands to the whole of morality the outlook within the context of law that law "covers" all behavior, allowing whatever it does not forbid and demanding compliance on all that it does forbid. But we generally recognize a distinction between law and morality and can well argue that morality has normative priority. Then, at the moral level, on my argument we have good reasons not to give priority to moral rules of impartiality but to acknowledge the claims of caring relations as at least no less fundamental. This view argues that at the moral level, justice is one value among others, not always the highest value. Care and its related values of relationship and trust are no less, and perhaps are more, important.

Susan Mendus, discussing Bernard Williams's argument about the man saving his wife, writes that the force of the argument is "that it is not merely impractical and politically inexpedient to force this extension of the scope of impartiality: it is also, and crucially, a deformation of concepts such as love and friendship, which are what they are precisely because they are not underpinned by completely justificatory explanations. In the example of the man saving his wife, willingness to pose the justificatory question is, in part, an acceptance of this deformed model."[36] This way of putting the point assumes that "justification" can only be in terms of impartial rules, whereas a broader concept of justification might not be limited to just such forms. But from the perspective of an ethic of care, Mendus is right to argue that accepting the demand to apply rules of impartiality is, in many cases of love and friendship and caring relations, to accept a "deformed model" of these.

Models of Morality

At the level of morality, we need to decide which "models" are appropriate for which contexts. Many of the arguments of recent decades about the priority of justice were developed against a background of utilitarian ascendancy. Rawls's theory of justice and its many offshoots are good examples.[37] Against utilitarian calculations subordinating all other considerations to the goals of general utility, or claiming that rights can only be justified on the basis of how well they serve overall welfare, arguments are persuasive that such views misunderstand what is inherent to rights. In Ronald Dworkin's memorable formulation, rights "trump" general utility, and just what we mean by a person having a right is that this claim is justified whether or not it promotes general utility: Rights must stand firm against such maximizing calculations.[38] Basic to democratic theory, for instance, is the view that individual rights must be respected even when this does not maximize the satisfaction of majorities. Similarly, it has been argued, at the moral level justice and rights have priority over general utility.

From the perspective of the ethics of care, however, this debate can be interpreted as being largely internal to the legal-political context. Rawls has explicitly confined his theory to the domain of the political and has argued that it should not be interpreted as a full-fledged moral theory.[39] Dworkin is explicitly a legal philosopher. Utilitarians have not shown comparable modesty, but one may argue, as I have done elsewhere, that utilitarian calculations can be useful and appropriate for recommending various public policy choices although they are inappropriate for judicial decisions and for a wide range of other kinds of choices.[40] Perhaps, then, neither rights theory nor utilitarianism has the capacity to be made into comprehensive moral theories. And many of those who have continued to argue for Kantian ethics have interpreted Kant in ways that move the theory far beyond rules of impartiality and into the domain of virtue theory.[41]

The moral supremacy of the state and its associated demands is an artifact of history. With a more satisfactory morality than one composed of rules of impartiality, the supreme state and its laws might shrink to more justifiable proportions. A culture liberated from commercial domination, for instance, might become the preferred domain of moral discourse out of which might come moral recommendations which could generally be accepted and acted on without the compulsions of legal enforcement.[42] These recommendations could include acceptance of the plurality of values, and of the primacy of trust and caring relations in various contexts.

The ethics of care suggests that the priority of impartial justice is at best persuasive for the legal-judicial context. It might also suggest that calculations of general utility are at best appropriate for some choices about public policy. Moral theories are still needed to show us how, within the relatedness that should exist among all persons as fellow human beings—and that does exist in many personal contexts and numerous group ones—we should apply the various possible models. We will then be able to see how the model of caring relations can apply and have priority in some contexts, and how it should not be limited to the personal choices made by individuals after they have met all the requirements of impartial rules. A comprehensive moral theory might show, indeed, how care and its related values are the most comprehensive and satisfactory model within which to locate more familiar components.

PART II

CARE AND SOCIETY

7

Care and the Extension of Markets

"The market" is often seen as the model according to which not only economic life but all sorts of human activity should be conducted. In the market, it is said, all exchanges are voluntary, and the workings of the market maximize the liberties and satisfactions of all who participate.

In the United States, more and more activities that used to be seen as public services are being "privatized" and "marketized." Health care, education, and the running of prisons are increasingly the province of for-profit corporations. The market's language and goals of efficiency and productivity are applied to more aspects of public as well as corporate institutions. Activities such as amateur sports and news reporting, which were once relatively independent of corporate involvement, are being overtaken by the market and its norms. The ever greater dominance of corporate influences in politics receives daily confirmation. And the entertainment media, commercial enterprises almost from their start and dependent on advertising and promotion, are increasingly dominated by a few corporate giants whose pursuit of economic gain and pervasive celebration of markets greatly outweigh their pursuit of aesthetic or noncommercial cultural values. The ideal of the free market does recommend against monopolies, but if there is competition, even if only between equally profit-driven corporations, the market offers no grounds for criticism.

As Robert Kuttner observes, "The ideal of a free, self-regulating market is newly triumphant.... Unfettered markets are deemed both the essence of human liberty, and the most expedient route to prosperity."[1] And "as the market vogue has gained force, realms that used to be tempered by extra-market norms and institutions are being marketized with accelerating force."[2]

What I will try to do in this chapter is sort out the relevant questions: What kinds of activities should or should not be in the market and governed by market norms? How does marketizing an activity change its character and what values are served or harmed by this transition? On what moral grounds can we best make such decisions and where should the limits (if any) of markets be drawn? I will show why this is an issue for feminists and why a feminist ethic of care is more promising than liberal individualism in enabling us to address these questions.

I will speak of the "extension" or "expansion" of the market and of its "boundaries," but this should not be understood in terms of a surface or territorial metaphor only, as when we might say that activities like the manufacturing and selling of jackets can appropriately be "in" the market, whereas an activity like the adoption of children should be kept "out of" or "outside" the market. The extension can be a matter of deeper or greater "marketization" of an activity that has both market and nonmarket features, as can be seen with labor markets. The production and distribution of culture is a good example of what can be done, more or less fully, for market objectives. I continue to use the language of extension, but the more complex meaning intended should be kept in mind.

Women and Markets

Women have a vast amount of experience of not being paid for all or much of the work they do. For many women, earning a wage—any wage—is progress, providing a glimpse of the kind of self-determination that income derived from work makes possible. For most feminists, it is progress when women "enter the labor market." Instead of being confined to unpaid work in the household and dependent on fathers or husbands or being limited to taking care of children and aged parents out of love or a sense of obligation, it is liberating for women to be able to earn their own paychecks and to decide how to spend them.

It can also be noted, however, that vast numbers of women have lived their lives as servants, earning little more than room and board for the housekeeping and childrearing tasks performed by "housewives" in households lacking servants. Relative to doing the same work as a servant, doing it in ways that are under one's own control, even though unpaid, may also be progress. But there may be agreement among women in both these situations that economic rewards for one's work, and more control over the conditions of it, are both desirable. They contribute to one's autonomy and well-being. Then, making of one's labor a commodity and using the market to obtain the best available reward and control it can buy appear to many to be appropriate routes to what women find satisfying. But the paid work they go into is often a version of the caring work they do at home—teaching the young, caring for the ill, managing an office—and they may resist the view that their work is simply a commodity. They may resist even more thinking of the unpaid work they do at home, caring for children out of affection and developing bonds of trust and family, merely in terms of the market value to which it would be equivalent if paid for.

This may lead feminists to views such as those of Paula England and Nancy Folbre who, noting that "work that involves caring pays less than other kinds of work," worry that opposition to the commodification or marketization of caring labor may be partly responsible.[3] "The belief," they claim, "that love and care are demeaned by commodification may, ironically, lead to low pay for caring labor."[4]

I take a very different view of the responsibilities here. Unless we have already let ourselves be misled by what Margaret Jane Radin calls "commodification as a worldview," in which the value of a commodity is defined as its market value, and almost everything is viewed as appropriately a commodity, the result of resisting the marketization of caring labor could be the opposite of what England and Folbre claim. We can and should recognize many values, of things and activities, other than their market value, and we can demand that what people are paid more nearly reflect the other-than-market value of their work. Elizabeth Anderson discusses the way we value things in accordance with different "modes of valuation." We should *respect* persons, not treat them as mere commodities. *Use* is a proper mode of valuing commodities, but many things are such that we should, for instance, appreciate their aesthetic or historical value, not merely use them. As Anderson argues, "Any ideal of human life includes a conception of how different things and persons should be valued. . . . We can question the application of market norms to the production, distribution, and enjoyment of a good by appealing to ethical ideals which support arguments that the good should be valued in some other way than use."[5]

We can recognize the intrinsic and not merely instrumental value of an activity. We can acknowledge the way much caring work expresses how persons care about, and are not indifferent to, others. And we can see caring work as enabling those cared for to know that someone values them. To be valued as a person is of value to every person; children cannot develop well without this.

We should, then, recognize the enormous value of caring work—in expressing social connectedness, in contributing to children's development and family satisfaction, and in enabling social cohesion and well-being (the list could go on). We should demand of society that such work, in all its various forms, be compensated more in line than it is with its evaluated worth, noting that its exchange or market value is one of the least appropriate ways in which to think of its value.

We can grant that of course caring labor deserves not only decent but excellent pay without agreeing that the expansion of the market is usually or inherently appropriate or justifiable or liberating. Often it is not.

Labor and Markets

A first clarification to make is that for persons to be paid for their work does not mean, as I use these terms, that their work is governed by market principles or is in the market in the standard sense. A teacher working in a public school or for a not-for-profit private school is in a sense in the labor market: The school must pay him to teach. But his work is not in the market in the sense that the principles under which he works are the market principles of the maximization of economic gain. Economic gain is not the primary aim of the school, and his primary goal is not economic gain if he could earn far more working for a corporation. The school's primary objective, and his, may be educating children well, not earning as much as possible. A doctor working for a not-for-profit hospital may have, as her governing principle, serving the health needs of the community, not increasing her own satisfaction, and the aim of the hospital may be the same, rather than increasing the profits of shareholders. And to reduce a motive like serving the needs of the community to satisfying a personal or institutional preference basically misinterprets such motives, which are to serve the needs of the community for the sake of the members of the community or for the sake of the community as a whole. Were the school or the hospital to be moved into the market or marketized, they would be governed by the market principle of all involved aiming to maximize their own economically quantifiable gains. To be guided by market principles is to be in the corporate sector of society.

As Kuttner notes, even corporate labor can be more marketized or less so. Labor markets are fundamentally different from markets for products. A pure market transaction is a single exchange at a moment of time, but "labor rarely behaves like a spot market because the workplace is not just a marketplace but a social organization with a certain institutional logic and institutional imperatives."[6] But, Kuttner notes, this is becoming an outmoded view, as the new labor market increasingly resembles a spot market. "The customary extra-market norms in worker-manager relationships, long thought to be institutionally efficient, have been substantially eroded by the resurgence of market forces.... Brutal downsizings have become normal. Relentless layoffs are not merely a temporary response to business cycles, but a way of life. Labor has come to be viewed not as a long-term resource but as an expendable cost center."[7] At a given moment, labor shortages may modify the effects of this increased marketization of labor markets, but the wider trend seems in place.

The issues to be kept foremost in mind, I argue, have to do with priorities. The issues are not working for nothing versus working for pay, or whether market imperatives such as efficiency have any place in an activity, but rather what has priority. Teachers and doctors need to pay the rent and feed their children, just as do those whose primary objective is as much wealth and individual satisfaction as possible. Schools and hospitals need to be run efficiently. But earning as much as one can as efficiently as possible easily may not be the primary objective of teachers and doctors and many others or of the entities organizing their work. The market, on the other hand, values teaching or the practice of medicine or the institutions organizing them only instrumentally for what they produce in economic gain.

The motives of most people are mixed: They want to both educate children or keep them healthy and earn a decent living doing so. Or they want to earn as much as possible so that they can provide well for their families and give generously to the charities of their choice. But we still can and should, I argue, sort out which values have priority and ask of people that they value things and activities and people in the mode of evaluation appropriate to them.

Moving an activity that was previously unpaid to the side of being paid is often a gain, not just for the person doing the work but also for others and for the quality of the work. As Nancy Folbre and Julie Nelson argue, having child care done by persons who are paid, rather than by unpaid housewives pressed into it by restrictive social norms, often improves the care. As women are increasingly employed outside the home, mothers with no talent for or interest in child care can do other work, and those with better skills and more understanding can be paid for the work of helping children thrive. For instance, a traditional stay-at-home mother is not likely "to have the knowledge of the developmental stage of four-year-olds possessed by a [good] nursery school teacher."[8] A frail old woman may receive more considerate care from a care worker who has chosen this kind of work than from a resentful daughter-in-law pressured into assuming the burden.

The issue on which I focus, then, is not whether the work is paid or not but the norms under which it is done and whether the values that have priority in its doing are market values or some others.

In many articles on the pluses and minuses of having caring labor in the market and paid for, rather than out of the market, unpaid, and done largely by women in traditional families, there is no discussion of the distinction between, say, a cooperative or not-for-profit community child care center and a chain of for-profit child care franchises. On my account, the former would not be governed by market principles, but the latter would be; the former might value child care in entirely appropriate ways, and the latter would evaluate it instrumentally and primarily for its market worth, which would be inherently inappropriate.

Economist Charles Wilber states that "under a system of allocation by markets, individuals pursue their own self-interest and the market coordinates their decisions. . . . Free market economists place almost complete reliance on markets, and a central thrust of their policies has been to extend the market allocation mechanism into all possible areas, from school lunches to the environment to civil rights. . . . Efforts to encourage allocation by moral values are seen as self-defeating."[9] Philosophers, accustomed to thinking of many other values than market ones, and feminists from any perspective, may be much less dismissive of the importance of moral values in personal and social choices.

Elizabeth Anderson defines a commodity as something to which the norms of the market, norms for regulating the production, exchange, and enjoyment of it, are applied.[10] As more and more things and activities are commodified, the norms of the market are applied to them and imagined to be appropriate for them. This, in my view, should be strongly resisted by feminists and others committed to human flourishing.

Ideal and Actual Markets

The idealized market assumes that everything has a price. Exchanges are made anonymously on grounds of rational self-interest. Neoclassical economic theorists of the Chicago school and the legal and political theorists they and their philosophical predecessors have influenced conceptualize all social interactions as free market exchanges and reflect the view that, in Margaret Radin's formulation, "all things desired or valued—from personal attributes to good government—are commodities."[11] Freedom, on this view, "is defined as free trade of all things," and the value of a commodity is defined as its market value—its exchange value in a free market.[12] All commodities are fungible and commensurable—interchangeable with every other commodity in terms of exchange value. Market enthusiast Richard Posner applies this analysis to law and to people's desire for children, exploring the advantages of a free market in babies.[13] Gary Becker straightforwardly considers children as commodities— "consumer durables," endorsing an extension of the market to everything.[14] In Becker's view, "The economic approach is a comprehensive one that is applicable to all human behavior."[15] His goal is explanation, not moral recommendation, but on the view of the economic approach, explanation is what matters. "The social ideal," in Radin's words, "reduces to efficiency."[16]

Actual markets are often very different. They include personal exchanges between persons who have social connections with each other and exchanges that incorporate various of the values other than market ones of the items or services being traded. But from the perspective of the ideal market, values that cannot be reduced to market values are flaws—interferences with rationality and free exchange. Social relations such as trust and caring are invisible. A person may have preferences that include making another person happy, but making another person happy for the other's sake rather than to satisfy the preference of the person doing so makes no sense in a market framework. In the ideal market, every social interaction is an exchange between individuals and the notion of a social tie disappears.

The appeal of this ideal needs to be understood. It is not merely an economist's abstraction but the standard that is being applied increasingly to ever wider domains of activity. Health care has already been largely pulled into the market; education at all levels could be next. Education has so far been largely out of the market, seen as a public service. But more and more schools run for profit and educational enterprises intended to reward their investors financially are being developed. The classroom is being commercialized as never before, and "privatization," which is often corporatization, is the predominant trend for more and more previously governmental activities. The media steadily reinforce the message that markets are better, freer, and more glamorous than any other ways of organizing human life. The ideal of everyone an entrepreneur is pervasive.

One might think there would be more resistance to the market. In a somewhat representative view, Jonathan Riley does not think that injustice under capitalism is inevitable, but he states that "the extent of measured economic inequality in the U.S. can only strengthen the conviction that capitalism is inherently unjust. . . . The pattern of wealth inequality in America is at odds with any reasonable distributional norm," including the norm that persons deserve to be rewarded on the basis of what they produce.[17] Yet the capitalist market becomes louder and apparently more popular all the time.

The results of the expansion of the market are often dismaying. In Kuttner's estimation, "as society becomes more marketized, it is producing stagnation in living standards for most people, and a fraying of the social fabric that society's best-off are all too able to evade. One thing market society does well is to allow its biggest winners to buy their way out of its pathologies."[18] Stagnation in the wages of nonwinners is especially harmful to women, who are disproportionately among those with meager earnings. At the global level, disparities between winners and losers are magnified still further.

The effects on justice and equality of the expansion of the market may be pernicious. According to Kuttner, "The main source of rising earnings inequality in the last quarter of [the 20th] century is greater marketization, in its multiple forms."[19] Wealth, even more concentrated than income, "has now reached its point of greatest concentration since the 1920's. All of the gains to equality of the postwar boom have been wiped out. This trend has multiple causes, but virtually every one is a variant on a single cause—the increased marketization of society."[20]

Of course we can agree that thinking in market terms need not always mislead us. Things can have multiple meanings or interpretations; for instance, to award monetary damages for the loss of a leg in a tort suit does not literally mean that a leg is "worth" that amount of money.[21] But we can be duly concerned when market modes of valuation are in fact taking over the ways in which health care and education and other activities are organized and practiced, as is happening. And if some kinds of work can be kept from being governed by market norms, perhaps some of these trends can be reversed.

The effects of thinking like an economist have been studied.[22] It has been found that students of economics, exposed for years to market assumptions that persons always act on self-interest, are significantly more likely to free ride and fail to cooperate than are other students. Men are also more likely to display these characteristics than women.[23] Of course it is not even in the economic self-interest of people to act on self-interest when cooperation is called for—as in building families and societies and protecting the common environment. But thinking in market terms can greatly obscure this. Various empirical studies show that where the economic approach would predict free riding, in fact, except for students of economics who score far lower, 40–60 percent of the subjects studied did not try to free ride but engaged instead in cooperative behavior to produce a social good.[24] Presumably, many people are not yet indifferent to values other than market ones, but it is unclear how long this will last.

Health Care and the Market

One of the best examples of the growing marketization of work in the United States is the health care sector. For years, bringing health care into the market was recommended as the way to increase efficiency and to restrain through competition its spiraling costs. The campaign to do so succeeded to such an extent that in the 1990s, profit-seeking health maintenance organizations (HMOs) overtook nonprofit HMOs in numbers of patients covered, and one nonprofit community hospital after another was taken over by a giant investor-owned chain. The profits of commercial HMOs result from not enrolling those most likely to get sick, thus driving the latter to the nonprofits, who are then threatened with financial insolvency and subjected to further disdain for their "inefficiency." A huge amount of governmental regulation of for-profit health care providers is needed to prevent the most serious abuses, but regulators are routinely one step behind the latest entrepreneurial idea to reward HMOs for risk selecting, nursing homes for reducing staff, or doctors for denying treatment or prescribing medications in which they have a financial interest.

The United States spends far more of its gross domestic product (GDP) on health care than countries with a universal system, yet has shorter life spans and lower patient satisfaction than most and more intrusion—often by insurance companies—into clinical decisions. In the estimation of some critics, "there is no realm of our mixed economy where markets yield more perverse results."[25] The triumphant ideology of the marketizers has produced a system where "well-insured people receive care that has become ever more technology-intensive and costly, with the costs driven by the entrepreneurial part of the system. Others, without insurance, get little or no care at all—a public health catastrophe."[26] By 2000, even enthusiasts of for-profit HMOs realized that they are not the answer to controlling health care costs and providing better care.[27]

The Market and Education

The expansion of the market into education is more nearly at its beginning, but "the education industry" seems to many market enthusiasts ripe for takeover. How far it will go remains to be seen. Following are a few examples of the plans of marketizers.

Ted Forstmann, a billionaire leveraged buyout specialist who is leading an effort to have business provide and run schools says, "I didn't get here without understanding supply and demand"; parents believe the schools are producing "a bad product at a high price. So why are no suppliers rushing forward to cater to them?"[28] His fellow corporate titan in this effort, John Walton, whose family gained its wealth through Wal-Mart, adds, "I will tell you that some people in this effort are actually going to make money . . . like everyone else who does a good job."[29]

Higher education is no less a target for corporate takeover supporters. The president of Teachers College quotes an entrepreneur as telling him, "You know, you're in an industry which is worth hundreds of billions of dollars, and you have a reputation for low productivity, high cost, bad management and no use of technology. You're going to be the next health care: a poorly managed nonprofit industry which was overtaken by the profit-making sector."[30] The University of Phoenix—a profit-making institution aiming to have 200,000 students, with uniform class syllabi, almost no full-time teachers, and lots of online learning—may well be the higher education of the future.

Here we can see the values of the market: The way the worth or value of an activity or product should be ascertained is by seeing the price it can command in the marketplace; those whose work is not rewarded with profits are not doing work that has worth; efficient management and high productivity take priority over, for instance, independent thought or social responsibility. Once an educational institution or activity has been taken over by the market, anything other than economic gain cannot be its highest priority, since a corporation's responsibility to its shareholders requires it to try to maximize economic gain.

Corporate influence in the university takes various forms. Universities are pressured into providing more of the technical training that corporations need their employees to have and less of the liberal arts that would foster independent thought. Universities adopt the corporate language and thinking of efficiency and productivity; workloads are increased and salaries decreased, except for the "stars" that make the university more competitive and the educational product they offer more marketable. Corporations see universities as promising targets for sales and contracts, ranging from providing them with maintenance services and soft drinks to licensing and patenting the knowledge they produce.

How close the commercialization of the classroom is to being a reality, rather than just a distant goal of market enthusiasts, may still be unclear. But here are some additional facts: Channel One, a commercial enterprise that now pervades a quarter of schools in the United States, offers a few minutes of poor-quality "news" and two minutes of commercials, which students are required to watch as part of their normal school day.[31] Edison Schools, a for-profit venture, now operates scores of schools around the country and seeks to expand to many more. In exchange for the computers they would otherwise be unable to afford, more schools in the United States are agreeing to the strings attached to the computers that various corporations provide, for instance, to a constant stream of advertisements on the lower left of the screen. Many schools that are short of funds are selling access to students to corporate sponsors, so that the halls of school buildings, walls of gymnasiums, and sides of school buses are filled with advertisements for Coca-Cola, Kellogg's Pop-Tarts, and other products that contribute to poor nutrition.[32]

These developments represent a reversal of the values that ought to have priority in education. We may lack the confidence in our ability to recognize the truth that led Socrates to berate the Sophists for selling their skills to the highest bidder, or putting economic gain ahead of devotion to knowledge. But just because we are more skeptical about truth and knowledge, there is reason to pay special attention to the motives with which various interpretations are offered. Entrepreneurs, pitchmen, advertisers, public relations manipulators, and corporate promoters might be among those least entrusted with decisions about what goes on in the classroom. Of course students should learn *about* markets and their values but also about how to *evaluate* these from positions outside the market.

Limits on Markets

What might the moral grounds plausibly be for deciding on the limits or boundaries of the market? An obvious place to begin is to consider what suggestions we might find in liberal individualism of either the more Kantian or of the more utilitarian kind.

On grounds of a Kantian respect for persons and their rights, informed and updated with understandings fundamental to welfare state liberalism, we might argue that the market fails to assure that all persons will have access to the resources they need to live, and hence that the assurance of rights to basic necessities (such as food, shelter, and health care) must be a responsibility of government. But such rights could be interpreted as rights to enter the market to obtain what is needed, with ability to enter the market provided through such mechanisms as food stamps, housing vouchers, health insurance, school vouchers, and now perhaps computers and so on. Liberal individualism does not seem to address such questions as whether the institutions providing the food, housing, medical care, and education should be private and profit-making or cooperative and socially responsible—whether, in other words, they should be in or out of the market and governed or not by its values. We get from the moral theories of liberal individualism no grounds for dealing with these sorts of questions, and indeed, the leading contemporary liberal individualist theorists with Kantian leanings have not, I think, adequately addressed these questions or provided useful insights as to how they ought to be decided, even in those areas in which we might have the most serious doubts that private, profit-making institutions can be guided by the appropriate values. Areas such as health care, child care, education, the informing of citizens, and the production of culture could all be thought of as domains in which values other than economic gain should be accorded priority. Yet if persons lacking the resources to do so are enabled to enter markets for these activities along with those already having such resources, the liberal individualist might conclude that the rights of all are thus respected and no further significant moral problems remain with such arrangements.

When these theorists have dealt with freedom of expression issues, they have interpreted them in terms of freedom from interference by government. The marketplace of ideas with its soapbox orators is still the reigning metaphor, with little attention to the resources needed to enter the current media marketplace. To the extent that the ways wealth can distort the political process have been considered, the suggested solution has been in terms of limiting expenditures, or of enabling those with less wealth to also enter the communications marketplace, by something that might be thought of as advertisement vouchers to be used on the commercial networks, rather than in terms of supporting and expanding the noncommercial avenues of communication, such as public television. Liberal theorists have a difficult time dealing with the inherent deficiencies of a purely commercial press, despite the crucial role played in a democracy by the press, which has the responsibility of providing citizens with the information they need to understand for what they are voting.

What about the eloquent Kantian injunction that because every person is a being worthy of respect, an end-in-himself, we ought not to use people, or reduce them to mere means to our ends? No one, Kant proclaims, should be treated as a thing with a price because every human being has intrinsic worth and is priceless. Does this give us grounds for limiting the market so that people's lives do not become commercialized and commodified?

The problem here is the word 'only' in Kant's formulation: "Act so that you treat humanity, whether in your own person or in that of another, always as an end and never as a means only."[33] Kant never suggested that the market should not be used to organize a great deal of human activity. We can employ people and use their labor for our purposes as long as we also respect their rights. What we must not do is treat them only as means to our ends, as things, as would happen if a person herself—a slave, say—would be bought and sold in a market. But if we respect the rights of persons, we can, consistently with Kant's principle, use their services and buy and sell such services in the marketplace. So Kant does not seem to give us grounds for deciding that some human activities, such as manufacturing and selling chairs, for instance, can appropriately be conducted through the market, whereas some others, such as providing the best education, should not be left to the market, even if the market is fair. Kant's principles provide the strong and important constraints of having to respect people's rights. They would rule out slave markets. But markets for many things would be allowed by Kantian principles, as long as people pursuing their interests in the market did so within the limits set by respecting people's rights. We do not get from Kant or his followers, I think, satisfactory grounds for deciding, within the constraints of rights, how wide or how narrow the reach of the market should be.

What of the liberal individualism that takes not a Kantian form but a utilitarian form of seeking to promote the general welfare? I have disagreed with those who hold that the goal of a legal system as a whole, on which judicial decisions should appropriately be based once the applicable rules of law have been taken into account, should be seen as a utilitarian goal.[34] The primary values of a legal system, which should be distinguished from a political system despite their overlap, should in my view be the rights and obligations of justice with their implied requirements of freedom and equality, better seen in deontological than in consequentialist terms.[35] But I have argued for a more utilitarian standard of promoting the general welfare and individual interests as appropriate for a wide range of political and economic decisions. Should the social decision, then, of whether to let an expanding market determine more and more activities or whether to promote alternatives to market determinations be decided on utilitarian grounds?

These utilitarian liberal individualist grounds are probably even less suitable for deciding these kinds of questions for the assorted kinds of activities at issue than are the more Kantian ones. Utilitarian arguments depend on the individual preferences that market mechanisms are so well designed to serve. In some cases, if a nonprofit public service enterprise does a better job at satisfying such individual preferences than a profit-making private enterprise, it will be recommended. But this is just to put an abstract higher level utilitarian market calculation ahead of an actual economic market determination; it doesn't take the question out of the market, which is the issue we are exploring. And it might easily suggest that the market would be the entirely suitable way to implement the abstract calculation, rather than show why a given activity or practice should be kept out of the market. The economic approach celebrated by market enthusiasts such as Becker explicitly build on the assumptions of Bentham and the utilitarians, as does neoclassical economics.

Consider how the arguments are frequently run concerning freedom of expression: Just about every political point of view is expressed out there somewhere; if people want a publication of any particular kind they can buy that publication and make it successful; therefore, those media products that get the most attention and have the dominant influence are those that people freely choose. But these arguments fail very seriously to take account of the corporate structures of the entertainment business.

The values of *shared* enjoyment or *social* responsibility, or *collective* caring may well be worth promoting in the realm of culture and in the activities or practices of communication, but these are values that cannot even be registered in calculations of maximizing individual preferences. Perhaps a nonprofit theater group in which a community shares in producing performances has greater value than a commercial TV program whose revenues go up with the numbers of its viewers and that produces a higher aggregate of preference satisfaction taken individually. Perhaps the former is deserving of public support. If so, this will need to be argued for on other than utilitarian grounds. So, too, will positions about many other activities that should be kept out of the market. To hold that the value of education, for instance, is other than the satisfaction of individual consumers requires more than a utilitarian aggregation can provide. For health care or child care to express the shared concern of a community for its vulnerable and dependent members requires that these services be more than commodities for individual consumption. And for civil society to nourish the sense of community on which political institutions depend, it must include more than market transactions (see chapter 8).

It is unlikely that rule-utilitarianism is better able than act-utilitarianism to decide where the boundaries of markets should be, not only because, in my view, rule-utilitarianism must inherently reduce to act-utilitarianism but because all forms of utilitarianism are restricted to taking account of individual benefits and burdens and cannot satisfactorily handle what we can take to be social values and values for social persons. Liberal individualism, then, whether Kantian or utilitarian, provides inadequate grounds for limiting the extension of the market. As Radin notes, "according to a traditional liberal view, the market appropriately encompasses most desired transactions between people, with a few special exceptions."[36]

The Ethics of Care

As we saw in part I of this book, a great deal has been done in recent years to develop more satisfactory conceptions than the earliest ones of what has come to be called "the ethics of care." In this ethics, relationships between persons, rather than either individual rights or individual preferences, are a primary focus. Persons are seen as "relational," rather than as the self-sufficient individuals of traditional liberal theory. Caring relations are seen as being of central value.

Relationships of family and friendship as well as of group and community can be valued on various grounds or evaluated as deficient. For instance, relationships can be trusting, considerate, and mutually empowering, or they can be hostile, exploitative, or oppressive. To characterize a relationship as satisfactory is to say something different from saying that the persons in it as individuals are satisfied with it. It is analogous to the difference between judging that a band plays well and judging that its separate members play well. Debates between liberal individualists and more communitarian theorists illustrate various of these views. Although differing from most communitarians on the values to be promoted, those advocating the ethics of care usually see care, as they see persons, in relational rather than in individualistic terms.

With the ethics of care and an understanding of its intertwined values, such as those of sensitivity, empathy, responsiveness, and taking responsibility, we could perhaps more adequately judge where the boundaries of the market should be. Those defending the ethics of care have successfully shown why it should be seen as applicable to political and social life and not limited to the "private" sphere of family and friendship, where the deficiencies of traditional moral theories are perhaps easiest to see. If we understand care as an important value and framework of interpretation for government as well as for the sphere of the personal, we will approach many of the issues involved in the relation between government and the economy differently from those for whom government should be only the protector of rights or the maximizer of preference satisfaction. We can see how government should foster caring connections between persons and limits on the markets that undermine them. The ethics of care provides grounds for arguing that we should care about one another as fellow members of communities, including gradually of the global community on which the future health of our mutual environments depends.

We should do so not by sacrificing individual children to the demands of traditional communities but by realizing that caring well for every child requires us to understand the social relations supporting the child's well-being and how they are in part constitutive of the personhood of that child.

From the point of view of the ethics of care we can say that fairness and the maximizing of individual utility should not be our only or always our overriding moral considerations. We can recognize domains in which the legal/juridical framework of traditional moralities and the assumption that we are free, equal, autonomous individuals are appropriate, but we can recognize how these ways of thinking should not be imagined to be suitable for all of human life. We can recognize domains in which the individual pursuit of self-interest and the maximization of individual satisfactions are morally permissible, but we can also see how this framework and these values should not be extended to the whole of human activity and society. In practices such as those involved in education, child care, health care, culture, and protecting the environment, market norms limited only by rights should not prevail, even if the market is fair and efficient, because markets are unable to express and promote many values important to these practices, such as mutually shared caring concern.

We should not preclude the possibility that economies themselves could be guided much more than at present by the concerns of care. Economies *could* produce what people really need in ways that contribute to human flourishing. But long before an economy itself is influenced by the values of caring, persons for whom care is a central value can and should affect the reach of the market through their government and their choices.

Drawing Lines

A helpful illustration of the sort of argument I have in mind can be found in discussions of "surrogate mothering," or, as it may more aptly be called, "contract pregnancy." From the point of view of liberal contractual or utilitarian thinking, why shouldn't this service be in the marketplace like any other? If a woman wants to contract to use her body in this way, if a couple wants to pay her to do so, and if appropriate safeguards are in place, why shouldn't the law recognize these contracts as it recognizes so many others? From the perspective of liberal individualism, must not the state be neutral as between the conceptions of the good of the proponents and the opponents of contract pregnancy?

Consider some other values we may take into account, especially the values involved in parental love. We are to value children for their own sakes, not to use or manipulate them for parental advantage. In Anderson's description, parental love can be understood as an "unconditional commitment to nurture one's child by providing her with the care, affection, and guidance she needs to develop her capacities to maturity. . . . Parents' rights over their children are trusts, which they must exercise for the sake of the children."[37]

Contract pregnancy undermines these values. In Anderson's words, it

substitutes market norms for some of the norms of parental love...it requires us to change our understanding of parental rights from trusts to things more like property rights—rights of use and disposal over the things owned. In this practice, the mother deliberately conceives a child with the intention of giving it up for material advantage.... She and the couple who pays her to give up her parental rights treat her rights as a partial property right. They thereby treat the child as a partial commodity, which may be properly bought and sold.[38]

I do not mean to imply that Anderson is an advocate of the ethics of care, but she is an advocate of various modes of valuation in addition to and often in conflict with market ones.

Mary Lyndon Shanley focuses on the labor involved in contract pregnancy. She argues that to view women's gestational labor as a commodity and contracts concerning it as enforceable ignore "the ways in which a woman's self, not simply her womb, may be involved in reproductive labor."[39] Mother and fetus are strongly interrelated, and a birth mother will never stop being the woman who gave life to a particular child, whether or not the child is raised by others. Such considerations lead Shanley to suggest that "pregnancy contracts might as usefully be compared to contracts for consensual slavery as to other kinds of employment contracts."[40] She argues, accordingly, that they should be seen as illegitimate.

In the view of many critics of contract pregnancy, the law should not enforce such contracts, which would then largely eliminate the practice except in rare cases where a woman might carry a child for a sister or very close friend with no payment or contract involved. These arguments can be persuasively developed on the basis of the ethics of care.[41]

We can see examples of how boundaries to the market can be drawn. We can discern areas of human activity and value in which commodification and commercialization should be avoided, and then consider other such areas where individual gain should not be the paramount value, even after rights have been respected. For instance, we can examine and come to understand what is wrong with the sale of human organs and the marketing of political power.[42] We can clarify the values that should be accorded priority in our different activities.

Commercialization should not be confused with competition itself. When musicians or artists compete to see which will be judged the best, we may get closer to promoting artistic values, not further from them. When Venus and Serena Williams compete in tennis, they need not undermine their closeness as sisters because their lives are not confined to the tennis court. If schools compete to see which can do the best job of educating children, this may be acceptable if it keeps in mind what values should be primary in education and that monetary gain should not be. If school systems compete to see which can do the best job with the smallest bureaucracy, that, too, may be beneficial. Hence I am not taking a position on, say, charter schools within a public school system as a way of increasing the possibilities for experimentation and of prodding tired educators in ineffective schools to try harder. Nor am I suggesting that vouchers should be opposed because they involve competition—though there may be other good reasons to oppose them. But any support of competition must also be evaluated in light of our priorities. One of the values that schools should teach is the cooperative exercise of one's civic responsibilities. This is a higher value than the ability to compete effectively for one's own economic gain. It is not inconsistent to argue that schools may compete in teaching cooperation. If competition between schools is needed, it should be for goals such as this as well as for improvement in test scores. It should not, I think, be for economic profit.

Commercialization should also not be confused with promoting efficiency or managing effectively. To apply some management techniques to schools to bring about improved performances by bureaucracies, teachers, and students, and at lower costs, may be appropriate. The same can be said about hospitals and nonprofit enterprises of most sorts.

The danger is that when we import the language and concepts of the marketplace and, for instance, evaluate schools in terms of productivity, efficiency, competition, and lower costs, we also import the foundations and goals of the marketplace, which sees these as means to economic gain. Education can also value efficiency and competition instrumentally and selectively, but it should never lose sight of the values that should inform its goals. It should clearly and explicitly make good education its highest priority, which might seem tautologous but in the present climate is not.

We should be able to argue that almost all education should be out of the market, and we should be able to draw firm lines against the massive inroads of the corporation into the public classroom and into systems of public education that are now taking place. Nonpublic educational institutions should see the reasons to zealously guard their nonprofit status. The ideology of the market is comparable to the ideology of religion. Since we are moderately successful at keeping the teaching of religion out of our public classrooms and in its appropriate secondary place in many of our private ones, we should aim to be as successful at keeping the ideology of the market—the proselytizing of market values—out of the classroom. Of course we do not have the U.S. Constitution and the courts to help, as they do in maintaining the separation of church and state. But if educators and their allies are firm in their beliefs, they can be fairly persuasive.

Contrary to recent developments, there are very good reasons to put most health care and almost all child care in this category of what should not be governed by market norms. And, in a vein that is even more utopian given current realities, I have argued for the liberation of culture from market domination.[43] Citizens should be informed and news should be produced primarily for the sake of democratic political values and true understanding, not principally for commercial gain as at present. Art and entertainment should be created and distributed primarily for the sake of aesthetic values and human enjoyment that has value, not overwhelmingly for the sake of private monetary advantage. The airwaves and the Internet should be subject to governmental controls enacted with a view to the public interest, not left entirely to a market whose only interest is maximizing economic gains. An ethic of care can provide the basis for asserting the relevant values that the market ignores.

As noted before, it is the issue of what has priority or primacy that must be stressed. Teachers, caregivers, news reporters, and musicians should be decently paid for the work that they do. Those who invest their own funds in various kinds of development can be justified in receiving appropriate compensation, though much more public investment for social purposes would often be better. Both public and private enterprises responsible for performing socially vital tasks, or influencing fundamentally the directions in which society will move, should not have commercial gain as their primary motive.

An article by John McMurtry described the current trend in Canada and England as well as in the United States of trying to justify excellence in education by showing how much it increases our ability "to compete effectively in the international marketplace." The author deplored the willingness of so many educators to subordinate the goals of education to the needs of global corporate capital and drew the following conclusion about the danger we face in where we are headed: "Because an educational process is required by its nature to reflect upon and question presupposed patterns of being, its absorption into one of these patterns, the global market system, must leave society in a very real sense without its capacity to think."[44] I, too, have written about how a culture, including its news media, that is subordinated to the demands of the market cannot perform the function that culture needs to perform to keep society healthy, the function of critical evaluation, of imagining alternatives not within the market, of providing citizens the information and evaluations they need to act effectively as citizens.

In trying to help educators see why they should resist submission to the market model, McMurtry conceptualized education and the market as almost totally opposed: opposed in their goals, opposed in their motivations, opposed in their methods, and opposed in their standards of excellence. I think, however, that seeing education and the market as totally opposed opens education to such misplaced criticism as that educators do not care at all about the inefficiency, mismanagement, and incompetence that can be found in their practices. It seems better to see education and the market as having different *priorities*, as *ordering* their values differently. Businesses can value educated, competent employees who can read and write well, but for their own businesses' purposes. Schools can value efficient management but should not do so at the expense of students' real learning. This way of seeing the differences seems more appropriate and capable of strengthening the resistance of education to takeover by market forces. Schools, for instance, should insist that they need the new technologies, but that educators, not corporations, should decide on the uses to which the technologies are put. This view of how we can appreciate multiple values in human activities while according them different priorities and of recognizing how important it is to order those priorities appropriately seems suitable also for the other activities considered, such as health care, child care, and cultural expression.

As a society, in the United States we ought to be trying to shrink rather than expand the market, so that other values than market ones can flourish. It seems to me that the moral theories built on liberal individualism are not well suited to help in this development. Those built on the foundations of moral pluralism and of virtue theory, with their recognition of the multiplicity of values, can do somewhat better, but many are still hampered by their individualism. Those built on the ethics of care that can acknowledge regions in which individual rights ought to be paramount and regions in which individual preferences ought to be given primacy but that do not lose sight of the ways these regions should be limited, can do best in my view. As we care for our children and their futures, we can become aware of the many values other than market ones we should try to encourage them to appreciate and heed. And we can argue for the kinds of social and economic and other arrangements that will reflect and promote these values.

8

Civil Society, Rights, and the Presumption of Care

There have been many discussions among feminists about women's rights: what rights are, what rights women have, what rights of women have not been but need to be recognized, and how to achieve respect for women's rights. It has been widely argued that conceptions of rights need to be revised to include various previously neglected rights of women, such as rights against marital rape and other forms of violence against women. How to interpret women's rights to equality within marriage and with respect to work and property have been discussed at length. And feminist theorists have suggested various reconceptualizations of rights.

Instead of adding to these considerations, what I will do in this chapter is examine what rights presume or what I am calling the presumption of care. I will consider what the preconditions of rights are and what rights presuppose, not just in a causal sense but also in a normative one. I will argue that empirically before there can be respect for rights there must be a sense of social connectedness with those others whose rights are recognized. I will argue that a relation of social connection, or a caring relation, is normatively prior and has priority over an acknowledgment of rights. We ought to respect the human rights of all persons everywhere, but first of all we ought to develop in everyone the capacity for and the practice of caring about all others as human beings like ourselves.

Civil Society, Community, and Citizenship

There has been in recent years much discussion of the neglected region between the personal and the legal-political-governmental. In the prior decade or so, the dominant focus of attention in political and social theorizing was squarely on rights and the realm of justice and law. The work of John Rawls, Robert Nozick, and Ronald Dworkin was decidedly at the center of attention. More recently, the focus has broadened to include what might be thought of as the preconditions of the realm of rights: the social cohesion that makes it possible for political institutions to exist, the social conditions that allow democratic institutions to work well, the background developments that promote the protection of rights and that foster progress toward justice. There has been much discussion of the need for a sense of community between citizens, of the cultivation of civic virtues, and of the components of a thriving civil society.

A wide variety of writings can be included in this discussion, from those advocating communitarian values to those reformulating liberal conceptions of citizenship and those dealing with civil society itself. For instance, in their review in 1994 of work on citizenship theory, Will Kymlicka and Wayne Norman concluded that such work is "quite hollow," lacking as it does any strong proposals to promote citizenship. But there was a new understanding that "citizenship is not just a certain status, defined by a set of rights and responsibilities. It is also an identity, an expression of one's membership in a political community."[1] Since many groups still feel excluded even when they have been accorded rights of citizenship, we can see that more is needed to incorporate diverse groups into a political community than recognizing their rights to citizenship.

A considerable literature has developed on how much "shared identity" is needed for political society. "Liberal nationalists" hold that a shared national identity is necessary for the viability of a state and the realization of liberal values.[2] This raises questions about how much assimilation is to be required or encouraged when the practices of a cultural minority conflict with those of the dominant group and how much multiculturalism can be permitted or celebrated. Some argue that the shared identity of a state need not be a national or ethnic one but that "a sense of belonging to their polity" may be sufficient.[3]

There has recently been an explosion of interest in the neglected concept of civil society and in how it should be understood. In his book *Civil Society*, John Keane describes how "for nearly a century and a half, the language of civil society virtually disappeared from intellectual and political life."[4] Since the 1990s, however, "in the European region and elsewhere, the term 'civil society' has become so voguish in the human sciences and uttered so often through the lips of politicians, business leaders, academics, foundation executives, relief agencies and citizens" that it is now a cliché.[5] There is even talk of a global civil society. Although they also specify other preconditions for a successful transition to democracy, Juan Linz and Alfred Stepan see the existence of "a free and lively civil society" as necessary.[6]

The meaning of 'civil society' has evolved far beyond Hegel's focus on economic exchanges. In the period prior to Hegel, the term was generally applied to political association; with the rise of capitalism and the development of the modern state, Hegel recognized a sphere between the familial and the political: civil society. The term as used now is closer to the "civic culture" sustaining democracy that was discussed in the 1960s, although it may focus on institutions rather than attitudes. In their book on civic culture, Gabriel Almond and Sidney Verba wrote that "attitudes favorable to participation within the political system play a major role in the civic culture, but so do such nonpolitical attitudes as trust in other people and social participation in general."[7] Jean Cohen and Andrew Arato say that "civil society refers to the structures of socialization, association, and organized forms of communication of the lifeworld to the extent that these are institutionalized or are in the process of being institutionalized."[8]

Civil society is often now taken to include attitudes, practices, and relations characterizing the ways members of a society interact in other than formal legal-political ways. In one description, "It is a coming together of private individuals. . . . It involves all those relationships which go beyond the purely familial and yet are not of the state. Civil society is about our basic societal relationships and experiences."[9] John A. Hall has examined the historical development of civil society and concludes that it is "a complex balance of consensus and conflict, the valuation of as much difference as is compatible with the bare minimum of consensus necessary for settled existence."[10] Keane explains that as he interprets it, civil society is "an ideal-typical category (an *idealtyp* in the sense of Max Weber) that both describes and envisages a complex and dynamic ensemble of legally protected non-governmental institutions that tend to be non-violent, self-organizing, self-reflexive, and permanently in tension with each other and with the state institutions that 'frame', constrict and enable their activities."[11]

Societies need civic virtues, although the tradition that advocates civic virtues held in common may be quite different from the acceptance of pluralism that the current interest in civil society includes.[12] To many writers, civil society requires practices of tolerance and abilities to work together, but that different groups will have different fundamental values is accepted. The cultivation of the needed civic virtues, it is argued, "must take place in families, neighborhoods, churches, the workplace, and voluntary associations of various sorts—in what has come to be called 'civil society.' "[13] Civil society teaches civic virtues as individuals "come to see how their interests depend upon and connect with those of others and thus develop a sense of community."[14]

Concern with the term is not limited to academic debates. In his book critical of the current overreliance on markets, Robert Kuttner writes of "reclaiming civil society," meaning "the voluntary sector, which is neither state nor market."[15] Rejecting the conservative picture of the welfare state crowding out voluntary associations, he holds that "there is good evidence that an excess of market, not state, is killing civil society" as more and more of what should have other than economic value is turned into a marketable commodity.[16] Others, such as Keane, more influenced by recent developments in Eastern Europe, believe that economic activity should not be excluded from what is thought of as civil society. The development of small businesses and economic activity independent of state control where such control has been pervasive can contribute greatly to the revival or growth of the civil society that makes possible a transition to democracy.[17] Cohen and Arato, however, argue that only if civil society is seen as distinct from both state and economy will the concept have the potential for critical analysis that should be sought in societies where market economies are already developed.[18]

Empirical work such as that of Robert Putnam on what makes democracy work lends support to the view that people need to learn to work together politically.[19] For democratic institutions to function well, citizens need to have contact with one another in nongovernmental associations, as de Tocqueville's nineteenth-century reports suggested.[20] A wide variety of such associations will do: They can be sports groups, arts groups, as well as civic associations. But where and when participation in such activities of civil society is high, democratic institutions seem to function well, and where and when it is low—as it is where traditions of leaving decisions to the aristocracy or the church or the mafia are strong, and as it is becoming in the United States where television watching replaces bowling or attending town meetings—democratic institutions seem endangered.[21] The writings of John Dewey on how democracy is a characteristic of much more than the political are gaining renewed appreciation.[22]

In a more normative and less empirical approach, there has been much discussion of the civic virtues that are needed for democracy to flourish and for rights to be honored.[23] Many writers have considered the kinds of education the state may or should require to foster such virtues: Can the government impose education in toleration and civic responsibility on its children even when a religious or cultural group wishes to educate its children as it sees fit in ways that exclude such civic tolerance?[24] Must civic virtue be taught for rights to have a chance of protecting us?

Those defending rational foundations for justice and rights and those building on liberal and social contract traditions in political philosophy often point out that rights and principles of justice are seen as appropriate for relations between strangers. In response to critics who cite the inappropriateness of rational choice theory or social contract theory for handling well the moral considerations that may be foremost in friendship and among family members, rational choice theorists and contractualists assert that they do not intend their arguments to apply to the contexts of family and friends but to the public, political realm, the context of relations between those not tied by sentiment or special relationship, the context of strangers. But it has been apparent to many of us that the political individuals of rational choice and contractualist theory are not really strangers: They already have sufficient connectedness to be part of the same society or group or nation. The problems of the appropriate boundaries within which rational persons can seek to agree on principles of justice, for instance, have merely been put aside, not solved or even addressed, in the major theories of rights and justice. The bloody and seemingly intractable ethnic conflicts and demands for secession and self-determination of the last decade of the twentieth century have brought to the fore the seriousness of these problems: Before hypothetical citizens can agree on the hypothetical terms of their self-government, they must agree on whom they seek agreement with. Thus, before rights can be specified, respected, and upheld, persons must agree on who the members of the group are within which they are to be specified and respected and upheld. In other words, they must see those others as belonging to the group of "us," as "we" seek agreement on our rights; all involved are thus actual or potential fellow citizens, not strangers. All must feel sufficiently connected to seek agreement among themselves and to be willing to respect each others' rights. In his analysis of transitions from authoritarian states to democratic ones and of the fragility of democracy in this process, Keane clarifies how "the democratic process *presupposes* the rightfulness of the political unit itself"; this cannot be decided on democratically. "Agreements about stateness," he argues, "are logically prior to the creation of democratic institutions."[25]

When boundary questions become problematic, we may become especially aware of such issues. We would do well to attend regularly to this prior realm of the preconditions for rights. When we do so we can conclude that for rights to be respected in any actual legal system or for principles of justice to be reflected in any actual constitution, there must be social relations of a fairly substantial kind connecting the members of the actual group of persons having this legal system and constitution. There is a presumption of civil society—of some degree of community and of civic virtue among citizens—within which rights are to be delineated and upheld.

The Ethics of Care

Along with the revived interest in civil society, there has been since the 1990s, as we have seen, a substantial development of the "care ethics" that originated in the 1980s. Care ethics emerged as the gender bias of such dominant moral theories as Kantian ethics and utilitarianism came under attack (see especially chapters 1 and 4). In contrast with the dominant views that give primacy to such values as autonomy, independence, noninterference, fairness, and rights, the ethics of care values the interdependence and caring relations that connect persons to one another. The ways many of the concerns of those interested in civil society are parallel to those of the ethics of care are apparent. Rather than rejecting the emotions as threats to the rationality and impartiality seen as the foundations of morality, the ethics of care attends to and values such moral emotions as empathy and shared concern. Rather than seeing morality as a struggle between individual self-interest and impartial universal principles, care ethics focuses on the region between the individual self and the universal "all rational beings." It seeks to evaluate the relations that connect actual persons and to deal with the moral issues involved, such as when trust is appropriate and when it is misplaced, and what is called for by mutual consideration. Here the issues are often not about one individual's interest versus another's but about the well-being of the relation between them where this depends on both together. In the ethics of care, the experiences of parents and children in their caretaking activities and of friends are thought to be highly relevant.[26]

Whereas the earlier forms of the ethics of care looked especially at relations between persons within the family and among friends, the later developments make very clear that care ethics is not to be limited to the domain of the "personal." Feminists have of course raised fundamental questions about the separation of public and private, pointing out how it has left men free to dominate, even violently, women and children within the patriarchal household. Some feminists emphasize that principles of justice and equality should be extended from the public sphere to the family.[27] Others emphasize that the caring relations most clearly understood and, thanks to an ethics of care, valued in the contexts of family and friendship should be extended into society's social and political structures. These relations will not be exemplified in the same kind of deeply involved caring activities as when a parent cares for a child, but caring social relations even in the political and legal domain will share some of the features of caring relations in the family or among friends: Persons will be valued for their own sakes as distinct, particular persons rather than as instances of abstract rational beings; relations of caring between persons will be morally evaluated and where appropriate cultivated as valuable; and close attention and responsiveness to persons' needs will be part of the caring relations being cultivated.

Many of those developing the ethics of care have shown its relevance for social life. Joan Tronto made clear why care ethics should not be thought to be confined to the personal; she argued that "the need to rethink appropriate [rather than exploitative] forms for caring raises the broadest questions about the shape of social and political institutions in our society."[28] Care, she notes, "is found in the household, in services and goods sold in the market, and in the workings of bureaucratic organizations in contemporary life."[29] Using care as a political concept "would change our sense of political goals and provide us with additional ways to think politically and strategically."[30] To aim to assure "that all people are adequately cared for is not a utopian question, but one which immediately suggests answers about employment policies, nondiscrimination, equalizing expenditures for schools, providing adequate access to health care, and so forth."[31] In my book *Feminist Morality* I discussed the implications of the ethics of care for the restructuring of social and political institutions, and this volume continues that project.

For instance, as the previous chapter argues, a society that cultivates caring relations between its members might limit rather than expand the kinds of activities, from health care to child care to cultural production, that it leaves to be determined by the market, where individual self-interest prevails.[32] And a society with well-functioning governmental practices to care for its members' needs would be able to expend far fewer of its resources and attention on legal remedies for illegal actions. In a caring society, for example, the realm of law would shrink, as will be argued in the next chapter. Noncommercial cultural production and public decision through moral discourse would grow. In the last chapter of this book, the ethics of care will be extended to the level of relations between nations, showing how this form of ethical theory has definite implications for global concerns.[33]

The Ethics of Care and Civil Society

There is wide agreement among those writing today on the ethics of care that care ethics should not be limited to the personal, but a connection has not yet been drawn between the ethics of care and civil society. I draw such a connection here. Most of the leading writers on communitarianism, citizenship, and civil society have said little or nothing about either feminism or that major strand of feminist ethics that is the ethics of care.[34] The ethics of care, however, is more suitable than traditional moral theories for dealing with many of the concerns of civil society.

Discussions of community, citizenship, and civil society focus on a domain that is neither the personal one of the family nor the neutral, impersonal one of liberal government. In civic associations, members develop enough empathetic feeling for one another to engage in common projects: to save a historical building, to send a soccer team to play in another county, to clean up a park. In a community, citizens develop such virtues as a willingness to listen attentively to others and to engage in respectful discussion of persons' needs and interests. These feelings and virtues also characterize caring relations in the contexts of family and friendship, though in stronger forms. In both cases, though to a different degree, what are most important are often the mutual relationships developed or maintained, not the outcomes for the separate individuals as assessed on a utilitarian calculation and not the strict following of deontological rules as might be the case in a legal context. The members of a civic association often think as much about maintaining the association and the connectedness it involves as about the individual gains or losses to them resulting from their membership. Communities are more than just instrumental mechanisms for the satisfaction of individual preferences. Although this is perhaps also true of the state, it is through fostering social trust and sentiments of solidarity, factors hardly visible in the liberal, rational choice, contractual firmament, that actual states can probably best maintain themselves. Actual states seem to be much less like what rational choice theorists or contractualists could provide than these theorists admit.

In both families and among friends, and in civic associations and political entities, there is a presumption of social relations holding the individual persons together. And in forming and maintaining these relations, empathetic feeling and a sense that what happens to the others in the group matters play important roles. Of course the feelings of affection and attachment and special relatedness are very much stronger in the case of families and among friends than in many social entities. However, caring relations between citizens can probably not be totally absent for any state not in danger of disintegration. Societies require that the grounds for social trust be adequately solid.[35] The rights a legal system can protect, then, presuppose the social interrelatedness of its members. These relations need to be evaluated.

Certainly some associations, like some families, promote the wrong values: racial discrimination, class oppression, gender domination. The ethics of care can evaluate wrongful as well as morally admirable aspects of relations and does not deprive us in any case of other moral grounds on which to judge associations and families.

Gradually, we can hope, feelings of solidarity will be extended to all persons everywhere, sufficiently to see their rights respected and their needs addressed. But it may be the value of care as much as the value of justice that can help this happen. Unless the presumption of care is met, people seem not to be concerned enough about others to care whether their rights are respected or even recognized. The history of disregard for and of domination and exploitation of those not strong enough to threaten the self-interest of rational contractors indicates how unpromising it may be to hope for respect for human rights to encompass the globe without building the caring relations such respect seems to presume.

Just as an effective legal system and well-functioning democratic institutions seem to rest on the social connectedness that civil society can provide, it can be argued that respect for human rights and for principles of justice presume some degree of caring relations between persons. We can see in the family and among friends the deepest and most compelling forms of care. But we can also see the relevance of the values of care and caring activities for the most comprehensive and global of moral concerns.

Keane observes that most discussions of civil society "seem uninterested in normative-philosophical questions."[36] He tries to reduce this "normative vulnerability," citing Hegel and Durkheim. He argues for "a post-foundationalist normative justification," and against the relativism that associates civil society only with "the West."[37] He thinks there must be a commitment to the institutional arrangements that protect an open, pluralistic civil society, but he is hard pressed to provide the moral arguments for it.

Much more promising than traditional moral theories for dealing with the issues of civil society would be the ethics of care. Unlike dubious claims that there will be a "natural" or rationally necessary global convergence on something like Western liberal contractualism, the ethics of care *is* based on universal experience: the experience of being cared for. It makes clear that persons need care or societies will not survive. It fosters appreciation for the ties of caring and demands that meeting the needs of the vulnerable be seen as valuable. It shows why violent conflict that damages persons and destroys practices of care must be rejected. It does not require cultural similarity, and care across cultural divides may succeed better than mere liberal toleration. As will be argued in the following chapter, the ethics of care is quite capable of responding to threats of violence and of evaluating violent conflict. It does not assume peace and harmony, though it knows their value.

The Priority of Care

I now turn to the question of how a precondition may be presumed and then to the question of how it may have normative priority. I focus first on the family to examine these issues.

Care as an actual, empirically observable activity is a precondition for anything else of value in a family. Without many years of at least a minimum of this kind of care, no child will survive. The caring activities of bringing up children and the moral values involved have long gone unnoticed by moral theorists. Such care has been dismissed as a "natural," biological process governed by maternal instinct and of no moral significance, or it has been seen, like tribalism, as motivated by emotions that are a threat to impartial, universal moral norms, as parents incline toward favoring their own children. The *values* of the caring activities of mothers and of all those who care for the young, the sick, and the old, have rarely (until recently in feminist ethics) been a topic for moral philosophy. But when we pay attention to these activities and the moral values they incorporate and exemplify, we see a new and important range of moral considerations. We see the enormity of what is presumed by dominant moral theories.

Care ethics, I have argued, is not merely a form of virtue theory (see chapter 3). The patriarchal assumptions built into the construction of the Man of Reason have had an analogue in the construction of the Man of Virtue. Virtue theory has focused on the individual and his dispositions. Care ethics, in contrast, focuses on relations between persons, on such relations as trust, mutual responsiveness, and shared consideration. It employs a concept of the person as relational and historically situated. But what of the priority of care? Should it be accorded a kind of priority over justice and rights? If so, should this priority be limited to contexts of friends and family, or can it be generalized to all moral contexts?

Empirically, in the context of the family, care has priority in the sense that without care, there will be no human beings. Infants will not survive, and, unless they receive much more than a minimum of food and shelter, children will not develop at all well, even if they survive. To grow into adequately healthy persons, children need to be valued for their own sakes, to experience relations in which large amounts of loving attention are shared between caretakers and children. They need to be cared for responsibly as they develop the social relations into which they are born. Adults need to be engaged in daily activities of caring for themselves and others to continue to exist or to live decently. But such a precondition for other activity, it might be said, need have no special moral primacy. Even if distributive justice presumes a condition of moderate scarcity, we need not find moderate scarcity morally superior to abundance. It might be thought that care, like the moderate scarcity that exists most of the time, is simply a fact of human existence. Whether it has moral primacy or even moral value remain to be argued.

How might we assess the moral priority (or not) of care in the context of the family? It has been suggested by theorists of justice that universal norms of impartiality always have priority, but that such norms can permit us in the case of family and friends to favor or care especially for the family members we love and the friends we choose (see chapter 6). This position evades the issue, since the question may be whether it can be morally defensible to care especially for our children and friends when the norms of universal, impartial morality are not silent but recommend otherwise. In such cases, do we question the kind of morality that makes these recommendations, or do we question our relations of care and what *they* seem morally to require (see chapters 5 and 6)?

When the ethics of care was first developed, it was often thought of as an ethic suitable for the family but not for the domain of political life where justice and rights should prevail. I have reviewed reasons to reject the view that care ethics lacks political implications. It has also been seen, even by those most interested in the ethics of care, that justice must not be confined to the political: It is also needed in the family and among friends, to overcome, for instance, the ways women are treated unequally in the household. When the realm of the "private" is off-bounds to justice and rights, women suffer a disproportionate diminishment of their rights.[38] Traditional arrangements about such personal matters as sex, marriage, reproduction, and household responsibilities seriously undermine the possibilities for girls and women to enjoy equal opportunities. But if justice should be extended into the household, should it then have priority, as when, for instance, legal requirements for an equal right to choose whom to marry are enforced on resisting families?

It makes good sense, I think, to see care as primary in the family. What matters most are the caring relations that sustain the family as a provider of care without which infants do not survive or children grow. Care seems the most basic moral value, as basic as the value of life. There can be no human life or families without the actual practice of care, but we need to recognize the *value* of such care to properly understand this most basic practice. There can be care without justice, but there can be no justice without the care that has value.

Within the caring relations of the family, questions of justice and rights should be pursued. Girls should be encouraged to seek equal treatment, and education and other social influences should lead families to provide girls with as much nourishment, education, and freedom as boys. But to the extent possible, the striving for equal rights should occur in ways that do not sunder family relations. Of course it is not always possible for a family member to assert his or her rights while remaining within the relations that form a set of persons into a family. If a father threatens to disown and permanently sever his ties to a daughter who refuses to marry the man he has chosen to be her husband, she may justifiably see her right to choose her husband as more morally compelling than her tie to her father. If a child is a victim of severe violence in his home, it will be morally better that he lose his ties to his family than that he lose his life. And so on. But these cases of what seem to be the priority of justice are as much failures to care as failures to respect justice. The threat of the father and the injuries of the child make this evident. Where a parent does care well for a child but fails to recognize the child's rights (to the extent that these can be separated, which is also questionable), the child morally ought to try to resolve the conflict through discussion and compromise within the network of family relations rather than breaking the relation with the parent altogether.

Concerns with rights and justice and fairness properly arise within caring relations. The suggestion that care has priority has sometimes been taken to have such unfortunate implications as that a wife with a violent and abusive husband should strive to maintain the relation even at the risk of her own safety. But this conclusion should not be drawn. To maintain a relation in conditions like these should be seen as a failure to properly care for oneself and for one's children if there are any. Given what is known about the likely progression of violence toward women who accept abuse, such acceptance should not be seen as the recommendation to be drawn from giving priority to caring relations. Caring for oneself in an existing or potential relation is part of what concerns those advocating an ethic of care for relational persons. So is the evaluation of relations *as* caring—or as abusive, damaging, and morally deleterious. Any priority given to caring relations presumes they are relations characterized by such values as trust and mutual consideration and that they are, indeed, caring relations. As care ethicists have made clear, care ethics does not advocate the actual family relations of patriarchal societies but the morally valuable aspects of human relationships of which we can sometimes get a glimpse when we pay attention to the relationships we experience.

The ethics of care works with a conception of the person as relational. It does not suggest that we are composed entirely of the relations we are in and virtually stuck with them. No feminist ethic could fail to recommend many changes in the relations in which many women find themselves. But the goal for persons in an ethic of care is not the isolated, autonomous, rational individual of the dominant, traditional moral theory. It is the person who, with other persons, maintains some and remakes other and creates still other morally admirable relations (see chapter 3). Such persons can and should evaluate and shape these changing relations autonomously, while recognizing that they are part of what we are. This conception of the person is compatible with the priority of care.

The Caring Society

Clearly, a case can be made that the value of caring relations has priority over rights and justice within the family, though not all feminists will agree with this position. Much more controversial will be the claim that care has priority over justice and rights at the social and political level, but I would like to argue in favor of it.

We have seen that a precondition for respecting rights and implementing justice seems to be enough social connectedness between people for them to be willing to agree on a scheme of rights and justice. The members of the society must care enough about one another and trust each other sufficiently to recognize them as also members of the same society. For a working legal system to protect their rights, citizens must acknowledge others as also citizens of the same system. But is this an empirical precondition only, a merely factual requirement, or does it have an analogue in a normative priority? I am starting to think that it does. Care and its related concerns of trust and mutual consideration seem to me to form and to uphold the wider network of relations within which issues of rights and justice, utility, and the virtues should be raised. This should not be taken to imply that all values and moral principles, or all practices they recommend, can be reduced to forms of care. Aiming at such reduction seems a mistaken goal (see chapter 4).

Not all relations are caring relations: Some are relations of mutual hatred or disdain or of violent antagonism. But the relations within which we can best raise other moral issues are caring ones. Within caring relations of family and friendship, we should make room for treating others equally and for respecting their rights, and the limited pursuit of self-interest should be permitted within these relations. And within the extended and thinner caring relations that make a group a society (which should gradually be extended to all members of a global society) we should make room for the agreements of rational contractors and for the legal and political arrangements that will uphold our rights, bring us justice, and increase our individual well-being. At both the level of the personal and the level of the social and political, we cannot dispense with the network of caring relations, and its values have priority. But within this network, considerations of care will not deal well with all issues, as reductionism would suggest they should. When an issue is one of rights and justice, we can appeal to the relevant principles, recognizing that although the background of care has priority (since otherwise the society will not cohere), it will not handle well the issue in question. At the same time we should remember that the morality of rights and justice is suitable only for a limited domain of concerns and not for the whole of morality as traditional moral theories have suggested. Dominant traditional theories have tended to generalize from understandings of legal rights and principles of justice to assertions of moral rights and moral principles of justice, supposing that these would provide a comprehensive morality covering all moral problems.

A caring society would attend to the health of the social relations between its members, rather than primarily promote the nearly boundless pursuit of individual self-interest restrained only by a few legal rulings forever straining to catch up with technological and other innovations making them perennially obsolete. The valid moral concerns of real families and of the associations of civil society would be of central rather than of merely peripheral importance.

In a caring society, attending to the needs of every child would be a major goal, and doing so would be seen to require social arrangements offering the kinds of economic and educational and child care and health care support that members of communities really need. Within the caring social relations that would characterize the kind of society the ethics of care would recommend, members should concern themselves with issues of rights and justice, utility and virtue. These are of great importance but should not be thought to occupy the whole or even the center of morality.

Within the caring relations of family and friendship there can certainly be room for competition and the pursuit of self-interest and for the assertion of rights to be treated with equal respect. But if the pursuit of self-interest and the assertion of individual rights dominate all their interactions, persons will not long be genuine friends or members of caring families, if the group of which they are members survives at all. Comparably, if those composing a society give priority to the pursuit of economic and political and cultural self-interest, and to the assertion of individual rights against others, over the whole of their interactions, the society will not long cohere. These pursuits need to occur within social relations of a sufficiently caring kind, and with enough recognition of the moral values of such relations, for the society to have a functioning political or legal or economic system.

The sufficiency of caring relations for political institutions may be quite minimal, however. In a caring society, in contrast, the caring relations would have a far greater influence, leading to arrangements that would reduce the pressures for political conflict and legal coercion. A caring society would limit the commodification of and the commercial competition over much that has value. It would cultivate practices that promote caring activities and considerate discourse throughout the society.

How will civil society fit in with what Keane calls "the growing mismatch between the scale of markets and the territorially bound state?"[39] Perhaps the organizations and associations of a global civil society guided by the ethics of care could provide the conditions for effective respect for human rights, including rights to a peaceful world.

Rights, I have argued, presume a background of social connectedness. The most appropriate basis for such connectedness or solidarity is the caring that has value. At the very least, human beings can and ought to care enough about other human beings to sustain the relations between them within which rights can be respected. Potentially they can strive to make their societies far more caring than they have been.

9

Power, Care, and the Reach of Law

Critics of the ethics of care sometimes associate it with rosy images of family warmth, and wonder how care ethics can possibly deal adequately with violence. They suppose that the ethics of care presumes peace and harmony while the reality of much human life is conflict and war. Feminists have called attention to the vast amount of violence that exists against women and children in intimate relations and in wartime rapes and expulsions. Many doubt that the ethics of care can appropriately address these issues. Claudia Card, for instance, praises the theorizing that grows out of taking seriously violence against women and that centers on resistance rather than on caretaking. She sees "women's care-taking of those who benefit from sex oppression" as "part of the problem that a feminist ethic needs to address."[1] She also thinks that "attending to the kinds of violence women have suffered historically is thus important for identifying limitations of care ethics."[2]

Although we can agree that versions of the ethics of care that do not pay attention to violence against women and violence between groups and states need to be improved, it is a misunderstanding of the ethics of care, I think, to interpret it as presuming anything like harmony and an absence of violence. It can perfectly well recognize the extent of violent conflict that exists in families, in societies, and between groups and states. As Sara Ruddick made clear in her original examinations of mothering and has expanded on since, conflict is part of the everyday experience of maternal life. The temptation to become violent toward children, and toward children who become violent, are part of the daily realities of maternal practice. But in their daily practice, mothers uphold standards of nonviolence even if they do not always succeed in meeting them.[3]

The ethics of care is not built on faulty images of peace. It can fully acknowledge that parents sometimes kill their children, mothers often strike them, friends can fall into lethal rivalries, and that human affairs are rife with war and violence. Even if we examine the ethics of care as developed in the primary contexts of families and friendship before it is developed for wider contexts, it is not unable to handle violent conflict. But the ethics of care upholds standards of care. It understands those who use violence, even in ways usually considered justifiable, as having morally failed to develop appropriate ways to avoid needing to do so. The ethics of care does not turn violent conflict into a Hobbesian assumption of normal relations between self-interested individuals in a state of nature. It highlights the ways parents can learn restraint, can channel their anger into effectively teaching a child appropriate behavior rather than letting the child erupt in violence. It emphasizes the way practices of care can overcome violence, rather than merely respond to it in kind.

What the ethics of care offers is an appreciation of the possibilities for nonviolence and of countering violence in appropriate ways. Those engaged in care develop ways to deal with conflict that are consistent with the goals of care: Instead of seeking to damage or destroy those who become violent, they seek to move toward peace. Practices of care may need to include the use of coercion to restrain a person who is or is threatening to become violent, but the objective is to do so without damaging the person physically or psychologically. Ruddick explains that in her account of mothering she is "not attributing success to mothers. Almost all mothers remember actions of theirs that were violent."[4] What she is clarifying is an ideal that governs in maternal thinking and that does have weight, as can be seen in the enormous amount of "resilient, nonviolent mothering" that occurs "under considerable provocation in difficult circumstances."[5]

At the level of groups and states, the ethics of care would promote the exploration of nonviolent alternatives to the use of military force.[6] Nonviolent opposition is not acceptance. The ethics of care is quite capable of recommending the use of force when absolutely necessary, either to resist a state's aggression, a violent individual's crimes, or a child's destructive rampage. What it does not lose sight of, however, are the goals and standards of care that are to be maintained and the responsibilities that are to be met to prevent violence before it occurs. The ethics of care at every level provides the appropriate suspicion rather than glorification of violence, and constant resistance to practices that incite or predictably fail to prevent unnecessary violence.

Within practices of care, as we have seen, rights should be recognized, including rights to peace and security of the person. Force may sometimes be needed to assure respect for such rights. This does not mean that the background of care can be forgotten.

Law and the Assurance of Rights

All feminists share a commitment to equal rights for women. This has led many to emphasize legal remedies for the subordination of women,[7] and to look to the law as the major source of progress for women. The ethics of care has then seemed to some to be misguided, because its approach has seemed to conflict with that of justice, rights, and law.

Early contributors to the ethics of care were indeed often critical of the language and conceptualizations of rights. Carol Gilligan, for instance, said that "a morality of rights and noninterference may appear frightening to women in its potential justification of indifference and unconcern."[8] Others emphasized the ways law and rights reflect the interests of men and not of women, and how the concept itself of a "right" seemed to conflict with the concerns of caring (see chapter 5).

There is general agreement that rights, whether moral or legal, attach to persons as individuals, although some theorists argue also for group rights. Many think rights call attention to individuals even more strongly than other concepts in traditional moral and legal theory. In Annette Baier's view, "the language of rights pushes us, more insistently than does the language of duties, responsibilities, obligations, legislation and respect for law, to see the participants in the moral practice as single clamorous living human beings, not as families, tribes, groups, classes, churches, congregations, nations, or peoples."[9] The contrast between the contexts examined by the ethics of care and all the major traditional frameworks of justice, with their concepts of rights, obligations, interests, rules, and principles, seems clear. Care ethics' emphasis on relations between persons rather than on distinct individuals and their possessions, thus seems in conflict with a morality of rights. The value placed by the ethics of care on attending to particular persons and actual contexts in all their diversity, rather than positing abstract rational beings in an ideal or hypothetical realm, casts further doubt on the worth of moralities of justice and rights. Whether rights are based on deontological or utilitarian rules, they may be ill-suited to dealing with actual relations between actual persons. Hence the ethics of care may seem antagonistic to an approach that makes law and rights central to progress.

It has been recognized that women and other oppressed groups have used the language of rights to redress their grievances and will probably need to do so for the foreseeable future. But those interested in the ethics of care urge us to pay attention to whole domains of human experience—bringing up children, caring for the dependent and vulnerable, the trust and civic connectedness that hold persons together—where moral issues are ubiquitous but have gone unrecognized and unexplored by the ethics of rights and rules. If we are open to the arguments, it is easy to see why the ethics of care would be suitable not only for the domains of personal relations but for political and social contexts as well. Rules specifying constraints on our actions leave unevaluated the moral issues surrounding caring well and being well cared for, of cultivating good relationships whatever the level, of living well with others who live well with us. The ethics of care addresses these issues.

The liberal traditions in which rights have been developed have presupposed a context of social trust, but they have done little to contribute to that trust. Perhaps they have even contributed to undermining it. Those defending the ethics of care understand the centrality of trust and human connectedness, and that when trust breaks down or fails to exist, there can be little respect for rights. But what, then, does the ethics of care imply for law and rights? Traditional thinking about law and rights has been framed almost entirely by an ethic of justice, when morality has been brought in to provide foundations for or evaluations of existing legal systems or outlines of better ones. There have always been some critics who have seen legal systems as little more than the outcomes or upholders of power, whether military, political, or economic, in whatever combination. But those who have sought some role for morality within or underlying law, or by which to make moral evaluations of law, have conceptualized that morality in terms of an ethic of justice, with universal rules that treat persons equally, that accord or recognize persons' rights, and that look to law and its enforcement to ensure the protection of rights and the fulfillment of obligations. What should the stance of the ethics of care be toward law and rights?

The criticism of rights from the perspective of the ethics of care, in my view, is a criticism of the conceptually imperialistic role that law has played in moral thinking. It is not directed at overthrowing rights in the domain of law but at keeping legal thinking where it belongs: in the domain of law. It opposes the view that imagines law and legal ways of thinking to be suitable for all moral problems.

Feminist Critiques of Legal Rights

Many feminist legal scholars have been critical of rights analyses. As Elizabeth Schneider has written, "legal scholars, in particular CLS [Critical Legal Studies] and feminist scholars have debated the meanings of rights claims and have questioned the significance of legal argumentation focused on rights."[10] Patricia Smith observes that "the rejection of patriarchy is the one point on which all feminists agree," and holds that "feminist jurisprudence is the analysis and critique of law as a patriarchal institution."[11] Feminist analyses have shown how law and its schemes of rights support patriarchy.

Even where the law appears to accord women equal rights, police, prosecutors, and judges often apply the law in ways that uphold patriarchal power. The state has traditionally done little to prevent violence against women and children in the "private" domain in which a male citizen has been the "head" of a household and effectively its ruler. When violent actions that would have been prohibited among strangers have occurred within the family, the law has been reluctant to intervene, thus reinforcing male supremacy in the family.[12] The judicial system has been more concerned with protecting white men from unjust accusations than with protecting women, especially women of color, from the real harm of rape.[13]

Not only does the law in fact support the subordination of women, but in the view of various feminist legal scholars, so does the whole of modern legal theory, whether liberal or not. Robin West, for instance, sees it as "essentially and irretrievably masculine" in its acceptance of the thesis "that we are individuals 'first,' and . . . that what separates us is epistemologically and morally prior to what connects us."[14]

Some feminists see rights as inherently abstract and reflective of a male point of view. Some think the use of rights discourse requires a social movement to adapt its goals unduly to what an existing legal system will permit, fostering conflict within the movement and diverting its strengths.[15] And feminists allied with Critical Legal Studies and postmodern approaches, subjecting rights claims to critical analysis, have deeply questioned the utility of legal argumentation focused on rights. Seeing law as an expression of power rather than of morality or reasoned argument, they are skeptical of all claims, including any about rights, to truth or objectivity.

Such fundamental critiques do not, however, constitute a rejection of rights and law by most feminists, including those advocating the ethics of care. Rather, they can be interpreted as (1) demands for reformulations of existing schemes of rights, (2) calls to reconstruct the concept of rights, and (3) moral recommendations for limiting the reach of law to its appropriate domain and placing that domain in its appropriate context.

Feminist Reformulations of Rights

Feminist jurisprudence has contributed many detailed analyses of what equal rights for women would require.[16] It is examining when differences between men and women, and differences between some women and others, need to be taken into account. It is questioning the practice of taking male characteristics as the norm according to which women's characteristics, such as the capacity to become pregnant, are seen as different and hence present a problem. "Why," Patricia Smith asks, "should equal protection of the law depend on being relevantly similar to men?"[17] Men, it is noted, are as different from women as women are from men.

Christine Littleton argues that what should often be required by the equal protection clause of the U.S. Constitution is not sameness of treatment but equality of disadvantage brought about by the treatment. Thus, if a pension scheme that excludes part-time workers and appears to be gender-neutral actually affects women much more adversely than men, it is discriminatory. Littleton's argument is that difference should not lead to disadvantage but should instead be costless.[18] A similar argument can be used with respect to racial disadvantages. Achieving equality may well require positive action, including governmental action, rather than merely ignoring differences. Arguments for pregnancy leave, child care provision, and affirmative action programs all combine a recognition of equality and difference and deny that we must choose between them. The ethics of care makes clear how activities of care must be kept in mind in thinking about rights and equality.

Legal rights often help bring about aspects of the social change needed. The area of sexual harassment shows well the potential of legal rights to improve the lives of women. The injuries that women had long experienced were turned by feminist jurisprudence into a form of discrimination from which legal protection could be sought. Catharine MacKinnon writes that the law against sexual harassment is a test of the "possibilities for social change for women through law."[19] Women subject to harmful and demeaning sexual pressure in the workplace gained a means to seek relief they had not previously had.

There are many examples of the uses of rights to reduce the subordination of women, but there are often drawbacks in these uses. Acknowledging differences between women and men, for instance, in protecting girls through statutory rape laws, has advantages and disadvantages. Frances Olsen has examined how statutory rape laws "both protect and undermine women's rights, and rights arguments can be used to support, attack, or urge changes in the laws."[20] Although such laws do provide young women some protection against coerced sex, they violate the privacy and sexual freedom of young women compared to young men, and they perpetuate sexist stereotypes. Olsen writes that "any acknowledgment of the actual difference between the present situation of males and females stigmatizes females and perpetuates discrimination. But if we ignore power differences and pretend that women and men are similarly situated, we perpetuate discrimination by disempowering ourselves from instituting effective change."[21]

Yet reforms can and do take place and do change people's lives, and some of the proposed changes can be seen as better than others. The perspective of the ethics of care helps distinguish them. Some recommended changes in statutory rape laws considered by Olsen include allowing underage women to control the decision of whether to prosecute and taking the young woman's characterization of the sexual encounter as voluntary or coerced as determinative. Although the major efforts must be beyond the law—empowering women generally and transforming sexuality from sexualized violence and domination to eroticized mutuality—changes law can bring about can be significant.

Feminists have been demanding reform in many aspects of law. In the area of rape law, for instance, they ask why women should be expected "to fight like men" to demonstrate nonconsent in potentially life-threatening circumstances where their attackers are often far stronger than they are. Feminist jurisprudence has clarified how statutes and the courts use standards about rape, consent, force, resistance, and reasonable belief that fail to take account of the perspectives of women. The law's standard "reasonable person" is one who fights back, although many women typically do not respond to threatening situations by fighting. As Susan Estrich put it, "the reasonable woman, it seems, is not a schoolboy 'sissy.' She is a real man."[22] The need to change such standards is obvious.

The backlash against affirmative action has made it more difficult politically to argue for positive efforts to overcome gender and racial disadvantages. But there is a strong determination on the part of feminists, including advocates of the ethics of care, to maintain the rights achieved. Of utmost importance to women are reproductive rights. It is generally agreed that reproductive rights are a precondition for most other rights for women, yet they are continually threatened. Because the ability to bear children is such an important capacity that women have and men lack, and because throughout history it has been under the control of men, the unwillingness of many to accord reproductive rights to women seems especially deep. No matter how they criticize the inadequacies of the language of rights for addressing the full range of moral concerns, advocates of the ethics of care share a determination to advance and protect women's rights to control their own sexuality and reproductive capacities and to avoid the commodification of women as sexual or reproductive objects.[23]

There are many ways in which law itself could be more receptive to care-based values, for instance, in dealing with the harms of hate speech or devising more satisfactory ways than those previously available for handling the sexual abuse of children.[24] Selma Sevenhuijsen shows how inadequate legal approaches are in dealing with conflicts over the custody of children and how much better would be arguments informed by the ethics of care.[25] Family law, she says, "provides a perfect illustration of the limitations and pitfalls of equal rights reasoning."[26] Legal discourse often leads to a one-sided "juridification of daily life," and "the illusion that issues of parenting can be decided in a power-free space."[27] It "closes itself off" from arguments having to do with care, affectivity, and relationship, finding no moral space for notions of connectedness to others. "The ethics of care," she concludes, "is a condition for a viable and creative politics in which the interests of women and children are not submerged under a universalistic ethics of equal rights and in which the masculine legal subject does not, implicitly or explicitly, continue to serve as the privileged point of reference."[28]

Advocates of the ethics of care, however, wish to contain and reform law, not dispense with it. Various strong voices have also reminded feminists of the centrality of rights arguments to movements for social justice. As the experience of many women and minority members affirms, persons suffering domination on grounds of race, gender, or sexual orientation usefully think in terms of rights to counter the disrespect they encounter.[29] Taking issue with the Critical Legal Studies critique of rights, Patricia Williams has argued that the rhetoric of rights has been an effective form of discourse for blacks.[30] Subordinate groups can describe their needs at length, but doing so has often not been politically effective, as it has not been for African Americans. Williams asserts that what must be found is "a political mechanism that can confront the denial of need," and rights have the capacity to do this.[31] Uma Narayan also warns against a weakening of feminist commitments to rights. She describes the colonialist project of denying rights to the colonized on grounds of a paternalistic concern for their welfare. Resisting this, the use of rights discourse by the colonized to assert their own claims contributed significantly to their emancipation. Then in turn, asserting their rights was important for women in opposing the traditional patriarchal views often prevalent among the previously colonized.[32]

It is widely understood among feminist critics of rights that rights are not timeless or fixed but contested and developing. Rights reflect social reality and have the capacity to decrease actual oppression. Achieving respect for basic rights is often a goal around which political struggles can be organized, and many of the most substantial gains made by disadvantaged groups are based on a striving for justice and equal rights. Advocates of the ethics of care do not suggest that these gains and goals be abandoned. On the other hand, rights arguments may not serve well for the full range of moral and political concerns that feminists have, and the legal framework of rights and justice should not be the central discourse of morality and politics. Rights are one concern among others, not the key to overcoming the subordination of women and building better societies. From the perspective of care, the person seen as a holder of individual rights in the tradition of liberal political theory is an artificial and misleading abstraction. Accepting this abstraction for some legal and political purposes may be useful.[33] But we should not suppose that it is adequate for morality or even political theory in general.

Reconceptualizations of the Concept of Rights

Some feminist legal theorists have argued that rights need to be fundamentally reconceptualized. Related to the previous argument about the utility of rights for social movements is an argument that rights need to be reconceptualized as nonideal. Instead of thinking of rights as belonging to a consistent scheme of rights and liberties worked out for an ideal world of perfect justice, we should think of rights as reflecting social reality and as capable of decreasing actual oppression and injustice.[34]

Martha Minow criticizes rights rhetoric for ignoring relationships and argues that we should never lose sight of the social relations of power and privilege within which individual rights are constructed. She advocates a conception of "rights in relationships" that can be used against oppressive forms of both public and private power. We need, she writes, "a shift in the paradigm we use to conceive of difference, a shift from a focus on the distinctions between people to a focus on the relationships within which we notice and draw distinctions."[35] In the family, for instance, rights rhetoric has "assigned the burdens of difference to women and children,"[36] but merely extending existing rights from the male head to others in the family "fails to acknowledge the special situations and needs of women and children—and neglects the significance of relationships within the family."[37] She wants, however, to "rescue" rights, not abandon them, seeing that "there is something too valuable in the aspiration of rights, and something too neglectful of the power embedded in assertions of another's need, to abandon the rhetoric of rights."[38]

Also needed are reconceptualizations of the ways rights are formulated with respect to given categories. Kimberle Crenshaw has analyzed the way antidiscrimination law proceeds by identifying a category such as race or sex on the basis of which wrongful discrimination has occurred and then seeking remedies. She shows how this overlooks what she calls the "intersectionality" of categories. Black women, for instance, have been marginalized not only by the courts but also in feminist theory and antiracist politics because their experience of race and sex intersects, and they are covered by neither the paradigms of sex discrimination against white women nor of race discrimination against black men.[39] Such distortions need to be corrected, and they occur for many categories.

Limiting the Reach of Law

At the level of moral theory, as we have seen, there has been an appreciation of rights and justice along with the development of the ethics of care.

Moralities of justice can well be interpreted as generalizations to the whole of morality of ways of thinking developed in the contexts of law and public policy. Advocates of the ethics of care do resist such expansion of legalistic approaches, seeing them as unsatisfactory for many contexts. But this does not imply that justice and moral rights are dispensable. Although it may be argued, as I have suggested, that the context of care is the wider one within which justice must be developed, it can be acknowledged that justice is essential for any adequate morality.

It can be understood that more than the ethics of care as first developed is needed to evaluate oppressive social arrangements and to deal with various types of problems.[40] Alison Jaggar has argued that the weakness of care thinking "is that its attention to situations' specificity and particularity diverts attention away from their general features such as the social institutions and groupings that give them their structure and much of their meaning."[41] Marilyn Friedman has shown why she thinks that "traditional concepts of justice and rights may fare better than care ethics in handling problems of violence."[42] Others have argued that justice must be extended to the family,[43] and reconceptualized for families,[44] but certainly maintained.

As conceptions of how justice and care ought to be integrated become more developed, there may be possibilities for agreement on the priorities that ought to govern in different domains. I have argued for the overall priority of care, but for the priority of justice in the legal domain. In her book *Autonomy, Gender, Politics*,[45] Marilyn Friedman suggests a version of such prioritizing of different values for different domains that is quite compatible with what I have argued.[46] She argues that in dealing with battered women who "choose" to stay with the partners who abuse them, the liberal state should through its legal system treat domestic violence, like other violence, as a crime against society. Although it might seem to further victimize the victim, the legal system should prosecute batterers whether or not their victims press charges, because this has been shown to decrease overall levels of violence against women. The law should require victims to testify, even against their will, for the same reasons. In its social services, however, it should be guided by different values, Friedman argues. Professional caregivers should aim to help the actual victim of domestic violence, should presume she knows what she wants better than they do, and should accept her interpretation of the situation without attempting to override her decisions.

Much of the criticism of rights from the perspective of the ethics of care can perhaps best be seen as resistance to the idea that the approaches and concepts of law and rights should be expanded to cover the whole of morality and political thinking. It is not directed at overthrowing rights in the domain of law but at limiting legalistic interpretations to the domain of law rather than supposing them to be suitable for all other moral problems as well. Once we think of the framework of law and rights as one to be limited to a somewhat narrow range of human concerns rather than as the appropriate one within which to interpret all moral and political problems, other moral approaches can become salient, and social and political organization can be based on other goals and concerns as well as on those of rights.

Furthermore, there is an understanding that the relational self conceptualized by advocates of the ethics of care in place of the abstract individual of traditional theories of justice must still allow the person enmeshed in relationships to change her situation: to break free of patriarchal communities and to alter oppressive social ties. Appeals to autonomy and rights need to be reformulated but not ignored (see chapter 3).

Some of these issues may be illustrated in current efforts to implement human rights at the international level. These efforts may benefit women in concrete ways by demanding an end to such human rights violations as denying women the vote or forcing women to marry against their will. But the dominant discourse of human rights may also draw attention away from pressing issues not best formulable in terms of human rights, such as the needs of women for more status and consideration within their families and communities, for cooperative economic development in common with other women, or for more empowering images in the media productions that shape their society's attitudes.[47]

Choices need constantly to be made about whether to interpret various issues as primarily matters of justice and rights or primarily matters to be approached from the perspective of care. Care advocates may believe that persons are not actually the individualistic, self-contained abstract entities that the law and traditional moral theories imagine them to be, and that they should not be thought to be such entities any more than is necessary for limited, legal purposes. If more satisfactory conceptions of persons and human relationships and morality are adopted, as they urge, then interpretations other than those of justice and rights often seem more appropriate. Greater attention may come to be paid, for instance, to social arrangements for the care and education of children and to the ways in which culture shapes society and can bring about social change. This does not imply that rights will be unimportant, but it may move them from the center of attention. The ethics of care may in time bring about a shift such that the legal system itself will be a far less central form of social organization and influence than in the past, as other ways of influencing attitudes and actions and practices play larger roles.

The Ethics of Care and Privacy

Fundamental to feminist theorizing have been questions about what is political and how the distinction between the public and political on the one hand, and the private and personal on the other, should be drawn.[48] There has been some concern that as the ethics of care and other feminist rethinking blurs the boundaries between the public and the private, privacy might be threatened.

An early slogan of the women's movement that began in the United States in the late 1960s was "the personal is political." It accompanied the insight that the greater power of men—politically, economically, and socially—affected the ways women suffered domination in what had been imagined to be the personal and private and nonpolitical domain of the household and the ways that this effect of men's power on women's personal lives in turn limited women's capacities and undermined their development in the workplace and in the public domain.

Feminists have been reexamining and rethinking the public/private distinction ever since. There is widespread agreement that the traditional conception is unsatisfactory. At the very least, women and children need public protection from violence. Traditional views that the home is a man's castle into which the law should not intrude, and that a man will be the protector of "his" family, have left women and children vulnerable both in the home and outside it. Women have been criticized for appearing in public, especially after dark, without adequate male "protection," thus restricting their activities. In many parts of the world, women are still subject to domestic and other violence on a massive scale because the public realm of law fails to protect them.

On the other hand, law often interferes with women's private decisions concerning reproduction and with the private sexual behavior of both women and men, and law orders marriage and the family in all sorts of ways.[49] Rethinking is needed to achieve greater consistency, fairness, and care in how law protects privacy, and families and their members. And much more than law is needed to promote gender equality generally.

The ethics of care goes further than feminist liberalism in questioning the boundaries between household and political spheres, arguing as it does that the values and practices of care most discernible in personal relations have fundamental implications for social life and political organization.

However, feminists generally and advocates of the ethics of care seek reconceptualizations of privacy, not, as sometimes charged, the abolition of the private.[50] Women have traditionally had very little privacy, even at home. Women do not want to sacrifice the ideals of affiliation and caring to self-centered demands to be left alone, but the subordinate and caretaking roles imposed on them have largely deprived them of the experience of privacy. To be confined to the "private sphere" is not to enjoy privacy; the many women now in the labor force are still unfairly burdened by household responsibilities that deny them equal opportunities to take advantage of privacy.[51]

A number of feminist theorists who can be characterized as radical feminists believe that sexuality and the way it is socially constructed is the deepest cause of women's secondary status. Male sexuality, on this view, has been developed in such a way that the domination of women is inherent to it, and violence, often against women, has been sexualized. To many radical feminists, the pornography that feeds this construction and the violence against women that indicates it are strong contributors to male domination and female disempowerment. Accordingly, the sexuality that is often thought of as most private is seen as actually the most important factor in the gender structure that pervades all societies and gives men the power to dominate women in most areas of life, public as well as private. As Catherine MacKinnon puts it, "Women and men are divided by gender, made into the sexes as we know them, by the requirements of its dominant form, heterosexuality, which institutionalizes male sexual dominance and female sexual submission. If this is true, sexuality is the linchpin of gender inequality."[52] Others, however, doubt that any one factor is vastly more important than many others.

Many feminists do far more than criticize the way the traditional lines between public and private have been drawn. This is connected with the feminist revaluation of the moral values of the personal realm and the rethinking of moral theory involved. Then, with a transformed view of moral theory and of persons, values, and social relations, the view of "the political" is transformed. It will surely make room for new and more adequate supports for reconceptualized realizations of personal privacy.

Postmodernism and the Ethics of Care

Feminist theorists of many kinds,[53] including some developing the ethics of care,[54] have been influenced by postmodernism. Critiques by such writers as Foucault, Derrida, Richard Rorty, and Lyotard of Enlightenment claims to rational and universal truths have helped many feminists dismantle gendered concepts and assumptions taken as certainties. In place of biased claims to universal and timeless rational understanding, postmodernism and many feminists offer social criticism, from many different cultural and racial perspectives, that is fractured, contextual, pluralistic, and ad hoc. Glimpses, images, and collages of observations are often thought to provide more insight than misleading totalizing abstractions.

In the project of reconstruction, however, many feminists have found a postmodern stance less helpful. Attempts to delineate normative recommendations and a social order more hospitable to women and other disadvantaged groups fall prey to the same weapons of irony and deconstruction used on the theory and order they aim to displace. To a number of feminists, postmodern approaches are seen as contributing less than adequately to the political goals of feminism. These theorists fear that postmodern celebrations of disunity undermine political efforts to resist the hegemony of corporate capitalism and achieve progress. Some fear that they subvert efforts to develop the ethics of care.

What feminists need, Nancy Hartsock argues, is not a wholesale and one-sided rejection of modernity, but a transformation of power relations, and for this "we need to engage in the historical, political, and theoretical process of constituting ourselves as subjects" engaged in making a different world. She acknowledges that some will dismiss her view as "calling for the construction of another totalizing and falsely universal discourse," but she rejects the view that Enlightenment thought and postmodern disassemblings are the only alternatives. Members of marginalized and oppressed groups are not "likely to mistake themselves for the universal 'man,'" but they can still name and describe their experiences and work to transform the political processes in which they are embedded.[55] Many other feminists appreciate postmodern contributions but are similarly aware of their political weaknesses. Selma Sevenhuijsen concludes that "postmodern philosophy has offered an important warning against the risks and pitfalls inherent in a feminist ethics of care," if it confirms women in a traditional, one-sided identity. On the other hand, "the feminist ethics of care can also make us aware of the limitations of postmodernism as a normative idiom for feminism."[56] Advocates of the ethics of care aim their progress in normative understanding to have an impact on political and social and personal life.

The Ethics of Care and Power

The ethics of care must not, and in my view does not, lose sight of power as the very real capacity to oppose what morality, even if persuasive, recommends, nor of the power of the structures that keep oppression in place. But the concern that a focus on care obscures the realities of power brings some feminists back to political theory in the more traditional sense, seeing politics as inherently about power and concentrating on it. As Christine DiStefano says, "power, along with its associated concept, the political, is the subject matter of feminist political philosophy."[57] However, power is itself one of the concepts undergoing feminist reconceptualizations, often with the help of perspectives of care. In an early treatment, Nancy Hartsock analyzed what she took to be a feminist alternative to the standard conception of power as the capacity to dominate, of power over others. She found a number of women theorists writing of power as energy and competence, or "power to" rather than "power over," and she developed this alternative idea.[58] Feminists have also explored the power to empower others, and the power involved in caring, of those who provide care and those whose needs call forth such care.

More recently, Amy Allen examines three conceptions of power with which feminists have been working. They recognize power as resource, power as domination, and power as empowerment. She finds the first inadequate because it suggests that power can be "possessed, distributed, and redistributed, and the second and third are unsatisfactory because each of these conceptions emphasizes only one aspect of the multifaceted power relations that feminists are trying to understand."[59] She discusses the work of Foucault, Judith Butler, and Hannah Arendt and develops her own conception that construes power as "a relation rather than as a possession," but avoids the tendency "to mistake one aspect of power," such as domination or empowerment, for the whole of it.[60]

Feminist critics of the project of bringing the values of care and concern, trust and relatedness to public and political life worry that doing so may lead us to lose sight of the power, especially in the sense of power to dominate, that may be arrayed against progress. There is no doubt that a backlash against women's advances has occurred in many forms along with the gains women have made in recent decades. But advocating that political life ought to be guided much more than at present by the values of care and trust in no way entails soft-headedness about the obstacles feminists must expect in transforming society.

There are many conflicts of an economic, religious, and ethnic kind wracking the globe that nonfeminist and some feminist critics see a politics of care as unsuitable for addressing. But the ethics of care is quite capable of examining the social structures of power within which the activities of caring take place.[61] There is nothing soft-headed about care. As various writers emphasize, family life and bringing up children are rife with conflict. Sometimes rules must be established and enforced and punishments meted out. But those adept in the skills of care, of defusing conflicts before they become violent, of settling disputes among those who cannot just leave but must learn to get along with one another, have much to teach peacemakers and peacekeepers in other domains.[62] As international mechanisms evolve for dealing with conflict and for persuading the uninvolved to contribute the funds and personnel needed to control violence and build tolerance, they will depend heavily on citizens caring about potential victims, wanting to prevent their suffering, and understanding what needs to be done.[63] And this factor of relatedness to other human beings may be more important than a mere rational recognition of abstract liberal rights, though progress in understanding and respecting human rights is surely important also.

Furthermore, in countering the corporate power that threatens to overwhelm politics as well as all other aspects of global life with its ideology of social Darwinism, liberal individualism offers weak defenses (see chapter 7). Corporate power is often exercised through enticement rather than coercion. It can increase its reach and the influence of its values in many ways without violating liberal rights. What is needed to restrain its imperialistic expansion is an assertion of alternative values, such as care and trust and human solidarity.

The Prospects For Political Change

Feminism seeks to overturn the gender hierarchy that has in various forms maintained its power and permeated almost all aspects of every known society throughout human history and to replace it with equality. This will require the transformation of what is thought of as knowledge, of the ways people think and behave at almost all levels, of almost all institutions, of culture, of society. Doing this is certainly revolutionary and cannot be imagined to be a historical change to be accomplished rapidly. Feminists do not seek to simply replace men with women in the existing positions of power determining how society will develop, they seek to change the way these positions are thought about and structured. The ethics of care seeks to change dominant normative evaluations and recommendations.

Advocates of the ethics of care who reject postmodern warnings about positing any alternatives to the failed ones of modernism suggest such imaginable though distant goals as an end of domination, exploitation, and hierarchy as inherent features of society. They seek an ordering of society along cooperative lines that foster mutual trust and caring. As an ideal, a democratic political system may seek to treat citizens equally, but it may presume conflicting interests between them and may allow an economic system that promotes conflict and self-interest far more than cooperation. As the economic system dominates more and more of the society, as in capitalist societies at present, cooperation is more and more marginalized. The ideal of democracy suggested by the ethics of care is often different.

The dominant way of thinking about democracy since the seventeenth century has seen it as what Jane Mansbridge calls "adversary democracy," in which conflicting interests compete, limited only by contractual restraints, and the strongest win.[64] She notes that in practice, citizens in actual democratic systems have often sought to persuade rather than merely overpower their opponents. But the leading views of the past several decades continue to see democracy as adversarial, and political practices seem increasingly to accord with such views.

Mansbridge would like to see this kind of democracy replaced by one "where mutual persuasion helps realize shared goals and interests."[65] She thinks that feminist understandings of maternal and other forms of connectedness can help us bring about the more consultative and participatory processes that many theorists advocate,[66] and that she sees as "unitary democracy." Many leading theorists of democracy think of deliberation as limited to what is "reasoned" and impartial, but feminists examine how activating feelings of empathy and responsibility is also needed to reach shared objectives. Of course, some emotions are dangerous, but others ought to be included in our understanding of what democracy requires and should be welcomed into democratic discourse.[67] Mansbridge notes that concern for ongoing relationships, listening, empathy, even common interests have been coded as female and therefore devalued by political theorists eager to be seen as tough-minded. Feminist theorists of the ethics of care are showing, in contrast, how these considerations are essential for acceptable uses of power, including democratic power. They understand at the same time that power is pervasive in human life and cannot be ignored. But it can be developed and used in morally appropriate ways.[68]

The extent to which the world is still wracked by ethnic, racial, and religious divisions that have not yielded to liberal universalism must be acknowledged. The ethics of care can greatly contribute to the understanding that makes civil society possible (see chapter 8). The feminist understanding of how both equality and difference can be respected can be useful in showing how politics can deal with group conflict. As we have come to see concerning women, members of groups can be both equal to but different from dominant groups. To be respected as an equal should not mean being reduced to sameness, which purported sameness has historically reflected the characteristics of the dominant group.[69]

In a society increasingly influenced by feminism and the values of care and concern, the need for law and coercion would not disappear, but their use might become progressively more limited as society would learn to bring up its children so that fewer would sink to violence or insist on pursuing their own individual interests at the expense of others or without reasonable restraints. Even in the most cooperative societies, politics would still be needed to make appropriate decisions and to determine suitable policies. But the terms of the contests might be political in the sense that the best arguments would be persuasive. They would not need to be political in the sense of the power to coerce, through political position or legal sanction or economic power or sheer numbers of votes, determining the outcome. Economic power would be limited so that it would not control political and cultural discourse. And we could foresee that much more public debate would be conducted in the domain of a culture freed from economic domination.[70] Such a culture could approach the free discourse on which democratic decisions ought to be based, along with the protections of basic rights. The outcomes might then much more nearly approach consensus than political coercion. Although using political power to coerce is progress over using violence or military force to do so, freely given accord is better still. The discourse influenced by feminist and care values would not be limited to the rational principles of traditional public and political philosophy. Images and narratives appealing to the moral emotions of empathy and caring would also contribute. The values of the ethics of care could incorporate traditional ones, such as justice, and go beyond them, as persons would seek cooperatively to provide for children and care for their global environment.

10

Care and Justice in the Global Context

The field of study known as international relations tries to guide our thinking about the world and relations between states. On the one hand it has had a normative component from the beginning, concerning itself with avoiding the mistakes that led, for instance, to World War I.[1] On the other hand, it has tried to be an empirical social science, and what is called "realism" has been dominant in international relations for a long time, at least since World War II.

It has sometimes been acknowledged that what people *think* about the morality of a state's behavior can influence that state's standing, and thus power. But the world has largely been seen as a global near-anarchy of rival states each pursuing its national interest. This national interest can sometimes be thought to include entering into agreements with other states. But trying to assess what really would be the moral course of action for states to pursue has usually been dismissed as pointless.

Of course, it has not seemed pointless to everyone, and a number of philosophers and others have concerned themselves with ethics and international affairs.[2] And, in the past decade or so, there seem to have been within the field of international relations more serious discussions than before of what morality—if it were taken seriously—would require of states. Also, international law, with its inherent or arguably normative aspects, has continued to grow despite serious challenges.[3] In short, much work has been done to develop the morality of justice, with its associated moral conceptions of individual rights, equality, and universal law, for the arena of international relations and politics. Global justice has come to be a familiar topic, along with just war.

This is sometimes seen as part of the "third debate" in international relations theory—after the idealism of the first debate, which was replaced by the realism of the second. Also in this third debate are the very different approaches of critical theory, postmodernism, and feminist theory.[4] From many such perspectives it is apparent how ideological the "realism" that passed for factual and scientific has been. Receptivity toward new ways of understanding international reality and what to do within it has grown.[5]

International relations has been among the last of the social sciences to be affected by the awareness of gender issues that made such strides in the last quarter of the twentieth century.[6] As J. Ann Tickner writes, "with its focus on the 'high' politics of war and Realpolitik, the traditional Western academic discipline of international relations privileges issues that grow out of men's experiences; we are socialized into believing that war and power politics are spheres of activity with which men have a special affinity" and to which women are irrelevant.[7] Gradually, however, as the equation of what is human with what is masculine is being questioned, the implications of attending to gender are becoming apparent for this field as for others. It is being shown how "the values and assumptions that drive our international system are intrinsically related to concepts of masculinity."[8] As two feminist scholars see it, "gender shapes our identification of global actors, characterization of state and nonstate actions, framing of global problems, and consideration of possible alternatives."[9] To take an only superficially frivolous example, it has been suggested that the disparagement of France engaged in by the administration of George W. Bush and many commentators over France's resistance to the U.S. invasion of Iraq and subsequent policies has been made easy by the strong identification of France as female. Entrenched stereotypes brand France as a woman, and thus the French as sissies.[10]

In international relations theory and practice, as feminist scholars show,

> the concept of "political actor"—the legitimate wielder of society's power— is derived from classical political theory. . . . Feminists argue that the models of human nature underpinning constructions of "political man," are not in fact gender neutral. . . . They are . . . claims about gendered divisions of labor and identity that effectively and sometimes explicitly exclude women from definitions of "human," "moral agent," "rational actor," and "political man."[11]

Corrections are being undertaken.

Meanwhile, within feminist theorizing in the area of moral theory, the major alternative to those ethics of justice routinely used in previous normative thinking about international affairs has been undergoing development. That alternative moral approach is the ethics of care examined in this book. It is beginning to influence how those interested in international relations and global politics see the world and our responsibilities in it, and it holds promise for new efforts to improve global relations.

The Ethics of Care and International Affairs

The ethics of care, as we have seen, offers a distinctive challenge to the dominant moral theories—Kantian moral theory, utilitarianism, and virtue ethics. The expression of Kantian moral theory as a morality of justice can easily be seen in much contemporary work in political theory, starting with John Rawls's *A Theory of Justice*. Many recent discussions of global justice illustrate the application of this sort of theory to international affairs. It can be seen, for instance, in the work of Charles Beitz, Onora O'Neill, and Thomas Pogge.[12] Theory of this kind relies on the view that all persons, assumed to be free, equal, autonomous individuals, could agree to certain impartial, abstract, universal principles of justice. Justice is taken to be the primary value in political and social arrangements. The goals of such theory are fair distributions of the products of economic activity and of positions of power. The theory demands that persons be respected through recognition of their rights and delineates the moral constraints within which individuals are permitted to pursue the interests they are presumed to seek. The implications of this kind of theory for the obligations of states are examined.

Utilitarian theories can also be interpreted as ethics of justice, as I have shown. They recommend maximizing the utility of all persons, assumed to be individuals pursuing their own interests though these interests need not be egoistic. Utilitarianism is less able to protect individual rights against majority interests, but it justifies the legal protection of rights as conducive to general utility. It aims to treat individuals fairly in its rational calculations of their interests. Utilitarian theories, like their Kantian counterparts, rely on impartial, universal principles. Their recommendations of moral requirements at the global level reflect these positions.[13]

The ethics of care differs with these theories in its assumptions, goals, and methods. It is closer to virtue ethics, which has enjoyed a recent revival, and it is sometimes thought to be a kind of virtue ethics. But the ethics of care is sufficiently different from virtue ethics as well as other theories to be counted, as I have argued, as a new and distinct kind of moral theory (see chapters 1 and 3). Of course it has precursors, but it is built on different foundations and has developed in distinctive ways.

Among the characteristics of the ethics of care is its view of persons as relational and as interdependent. Kantian and utilitarian moral theories focus primarily on the rational decisions of agents taken as independent and autonomous individuals. Even virtue theory focuses on individuals and their dispositions. In contrast, the ethics of care sees persons as enmeshed in relations with others. It pays attention primarily to relations between persons, valuing especially caring relations. Rather than assuming, as do the dominant moral theories, that moral relations are to be seen as entered into voluntarily by free and equal individuals, the ethics of care is developed for the realities as well of unequal power and unchosen relations; salient examples are relations between parents and children, but the ethics of care is not limited to such contexts. It understands how our ties to various social groups and our historical embeddedness are also part of what make us who we are. The relevance to international affairs of these alternative ways of thinking about moral issues are striking.

For the dominant moral theories, there is attention to individual aims and interests on the one hand and to universal moral norms on the other. Conflicts between the desires of the individual self and the moral claims of everyone seen from an impartial perspective are recognized. But anything between these extremes of individual self and all others is virtually invisible. To the ethics of care, in contrast, moral life is populated by caring relations in which the interests of self and other are mingled, and trust is crucial. In caring for her child, for instance, a mother may often be pursuing not her own individual interest, or altruistically her child's as if it were in conflict with her own, but the mutual interest of both together. She will characteristically value her child and her relation to the child for their own sakes, not to satisfy her own preferences. Her moral concern may well be not that of all persons universally but that of the particular others with whom she shares such caring relations. And such caring relations are not limited to the personal contexts of family and friends. They can extend to fellow members of groups of various kinds, to fellow citizens, and beyond. We can, for instance, develop caring relations for persons who are suffering deprivation in distant parts of the globe. Moral theories that assume only individuals pursuing their own interests within the constraints supplied by universal rules are ill-suited to deal with the realities and values of caring relations and of relational persons in a global context. The ethics of care has resources to understand group and cultural ties, and relations between groups sharing histories or colonial domination or interests in nonmarket economic development.

Ethics of justice focus on issues of fairness, equality, and individual rights, seeking impartial and abstract principles that can be applied consistently to particular cases. Individual persons are seen as instances of the general and timeless conception of person. In contrast, the ethics of care focuses on attentiveness to context, trust, responding to needs, and offers narrative nuance; it cultivates caring relations in both personal, political, and global contexts. Persons are seen as involved in relations and unique. An ethic of justice seeks fair decisions between competing individual rights and interests. The ethics of care sees the interests of carers and cared-for as importantly shared. While justice protects equality and freedom from interference, care values positive involvement with others and fosters social bonds and cooperation.

In trying to ascertain what we morally ought to do, Kantian moral theory and utilitarianism rely entirely on reason, though they conceptualize reason differently. The ethics of care, instead, appreciates the contribution of the emotions in helping us understand what morality recommends. For instance, empathy, sensitivity, and responsiveness to particular others may often be better guides to what we ought to do than are highly abstract rules and universal principles about "all men" or even all persons. In place of what has traditionally been thought of as "moral knowledge," the ethics of care advocates attention to particulars, appreciation of context, narrative understanding, and communication and dialogue in moral deliberation, suspecting that the more general and abstract the recommendation, the less adequate for actual guidance. With the ethics of care, global suspicion of Western claims about universal reason may be circumvented.

From the perspective of law, emotion is traditionally seen as a threat to the impartiality law requires; emotion is then to be discounted and dismissed. But from the perspective of care, the social relations that must exist before law can get off the ground can be seen, importantly, as a form of caring relations between, say, fellow citizens or potentially fellow members of regions or of the globe. Caring persons will draw on the understanding of care that can be developed from actual experiences of caring and being cared for, often across divergent cultures.

Dominant moral theories seem to have generalized to what they take to be the whole of morality the outlooks thought to be appropriate for the impartial decisions of judges and legislators or the pursuits of rational self-interest in the marketplace and in politics. With the rise of women's reliance on their own experiences and feminist insights, however, the relevance to morality of the concerns and responsibilities of caring, in the family and far beyond, can be appreciated. It is becoming apparent that this requires profound changes in the way morality is understood, including in the arena of international relations.

The ethics of care values caring relations and their associated concerns of trust and mutual responsiveness. Care is a practice involving the work of caregiving and the standards by which the practices of care can be evaluated. Care must concern itself with the effectiveness of its efforts to meet needs, but also with the motives with which care is provided. Recipients of care sustain caring relations through their responsiveness. Relations between persons can be criticized when they become dominating, exploitative, mistrustful, or hostile. Relations of care can be encouraged and maintained.

Care is also a value (see chapter 2). We value caring relations and caring persons. We can understand many aspects of how persons are interrelated through a constellation of moral considerations associated with care: mutual concern, trustworthiness, attentiveness, responsiveness. To advocates of the ethics of care, care involves moral considerations at least as important as those of justice. And, when adequately understood for various contexts, it is an ethics as appropriate for men as for women, and as appropriate for political and international relations as for personal ones.

This is not to say that care excludes justice. Justice should be incorporated into morally acceptable practices of care. It is plausible to see caring relations as the wider and deeper context within which we seek justice and, in certain domains, give it priority.[14] In the domain of law, for instance, the language and principles of justice ought to have priority, even though any justice system can and ought to be more caring than it almost surely is at present. At the same time, we should keep in mind how the domain of law, with justice its priority, should be a limited domain and *not* imagined to be the model for the whole of moral life (see chapter 9). The argument applies in the international context as well as in the national one.

The values of care are already roughly incorporated into existing practices of care; they need to be better reflected and the practices improved and expanded. With better and more extensive practices of care, the needs for law and the enforcement mechanisms of the state could shrink. Cultures could be liberated from the domination of commercial interests where it exists, and greatly enlarged opportunities could be made possible for social decisions to be arrived at through dialogue and discourse rather than through imposed governmental determination.[15] Environmental concerns would be accorded the importance they deserve. As cultures disapproved of those failing to take responsibility for the effects of their activities and for their failures to sustain caring relations, less enforcement would be required. These developments could have analogues in relations between states.

From the perspective of care, markets should be limited rather than ever more pervasive, as they undermine the caring relations in which persons and the relations between them are valued for their own sakes (see chapter 7). To the market, everything is a fungible commodity, and economic gain is the highest priority.[16] The ethics of care would enable us to evaluate and to criticize the current globalization that expands the market ever more insistently, at the expense of caring relations throughout the world.

We have seen how rights presuppose care. Respecting rights within a society requires that persons care enough about each other to be willing to think of each other as fellow members of whatever group or political entity is asserting or recognizing such rights (see chapter 8). As more attention has been paid in recent years to the practices of civil society on which satisfactory political institutions depend, the relevance of the ethics of care can be appreciated. The practices of civil society build connections between persons and ties that hold people together into groups capable of democratic self-government. They can foster caring relations.

Various advocates of the ethics of care explicitly include citizenship among the practices of care. Peta Bowden, for instance, examines four types of caring practice: mothering, friendship, nursing, and citizenship. Those who do not yet think of citizenship in terms of care can come to see why they should. Bowden resists undue generalizations and abstract theorizing about care but notes resemblances among its various forms. These include their emphases on the interdependence of persons and the quality of their relationships. All caring practices have been devalued; all should be accorded recognition of their enormous ethical significance. The arguments apply also to what we may come to think of as global citizenship.

Implications for Global Change

The ethics of care clearly implies that society must recognize its responsibilities to its children and others who are dependent, enabling the best possible bringing up and educating of its future generations, appropriate responses to its members in need of health care, and assistance with the care of dependents.

It clearly implies that the members of wealthy societies must recognize their responsibilities to alleviate the hunger and gross deprivations in care afflicting so many members of poor ones. A United Nations report for 2004 puts the number of chronically hungry people in the world at 852 million, an *increase* of 18 million since 2000, with 5 million children dying of hunger every year.[17] Few trends could be more obviously in conflict with the values of care than a trend toward increasing hunger.

Relying largely or entirely, as societies have traditionally done, on the unpaid labor of women in the household for the provision of care is inconsistent with the values of care as well as of justice. The ethics of care calls for increased state support of various forms of caring and for meeting people's needs in caring ways. It recommends the equal participation of men in caring activities and of women in the political and economic structures that affect the circumstances in which caring takes place. It guides the practices that encourage cooperation between persons and groups, and the caring that is needed to uphold the values of citizenship. It implies an increased taking of responsibility in privileged societies for enabling development in societies not yet able to care for their members.

Carol Gould considers the implications of the concept of care for globalizing democracy. She observes that "care translates into a responsiveness to the particular needs and interests of individuals or groups at the social level. It also has a political parallel in the concern for providing the economic and social means for the development of individuals and not only in refraining from impeding their choices."[18] The reciprocity that characterizes democratic community presupposes no personal affection among its members, but democracy does presuppose that people have shared ends "in pursuit of which their cooperation is voluntary and not merely constrained by law or habit or effected by coercion."[19]

The ethics of care calls for the transformation of the different segments of society, with caring values and cooperation replacing the hierarchies and dominations of gender, class, race, and ethnicity. It recommends families characterized by mutual care; educational, health care, and child care institutions well supported and developed; economies focused on actually meeting needs rather than enriching the powerful; military-industrial power under social constraints and decided about by women as well as men in diplomatic and political institutions, military services, and defense industries; legal and political systems more expressive of the values of care as well as justice; and cultures free to present imaginative alternatives and to inspire cooperative and creative solutions to contested issues. But in addition to transforming each of such given domains, the ethics of care would transform the relations between domains (see chapter 4 for further discussion). Instead of domination by military and economic and political power and the marginalization of caring activities, the latter would move to the center of attention, effort, and support. Bringing up new persons in caring relations that would be as admirable as possible would be seen as society's most important goal.

We can also begin to see how the ethics of care should transform international politics and relations between states as well as within them. Building on its feminist roots, the ethics of care notices rather than ignores the role of the cultural construct of masculinity in the behavior of states. This image of masculinity does not actually characterize many men, and it can be aspired to by women as well as by men. But it does shape what those in positions of power, including the voters who support them, aim to do. Among its influences are the overemphasis on the part of states on military security and economic preeminence, and the neglect of other aspects of security such as environmental and ecological concerns, the moral acceptability of policies to those affected, and the cultivating and maintaining of cooperative relations with others. The behavior of the United States under the administration of George W. Bush, in its nearly unilateral war against Iraq, its bullying of potential allies, its rejection of UN restraints and of the Kyoto and other treaties, illustrates the kind of foreign policies that almost certainly bear the influence of an exaggerated image of masculinity. The fear of being less than "tough," the prejudice that cooperation is for wimps, infects the possibilities for improving relations between states.

Feminists have demonstrated the gender bias in Hobbes's view of the political world.[20] "Hobbes's androcentrism is revealed simply when we ask how helpless infants ever become adults if human nature is universally competitive and hostile. From the perspective of child-rearing practices, it makes more sense to argue that humans are naturally cooperative: without the cooperation that is required to nurture children, there would be no men or women."[21]

Realists and neorealists in international relations have transferred the Hobbesian view to the international arena, advocating preparation for war and the avoidance of dependence on others as the road to security. For Hans Morgenthau and Kenneth Waltz, for instance, maximizing military power and maintaining effective autonomy lead to states' success.[22] The ethics of care, in contrast, understands the importance of cultivating relations of trust, listening to the concerns of others, fostering international cooperation, and valuing interdependence.

In the usual construal of the global context, states are thought of as regions of security and order, and the world beyond is seen as dangerous, anarchic, and frequently violent—Hobbes's war of all against all. This picture is analogous to that of the household as "haven in a heartless world." Military might is seen as analogous to the male "protector" of hearth and home. Feminists have cracked this picture of the household and its international counterpart, making visible the enormous amount of violence against women and children that occurs within families and states. They have noted the special ways in which women throughout the world are threatened: Women are subject to rape, forced marriage, female infanticide, and the denial of health care and nutrition, merely because they are female.[23] Feminists are also cracking the picture of military strength and the willingness to use it as offering protection. They note, for instance, that "civilians now account for about 90 percent of war casualties, the majority of whom are women and children."[24] From the perspective of the ethics of care, the militarized state may be more threat than protector. When in possession of overwhelming force, the temptation may be overwhelming to use it; the result may be arms races among all who feel threatened and ever less attention to the real sources of security.

Feminists have also examined the image of the citizen-warrior at the heart of so much political theory and international relations thinking.[25] They make explicit its devaluation of women and women's activities and call for the revision of this constructed social ideal and of the way it has been transferred to the international arena of imagined personified states.

When the needs for law and restraint are acknowledged in relations between states, and when justice is sought, the model that is then used is usually contractual, as it is within states. The gender bias of law within states is then magnified on the international stage. When relations between states are examined critically, it is apparent how far they are from the assumptions of those who imagine their liberal democracies to be based on freely chosen contracts between equal individuals,[26] and see this as the model for the world. In fact, states have been created and their boundaries determined primarily by force, and fraud has usually played a large role. Disparities between the global North and the global South are fraught with involuntary aspects and unequal power. Net capital flows during the 1980s and 1990s have been from South to North,[27] with the gaps between poor and rich not only morally inexcusable but growing. According to a United Nations report for 1996, in the prior three decades the gap between poor and rich had widened as follows: The share of global income going to the poorest 20 percent of the world's population decreased from 2.3 percent to 1.4 percent; the share going to the richest 20 percent rose from 70 percent to 85 percent.[28] Moreover, among the poor countries, women are increasingly the most vulnerable.[29]

Care and Political Economy

Alongside a gendered international law, the recommendations and requirements of economic development have also not been gender neutral.

Prior to Western colonization, according to various scholars, gender divisions of labor in many cultures had been fairly elastic and egalitarian, but colonization imposed more rigid gender differentiation. Land rights held by women were often transferred to men (when not usurped by Western plantation owners) and the conditions of women worsened.[30] By the 1980s women still performed between 40 and 80 percent of all agricultural labor throughout the developing world, but their control over farming decreased.[31] "Western efforts to develop or modernize the postcolonial developing world through aid, loans, and technical assistance have continued to favor landowning men as recipients of assistance," further weakening the situations of women and contributing to the problem of world hunger as mechanized farming for cash crops has undermined female farming systems.[32] In the mid-1990s, women in Africa received from formal banking institutions less than 10 percent of the credit to small farmers and 1 percent of total credit to agriculture.[33] "Even in areas of the world where economic growth has been rapid, economic progress has not been matched by improvements in the position of women. . . . Silence about gender occurs because it is invisible in the concepts used for analysis, the questions that are asked, and the preference for the state level of analysis."[34]

The effects of "restructuring" for the global market have often been especially harmful to women as well as to other marginalized groups. During the 1990s, feminist scholars began to show how "women have been, not the beneficiaries, but significant victims" of globalization "not only in the South but also in the North."[35] A paper from this period was called, appropriately, "Wealth of Nations—Poverty of Women."

For women in Central and Eastern Europe, for instance, globalization brought unprecedented unemployment rates and the loss of state-funded maternity health care, maternity leave, and child care. Women became "unattractive employees" to privatized industries that wanted to avoid providing benefits.[36] Restructuring has led to an intensification of propatriarchal family policies generally, pushing women out of the jobs they previously held and often into the sex trade.[37] The globalization so aggressively promoted by those with a neoliberal agenda has often been deleterious to many, but it has had an especially unfortunate impact on many women.[38]

Mainstream international relations theory, meanwhile, has paid inadequate attention to such global economic realities, or to the gross inadequacy of the way mainstream economics views social reality.

Consider the difference it would make if the essential nature and enormous value of the unpaid caring work that women do were recognized in the thinking of economists. It would help to undermine the assumed greater importance of "production" over "reproduction," "public" over "private," and male over female. If caring labor were appropriately valued and shared by men, the assumption that men's development should be promoted while women's can be overlooked and that men are more suited than women for high-status work in the economy and the polity would be superceded. V. Spike Peterson and Anne Sisson Runyan write that "by making the costs of current economic priorities visible and making visible who (women) and what (the environment) bear the brunt of these costs, states and corporations would find it hard to justify a great deal of what they claim is wealth-generating activity. . . . Keeping the reproductive and informal sectors undervalued is only 'functional' for those few at the top who reap greater profits as a result of this under- or devaluation."[39]

As a result of feminist criticism, development agencies have begun to consider the effects of their policies on women. But generally they resist upsetting the gendered division of labor that privileges the work that men do and renders many women increasingly impoverished and powerless. Changes in "cultural practices" concerning gender often do need to arise from women within developing cultures who can be assisted, rather than to be imposed by outside agencies. But this should not preclude the general economic revisioning of caring labor everywhere, and the recognition of the obstacles to doing so presented by the interests of capital and the economic theories that reflect them.

The policies that permit and promote the prosperity of the developed countries and the impoverishing of the "developing" countries can be attacked on grounds of justice. But the mechanisms to enforce anything remotely like global economic justice are almost entirely absent. Persuasive efforts such as those presently taking place to reduce the subsidies that governments in the richest countries provide their agribusinesses, rendering farmers in poor countries unable to compete, have made little progress. Arguments based on considerations of care and promoted through institutional and personal interconnections would be no more utopian and might be more effective. The ethics of care is more suited than the ethics of justice for understanding the particularities of different situations, groups, and cultures, to see what really will improve the lives of children, women, and men. And it can do so without incurring the liabilities of postmodernism's parallel appreciation of difference and suspicion of universalisms.

Imperialistic Approaches

Great care needs to be taken to avoid the imperialism in thinking and in programs that postcolonial feminists discern in many feminists from the global North. These warnings apply to those developing the ethics of care as well as to those with other approaches. Western radical feminists have so generalized about the centrality of sexuality in the oppression of women that in the view of a number of postcolonial feminists, they unduly overlook the differences between rich, white, Western women and those of the global South, and the differences between women in different classes, ethnic groups, and regions of the developing world. Liberal feminists, meanwhile, have been so intent on applying universal norms of equality that they, too, have failed to appreciate the different contexts in which they seek to rescue women from what they see as intolerable conditions. Feminists from the global North too often think of others as, in Chandra Mohanty's words, "the typical Third World woman . . . (read: ignorant, poor, uneducated, tradition-bound, family-oriented, victimized, etc.),"[40] whereas postcolonial women often see themselves as quite capable of exercising agency and influencing reform in their societies.

Alison Jaggar describes the dilemma she feels: "Morally and politically, I have strong sympathies with the anti-imperialist feminists, since it is evident to me that many Western feminist criticisms of third world practices are objectifying, patronizing and self-congratulatory. At the same time, I do feel a responsibility to help women (indeed, all citizens) in the poorer countries of the world. Is it possible to help while avoiding a colonialist stance?"[41] She expresses her concern that the literature preoccupied with how Westerners should respond to injustices in non-Western cultures "deflects attention away from the ways in which the citizens of the global North are implicated in many of the injustices from which women suffer in the global South."[42] The principles and policies of neoliberal globalization that the global North has imposed on the world "have increased inequality both among and within countries," such that "the suffering of women in the global South has been at least intensified by decisions made in the global North."[43] Western feminists can and should oppose the neoliberal globalization that has these results.

As I argue in chapter 7, the ethics of care is in a strong position to argue against the globalization that ignores other values than those of the market, but it must be attuned to the dangers of neocolonial insensitivities. Care needs also to be taken that morally admirable impulses to help are not naive and misplaced but really do lead to effective care. Natalie Brender develops these cautions specifically for the ethics of care and humanitarian relief, which is sometimes carried out in ways that do more harm than good.[44] The ethics of care has the resources to evaluate such efforts; they must be thoughtfully employed.

The Future of Care

Fiona Robinson argues that both mainstream international relations theory and mainstream normative theory about international relations have "resulted in the creation of a global 'culture of neglect' through a systematic devaluing of notions of interdependence, relatedness, and positive involvement in the lives of distant others."[45] A morality suited to unchosen relations between agents of unequal vulnerability, as is the ethics of care, might often have more relevance to global realities than have versions of social contract theory.

In addition, the ethics of care, with its attention to actual differences between persons and groups and its resistance to universalizing all into an abstraction of the ahistorical rational-individual-as-such, may be more suited to the realities of global differences of culture, felt identity, resources, and group exclusion, the sources of much recent conflict.

Within the ethics of justice, respect for human rights has played a central role, and this concern has been increasingly apparent at the global level. But as feminist scholars have shown, the human rights of women have been woefully neglected. Until recently, violence against women was not part of the international human rights agenda. The public/private distinction was reproduced at the international level, with the many forms of violence against women—from rape to patterned malnutrition to bride burning—considered "unfortunate cultural practices outside of the state's or international system's responsibilities."[46] The priority given to civil and political rights over economic and social rights, especially in U.S. foreign policy but also in much liberal theorizing about democratization, has been especially unfortunate for women. As work on the "feminization of poverty" shows, women have been disproportionately at the bottom of socioeconomic scales around the world;

UN research found that "of the 1.3 billion people estimated to be in poverty in the mid 1990's, 70 percent were women."[47]

In this and other ways it can be seen how international law has been deeply gendered. Issues traditionally of concern to men have been interpreted as general human concerns, whereas "women's concerns" have been relegated to a special category and marginalized. Strong efforts are now being made to extend justice to women—to recognize and to protect the human rights of women. In addition, feminist moral theorists have been showing how the ethics of justice itself is gendered, and as we have seen, they have been developing the ethics of care.

The ethics of care requires not only transformations of given domains—the legal, the economic, the political, the cultural, and so on—within a society but also a transformation of the relations between such domains. So would it in the global context. Taking responsibility for global environmental well-being would become among the central concerns of a caring global policy. Fostering the kinds of economic development that actually would meet human needs and enable the care needed by all to be provided would also be seen as of primary importance. Ecofeminists, for instance, offer an ethic of care for nature and call for a radically different kind of economic progress. They ask that development be sustainable, ecologically sound, nonpatriarchal, nonexploitative, and community oriented.[48]

As caring values would become more influential within a society, resolutions of conflict through the threat and use of force would decrease; so would they in the international context as relations between states would be influenced by the ethics of care. This would not mean that at this stage of development there should be less rather than more support for whatever restraints can be provided by international law. Where the use of force and violence restrained only by national interest is the norm, accepting legal restraints is more expressive of care than disregarding them. Although there should always be a presumption against the use of violence, and though the responsibility for restraint falls especially heavily on powerful states for whom other means than violence are available to respond to justifiable demands or to resist unjustifiable ones, violence as a last resort is not ruled out by the ethics of care and may sometimes be called for. As I argue in chapter 9, the ethics of care is quite capable of dealing with violence. Some enforcement of law may always be needed between states as within them, though international police actions should be carried out with international support, not unilaterally by superpowers. But where caring relations have been adequately developed within a society, the need for legal enforcement can be reduced. The same could be looked forward to in the global context.

At the current stage of development, efforts to achieve progress in respect for human rights are also certainly to be supported rather than neglected. But in a world in which the multiple ties of care would have expanded to encompass the whole human community, and poverty and exclusion really would be on the wane rather than, as at present, increasing, caring relations might make appeals to human rights less important.

A vast number of efforts, through nongovernmental organizations and state and international agencies, could do much to establish the ties of care between actual persons within and across state boundaries that can enable the decrease of violence and exploitation. Ties among poor women within a state, for instance, have potential for transforming economic and gender hierarchies.[49] Ties between persons from different states can contribute to decreasing international hostility and resort to violence. They should be far more adequately supported. Those from the global North need to listen and understand, as in friendship, rather than bestow limited benevolence. And those in the global South need to overcome humiliation and participate in the discourses that will determine their circumstances, enabling caring economic development rather than unfettered capitalism.

The ethics of care is compatible with several current trends: the increased influence of nongovernmental organizations,[50] and of the transnational movements that Richard Falk has seen as part of "globalization from below."[51] The networks of government officials described by Anne-Marie Slaughter as constituting a kind of "global governance" do not yet appear to be influenced by the ethics of care, but their activities could be enhanced by it. In Slaughter's view, government officials from agencies in different states often consult with their counterparts in other states to hammer out policies and put practices in place that will best address their common problems, such as improving environmental regulations, assuring the safety of food, or maintaining financial stability.[52] These networks, Slaughter writes, "build trust and establish relationships among their participants that then create incentives to establish a good reputation and avoid a bad one. These are the conditions essential for long-term cooperation."[53] States, in her view, are not likely in the foreseeable future to cede substantial power to any kind of global government, but she sees the global networks that are developing as able to foster compliance with norms: "They can bolster and support their members in adhering to norms of good governance at home and abroad.... They can enhance compliance with existing international agreements and deepen and broaden cooperation to create new ones."[54] Although Slaughter does not discuss the ethics of care, the kinds of values the members of such networks might often be best guided by could be the values of care.

Slaughter may be too optimistic about the motives of government officials— surely some will be more interested in promoting the interests of their employers than in pursuing the general good—but she shows the potential of networks guided by shared values.

In chapter 8, I discuss the potential affinities between the ethics of care and civil society. John Keane believes that "global civil society" is now bursting onto the scene.[55] He tries out a number of different metaphors to describe this promising reality that he sees emerging and that requires new ways of thinking. Rejecting the metaphors of levels of government and structures of international order, he prefers that of "a vast, dynamic biosphere" made up of "a bewildering variety of interacting habitats and species: INGO's, voluntary groups, businesses, civic initiatives, social movements, protest organizations."[56] Keane finds this metaphor misleading also, because the phenomena of global society are not the naturally occurring ones of a biosphere but are socially produced. Nevertheless, in avoiding the hierarchies of architecture or organizational charts, it conveys much about what he believes is developing.

Characteristics of the global civil society Keane discerns include that its elements are nongovernmental, that they are social, not organic or mechanistic processes, and that they are guided by norms of civility rather than produced by violent confrontation. Global civil society "champions the political vision of a world founded on non-violent, legally sanctioned power-sharing arrangements among many different and interconnected forms of socio-economic life that are distinct from governmental institutions."[57]

Slaughter's networks of governmental officials and Keane's civil society of nongovernmental organizations may both be more threatened than they acknowledge by global forces of devastation. A hypercapitalist superpower roused to concentrate on an endless "war on terrorism," and groups around the world intent on using political violence to promote their local aims may constitute formidable obstacles to global weavings of interconnectedness. But with progress in forestalling violence, among those open to cooperation, perhaps these obstacles may not be insurmountable.

Although they do not indicate awareness of each other's work, Keane, like Slaughter, sees a process of global interconnectedness developing and sees a vision of what it is and should be like as able to affect the process being considered. Slaughter holds that "to achieve a better world order, we must believe that one can exist and be willing to describe it in sufficient detail that it could actually be built."[58] Neither author gives any indication of having been influenced by the ethics of care, but both (and those they influence) might find their work enhanced by using the ethics of care to evaluate global developments and to promote the best of them. The aims of those working toward global cooperation could well be fostered by an increased awareness of the values of care. The dangers of more powerful agents imposing outcomes on the less powerful are great, as with many caring situations, but the ethics of care has resources for appropriate critiques.

Caring relations, rather than what persons do as individuals, exemplify the values of caring. The small societies of family and friendship embedded in larger societies are formed by caring relations. More attenuated but still evident caring relations between more distant people enable them to trust each other enough to form social organizations and political entities and to accept each other as fellow citizens of states. A globalization of caring relations would help enable people of different states and cultures to live in peace, to respect each other's rights, to care together for their environments, and to improve the lives of their children.

Notes

Chapter 1

1. I use the term 'ethics' to suggest that there are multiple versions of this ethic, though they all have much in common, making it understandable that some prefer 'the ethic of care.' I use 'the ethics of care' as a collective and singular noun. Some moral philosophers have tried to establish a definitional distinction between 'ethics' and 'morality'; I think such efforts fail, and I use the terms more or less interchangeably, though I certainly distinguish between the moral or ethical beliefs groups of people in fact have and moral or ethical recommendations that are justifiable or admirable.

2. See, for example, Annette C. Baier, *Moral Prejudices: Essays on Ethics* (Cambridge, Mass.: Harvard University Press, 1994), esp. chap. 1; Peta Bowden, *Caring: Gender Sensitive Ethics* (London: Routledge, 1997); and Margaret Urban Walker, "Feminism, Ethics, and the Question of Theory," *Hypatia: A Journal of Feminist Philosophy* 7 (1992): 23–38.

3. See, for example, Baier, *Moral Prejudices*; Virginia Held, *Feminist Morality: Transforming Culture, Society, and Politics* (Chicago: University of Chicago Press, 1993); Diana Tietjens Meyers, *Subjection and Subjectivity* (New York: Routledge, 1994); and Margaret Urban Walker, *Moral Understandings: A Feminist Study in Ethics* (New York: Routledge, 1998).

4. See, for example, Seyla Benhabib, *Situating the Self: Gender, Community, and Postmodernism in Contemporary Ethics* (New York: Routledge, 1992); Marilyn Friedman, *What Are Friends For? Feminist Perspectives on Personal Relationships* (Ithaca, N.Y.: Cornell University Press, 1993); Held, *Feminist Morality*; and Eva Feder Kittay, *Love's Labor: Essays on Women, Equality, and Dependency* (New York: Routledge, 1999).

5. See Brian Barry, *Justice as Impartiality* (Oxford: Oxford University Press, 1995); Diemut Bubeck, *Care, Gender, and Justice* (Oxford: Oxford University Press, 1995), pp. 239–40; and Susan Mendus, *Impartiality in Moral and Political Philosophy* (Oxford: Oxford University Press, 2002). See also chapters 5 and 6 this volume.

6. It is often asserted that to count as moral, a judgment must be universalizeable: If we hold that it would be right (or wrong) for one person to do something, then we are committed to holding that it would be right (or wrong) for anyone similar in similar circumstances to do it. The subject terms in moral judgments must thus be universally quantified variables and the predicates universal. "I ought to take care of Jane because she is my child" is not universal; "all parents ought to take care of their children" is. The former judgment could be universalizeable if it were derived from the latter, but if, as many advocates of the ethics of care think, it is taken as a *starting* moral commitment (rather than as dependent on universal moral judgments), it might not be universalizeable.

7. Baier, *Moral Prejudices,* p. 26.

8. Margaret Urban Walker, "Moral Understandings: Alternative 'Epistemology' for a Feminist Ethics," *Hypatia* 4 (summer 1989): 15–28, pp. 19–20.

9. Good examples are Stephen L. Darwall, *Impartial Reason* (Ithaca, N.Y.: Cornell University Press, 1983), and David Gauthier, *Morals by Agreement* (Oxford: Oxford University Press, 1986).

10. Brian Barry, *The Liberal Theory of Justice* (London: Oxford University Press, 1973), p. 166.

11. Michael Sandel, *Liberalism and the Limits of Justice* (Cambridge: Cambridge University Press, 1982), p. 133. Other examples of the communitarian critique that ran parallel to the feminist one are Alasdair MacIntyre, *After Virtue: A Study in Moral Theory* (Notre Dame, Ind.: University of Notre Dame Press, 1981), and *Whose Justice? Which Rationality?* (Notre Dame, Ind.: University of Notre Dame Press, 1988); Charles Taylor, *Hegel and Modern Society* (Cambridge: Cambridge University Press, 1979); and Roberto Mangabeire Unger, *Knowledge and Politics* (New York: Free Press, 1975).

12. Martha Nussbaum, *Sex and Social Justice* (New York: Oxford University Press, 1999), p. 62.

13. See, for example, Diana T. Meyers, *Self, Society, and Personal Choice* (New York: Columbia University Press, 1989); Grace Clement, *Care, Autonomy, and Justice* (Boulder, Colo.: Westview Press, 1996); Diana T. Meyers, ed., *Feminists Rethink the Self* (Boulder, Colo.: Westview Press, 1997); and Catriona MacKenzie and Natalie Stoljar, eds., *Relational Autonomy: Feminist Perspectives on Autonomy, Agency, and the Social Self* (New York: Oxford University Press, 2000). See also Marina Oshana, "Personal Autonomy and Society," *Journal of Social Philosophy* 29(1) (spring 1998): 81–102.

14. This image is in Thomas Hobbes's *The Citizen: Philosophical Rudiments Concerning Government and Society,* ed. B. Gert (Garden City, N.Y.: Doubleday, 1972), p. 205. For a contrasting view, see Sibyl Schwarzenbach, "On Civic Friendship," *Ethics* 107(1) (1996): 97–128.

15. Kittay, *Love's Labor.*

16. Baier, *Moral Prejudices,* p. 29.

17. See Robert A. Frank, Thomas Gilovich, and Dennis T. Regan, "Does Studying Economics Inhibit Cooperation?" *Journal of Economic Perspectives* 7(2) (spring 1993): 159–71; and Gerald Marwell and Ruth Ames, "Economists Free Ride, Does Anyone Else?: Experiments on the Provision of Public Goods, IV," *Journal of Public Economics* 15(3) (June 1981): 295–310.

18. See Virginia Held, *Rights and Goods: Justifying Social Action* (Chicago: University of Chicago Press, 1989), chap. 5, "The Grounds for Social Trust," and chapter 8 in this volume.

19. Carol Gilligan, *In a Different Voice: Psychological Theory and Women's Development* (Cambridge, Mass.: Harvard University Press, 1982), and "Moral Orientation and Moral Development," in *Women and Moral Theory*, eds. Eva Feder Kittay and Diana T. Meyers (Lanham, Md.: Rowman and Littlefield, 1987).

20. Sara Ruddick, "Injustice in Families: Assault and Domination," in *Justice and Care: Essential Readings in Feminist Ethics*, ed. Virginia Held (Boulder, Colo.: Westview Press, 1995), p. 217.

21. Bubeck, *Care, Gender, and Justice*, p. 11.

22. Ibid., p. 206.

23. This is not to deny that justice includes responding to needs in the general sense. For instance, any decent list of human rights should include rights to basic necessities, despite the peculiar backwardness of the United States, which fails to recognize this. Most of the world rightly accepts, at least in theory, that economic and social rights providing basic necessities are real human rights along with civil and political rights. But justice and fairness require such rights because it is unfair as a matter of general principle for some to have the means to live and act, while others lack such means. Care, in contrast, responds to the particular needs of particular persons regardless of general principles. See, for example, Henry Shue, *Basic Rights* (Princeton, N.J.: Princeton University Press, 1980); Held, *Rights and Goods*; James W. Nickel, *Making Sense of Human Rights* (Berkeley: University of California Press, 1987); and Louis Henkin, *The Age of Rights* (New York: Columbia University Press, 1990). See also David Copp, "Equality, Justice, and the Basic Needs," in *Necessary Goods*, ed. Gillian Brock (Lanham, Md.: Rowman and Littlefield, 1998).

24. See Clement, *Care, Autonomy, and Justice*.

25. Stephen Darwall, *Philosophical Ethics* (Boulder, Colo.: Westview Press, 1998), chap. 19, "Ethics of Care."

26. Nel Noddings, *Caring: A Feminine Approach to Ethics and Moral Education* (Berkeley: University of California Press, 1986).

27. See Held, *Rights and Goods*, and chapter 4 in this volume.

28. Sara Ruddick, *Maternal Thinking: Toward a Politics of Peace* (Boston: Beacon Press, 1989).

29. See Held, *Feminist Morality*, esp. chap. 5.

30. Joan C. Tronto, *Moral Boundaries: A Political Argument for an Ethic of Care* (New York: Routledge, 1993), p. 175.

31. Ibid., p. 113.

32. Bubeck, *Care, Gender, and Justice*; Kittay, *Love's Labor*; see also Mona Harrington, *Care and Equality: Inventing a New Family Politics* (New York: Knopf, 1999); and Nancy Folbre, *The Invisible Heart: Economics and Family Values* (New York: New Press, 2001).

33. Nel Noddings, *Starting at Home: Caring and Social Policy* (Berkeley: University of California Press, 2002).

34. See, for example, Maria C. Lugones, "On The Logic of Pluralist Feminism," in *Feminist Ethics*, ed. Claudia Card (Lawrence: University Press of Kansas, 1991).

35. Peggy DesAutels and Joanne Waugh, eds., *Feminists Doing Ethics* (Lanham, Md.: Rowman and Littlefield, 2001). See contributions by Lisa Tessman, Margaret McLaren, Barbara Andrew, and Nancy Potter.

36. Michael Slote, *Morals from Motives* (Oxford: Oxford University Press, 2001).

37. For another view, see Richmond Campbell, *Illusions of Paradox: A Feminist Epistemology Naturalized* (Lanham, Md.: Rowman and Littlefield, 1998).

38. See Jürgen Habermas, "Discourse Ethics," in his *Moral Consciousness and Communicative Action* (Cambridge, Mass.: MIT Press, 1995); and Benhabib, *Situating the Self.*

39. See especially Baier, *Moral Prejudices.*

40. Chenyang Li, "The Confucian Concept of *Jen* and the Feminist Ethics of Care: A Comparative Study," *Hypatia* 9(1) (1994): 70–89; and "Revisiting Confucian *Jen* Ethics and Feminist Care Ethics: A Reply to Daniel Star and Lijun Yuan," *Hypatia* 17(1) (2002): 130–40.

41. Daniel Star, "Do Confucians Really Care? A Defense of the Distinctiveness of Care Ethics: A Reply to Chenyang Li," *Hypatia* 17(1) (2002): 77–106.

42. Lijun Yuan, "Ethics of Care and Concept of *Jen*: A Reply to Chenyang Li," *Hypatia* 17(1) (2002): 107–29.

43. Chan Sin Yee, examining Confucian texts, finds the traditional neo-Confucian denigration of women a misinterpretation. She acknowledges that even a reformed Confucian ethics might subscribe to a gender essentialism in which appropriate (though not necessarily unequal) roles based on gender would be promoted, but suggests how a return to early Confucianism could avoid this. Chan Sin Yee, "The Confucian Conception of Gender in the Twenty-First Century," in *Confucianism for the Modern World*, eds. Hahm Chaibong and Daniel A. Bell (Cambridge: Cambridge University Press, 2002).

44. For a thoughtful account of various ways in which the ethics of care and Christian and Jewish ethics "converge" from very different starting points, see Ruth E. Groenhout, "Theological Echoes in an Ethic of Care," Erasmus Institute Occasional Paper 2003, no.2 (University of Notre Dame, Notre Dame, Ind., 2003).

45. See, for example, Susan Moller Okin, *Justice, Gender, and the Family* (New York: Basic Books, 1989), and Nussbaum, *Sex and Social Justice.*

46. For example, see Barbara Houston, "Rescuing Womanly Virtues: Some Dangers of Moral Reclamation," in *Science, Morality and Feminist Theory*, eds. M. Hanen and K. Nielsen (Calgary: University of Calgary Press, 1987); Claudia Card, "Gender and Moral Luck" and Alison Jaggar, "Caring as a Feminist Practice of Moral Reason," in *Justice and Care*, ed. V. Held; but see also Cynthia Willett, *Maternal Ethics and Other Slave Moralities* (New York: Routledge, 1995).

47. Onora O'Neill, "Justice, Gender, and International Boundaries," in *International Justice and the Third World*, eds. Robin Attfield and Barry Wilkins (London: Routledge, 1992), p. 55.

48. Fiona Robinson, *Globalizing Care: Ethics, Feminist Theory, and International Affairs* (Boulder, Colo.: Westview Press, 1999), p. 164.

49. See, for example, Elizabeth V. Spelman, *Inessential Woman* (Boston: Beacon Press, 1988); Sara Lucia Hoagland, *Lesbian Ethics: Toward New Value* (Palo Alto, Calif.: Institute of Lesbian Studies, 1989); Patricia Hill Collins, *Black Feminist Thought: Knowledge, Consciousness, and the Politics of Empowerment* (Boston: Unwin Hyman, 1990); Patricia J. Williams, *The Alchemy of Race and Rights* (Cambridge, Mass.: Harvard University Press, 1991); and Uma Narayan, *Dislocating Cultures: Identities, Traditions and Third World Women* (New York: Routledge, 1997).

50. I share Stephen Darwall's view that normative ethics and metaethics are highly interrelated and cannot be clearly separated. See his *Philosophical Ethics*, esp. chap. 1.

51. See Alasdair MacIntyre, *After Virtue: A Study in Moral Theory* (Notre Dame, Ind.: University of Notre Dame Press, 1981). A virtue theorist who was fairly widely read in the period before this was Philippa Foot; see her *Virtues and Vices* (Berkeley: University of California Press, 1978). See also Amelie Rorty, ed., *Essays on Aristotle's*

Ethics (Berkeley: University of California Press, 1980). Other work contributing to the revival of virtue ethics includes Michael Slote's; see especially his *Goods and Virtues* (Oxford: Oxford University Press, 1983) and *From Morality to Virtue* (New York: Oxford University, 1992). See also Owen Flanagan and Amelie Oksenberg Rorty, eds., *Identity, Character, and Morality: Essays in Moral Psychology* (Cambridge, Mass.: MIT Press, 1992); and Julia Annas, *The Morality of Happiness* (New York: Oxford University Press, 1995). Martha Nussbaum's work, for example, *The Fragility of Goodness* (Cambridge: Cambridge University Press, 1986), has contributed to virtue theory, but she argues against the ethics of care.

52. Lawrence A. Blum, *Friendship, Altruism and Morality* (London: Routledge, 1980); and Bernard Williams, *Ethics and the Limits of Philosophy* (Cambridge, Mass.: Harvard University Press, 1985).

53. See, for example, Charles Taylor, *Philosophical Papers* (Cambridge: Cambridge University Press, 1985); Michael Stocker, *Plural and Conflicting Values* (New York: Oxford University Press, 1990); and Elizabeth Anderson, *Value in Ethics and Economics* (Cambridge, Mass.: Harvard University Press, 1993).

54. Walker, *Moral Understandings*, p. 1.

55. Robinson, *Globalizing Care*, p. 7.

56. Walker, *Moral Understandings*, p. 21.

57. See especially Alison M. Jaggar, "Feminist Ethics: Some Issues for the Nineties," *Journal of Social Philosophy* 20 (spring–fall 1989): 91–107.

58. For example, Marcia Baron, *Kantian Ethics Almost without Apology* (Ithaca, N.Y.: Cornell University Press, 1995); and Barbara Herman, *The Practice of Moral Judgment* (Cambridge, Mass.: Harvard University Press, 1993).

59. For example, Laura M. Purdy, *Reproducing Persons: Issues in Feminist Bioethics* (Ithaca, N.Y.: Cornell University Press, 1996).

60. For example, Jean Hampton, "Feminist Contractarianism," in *A Mind of One's Own: Feminist Essays on Reason and Objectivity*, 2nd ed., eds. Louise M. Antony and Charlotte Witt (Boulder, Colo.: Westview Press, 2002); and Okin, *Justice, Gender, and the Family*.

61. For example, Nussbaum, *Sex and Social Justice*.

62. See Okin, *Justice, Gender, and the Family*.

63. Sara Ruddick, "Maternal Thinking," *Feminist Studies* 6 (summer 1980): 342–67.

64. For some early feminist thinking, see Joyce Trebilcot, ed., *Mothering: Essays in Feminist Theory* (Totowa, N.J.: Rowman and Allanheld, 1983).

65. Carol Gilligan, "Moral Orientation and Moral Development," in *Women and Moral Theory*, eds. Kittay and Meyers, p. 25.

66. See, for example, Lawrence J. Walker, "Sex Differences in the Development of Moral Reasoning: A Critical Review," *Child Development* 55 (June 1984): 677–91; and Sandra Harding, "The Curious Coincidence of Feminine and African Moralities," in *Women and Moral Theory*, ed. Kittay and Meyers.

67. See, for example, Kathryn Pauly Morgan, "Women and Moral Madness," in *Science, Morality and Feminist Theory*, eds. Hanen and Nielsen; and Kittay and Meyers, eds., *Women and Moral Theory*.

68. Annette Baier's influential essay "Trust and Anti-Trust," appeared in *Ethics* in January 1986; it and other essays on trust and other matters are collected in Baier, *Moral Prejudices*.

69. Among major titles, arranged chronologically, are Ruddick, *Maternal Thinking*; Jeffrey Blustein, *Care and Commitment* (New York: Oxford University

Press, 1991); Card, ed., *Feminist Ethics*; Kathryn Pyne Addelson, *Impure Thoughts: Essays on Philosophy, Feminism, and Ethics* (Philadelphia: Temple University Press, 1991); Benhabib, *Situating the Self*; Eve Browning Cole and Susan Coultrap McQuin, eds., *Explorations in Feminist Ethics: Theory and Practice* (Indianapolis: Indiana University Press, 1992); Rita Manning, *Speaking from the Heart: A Feminist Perspective on Ethics* (Lanham, Md.: Rowman and Littlefield, 1992); Susan Sherwin, *No Longer Patient: Feminist Ethics and Health Care* (Philadelphia: Temple University Press, 1992); Friedman, *What Are Friends For?*; Held, *Feminist Morality*; Mary Jeanne Larrabee, ed., *An Ethic of Care: Feminist and Interdisciplinary Perspectives* (New York: Routledge, 1993); Rosemarie Tong, *Feminine and Feminist Ethics* (Belmont, Calif.: Wadsworth, 1993); Tronto, *Moral Boundaries*; Linda A. Bell, *Rethinking Ethics in the Midst of Violence* (Lanham, Md.: Rowman and Littlefield, 1993); Baier, *Moral Prejudices*; Meyers, *Subjection and Subjectivity*; Bubeck, *Care, Gender, and Justice*; Susan J. Hekman, *Moral Voices, Moral Selves* (University Park: University of Pennsylvania Press, 1995); Held, ed., *Justice and Care*; Clement, *Care, Autonomy, and Justice*; Bowden, *Caring: Gender Sensitive Ethics*; Meyers, ed., *Feminists Rethink the Self*; Selma Sevenhuijsen, *Citizenship and the Ethics of Care* (London: Routledge, 1998); Walker, *Moral Understandings*; Claudia Card, ed., *On Feminist Ethics and Politics* (Lawrence: University Press of Kansas, 1999); Julia E. Hanigsberg and Sara Ruddick, eds., *Mother Troubles: Rethinking Contemporary Maternal Dilemmas* (Boston: Beacon Press, 1999); Mona Harrington, *Care and Equality: Inventing a New Family Politics* (New York: Knopf, 1999); Kittay, *Love's Labor*; Robinson, *Globalizing Care*; Margaret Urban Walker, ed., *Mother Time: Women, Aging, and Ethics* (Lanham, Md.: Rowman and Littlefield, 1999); Catriona MacKenzie and Natalie Stoljar, eds., *Relational Autonomy: Feminist Perspectives on Autonomy, Agency, and the Social Self* (New York: Oxford University Press, 2000); Julie Anne White, *Democracy, Justice, and the Welfare State: Reconstructing Public Care* (University Park: Pennsylvania State Press, 2000); Des-Autels and Waugh, eds., *Feminists Doing Ethics*; Slote, *Morals from Motives*; Diana Tietjens Meyers, *Gender in the Mirror: Cultural Imagery and Women's Agency* (New York: Oxford University Press, 2002); Noddings, *Starting at Home*; Margaret Urban Walker, *Moral Contexts* (Lanham, Md.: Rowman and Littlefield, 2003). Not all of the authors or editors on this list consider themselves advocates of the ethics of care, but these works have contributed to the development of such ethics.

Chapter 2

1. See, for example, Jeffrey Blustein, *Care and Commitment* (New York: Oxford University Press, 1991), and Harry G. Frankfurt, *The Importance of What We Care About* (Cambridge: Cambridge University Press, 1988).

2. Nel Noddings, *Caring: A Feminine Approach to Ethics and Moral Education* (Berkeley: University of California Press, 1986), esp. pp. 14–19.

3. Ibid., pp. 42, 80.

4. Nel Noddings, *Starting at Home: Caring and Social Policy* (Berkeley: University of California Press, 2002), p. 13.

5. Joan C. Tronto, *Moral Boundaries: A Political Argument for an Ethic of Care* (New York: Routledge, 1993), p. 103; and Berenice Fisher and Joan Tronto, "Toward a Feminist Theory of Caring," in *Circles of Care*, eds. E. Abel and M. Nelson (Albany, N.Y.: SUNY Press, 1990), p. 40.

6. See Virginia Held, *Feminist Morality: Transforming Culture, Society, and Politics* (Chicago: University of Chicago Press, 1993).

7. Diemut Bubeck, *Care, Gender, and Justice* (Oxford: Oxford University Press, 1995), p. 129.

8. Ibid., p. 133.

9. Sara Ruddick. "Care as Labor and Relationship," in *Norms and Values: Essays on the Work of Virginia Held*, eds. Joram C. Haber and Mark S. Halfon (Lanham, Md.: Rowman and Littlefield, 1998), pp. 13–14.

10. Peta Bowden, *Caring* (London: Routledge, 1997), p. 1.

11. Selma Sevenhuijsen, *Citizenship and the Ethics of Care: Feminist Considerations on Justice, Morality and Politics* (London: Routledge, 1998) p. 83.

12. Ibid., p. 83.

13. Ibid., p. 85.

14. Ibid., p. 82.

15. Ibid., p. 84.

16. Michael Slote, *Morals from Motives* (Oxford: Oxford University Press, 2001), p. ix.

17. Ibid., p. 30.

18. See chapters by Lisa Tessman, Margaret McLaren, and Barbara Andrew in *Feminists Doing Ethics*, eds. Peggy DesAutels and Joanne Waugh (Lanham, Md.: Rowman and Littlefield, 2001).

19. Lawrence Blum, *Moral Perception and Particularity* (New York: Cambridge University Press, 1994), p. 199.

20. Ibid., p. 175.

21. Ibid., pp. 173, 179–80.

22. Ibid., p. 195.

23. Ibid.

24. Eva Feder Kittay, *Love's Labor: Essays on Women, Equality, and Dependency* (New York: Routledge, 1999), p. ix.

25. Ibid., p. 30.

26. Ibid., p. 35.

27. Ann Ferguson and Nancy Folbre, "The Unhappy Marriage of Patriarchy and Capitalism," in *Women and Revolution*, ed. Lydia Sargent (Boston: South End Press, 1981), p. 314.

28. Ruddick, "Care as Labor and Relationship," p. 4.

29. Ibid.

30. Ibid., pp. 20–21.

31. Ibid., p. 14.

32. I thank Tucker Lennox for his comment on this issue in connection with a different paper.

33. Diana Tietjens Meyers, *Gender in the Mirror: Cultural Imagery and Women's Agency* (New York: Oxford University Press, 2002), p. 65.

34. Virginia Held, "Moral Subjects: The Natural and the Normative," presidential address, American Philosophical Association, Eastern Division. *Proceedings and Addresses of the American Philosophical Association* (Newark, Del.: APA, November 2002).

35. Sara Ruddick, "Injustice in Families: Assault and Domination," in *Justice and Care: Essential Readings in Feminist Ethics*, ed. Virginia Held (Boulder, Colo.: Westview, 1995).

36. See Virginia Held, *Rights and Goods: Justifying Social Action* (Chicago: University of Chicago Press, 1989), esp. chap. 8.

37. Blum, *Moral Perception and Particularity*, chap. 7, "Virtue and Community."

Chapter 3

1. Edmund Pincoffs, *Quandaries and Virtues: Against Reductivism in Ethics* (Lawrence: University Press of Kansas, 1986).

2. Alasdair MacIntyre, *After Virtue: A Study in Moral Theory* (Notre Dame, Ind.: University of Notre Dame Press, 1981).

3. James D. Wallace, *Virtues and Vices* (Ithaca, N.Y.: Cornell University Press, 1978).

4. Rosalind Hursthouse, Gavin Lawrence, and Warren Quinn, eds., *Virtues and Reasons: Philippa Foot and Moral Theory* (Oxford: Clarendon Press, 1998).

5. Alasdair MacIntyre, *Dependent Rational Animals: Why Human Beings Need the Virtues* (Peru, Ill.: Open Court, 1999).

6. Sydney Shoemaker, "Parfit on Identity," in *Reading Parfit*, ed. Jonathan Dancy (Oxford: Blackwell, 1997), pp. 138–39.

7. Hilde Lindemann Nelson, "Identity and Free Agency," in *Feminists Doing Ethics*, eds. Peggy DesAutels and Joanne Waugh (Lanham, Md.: Rowman and Littlefield, 2001), p. 45.

8. Diana Tietjens Meyers, "Narrative and Moral Life," in *Setting the Moral Compass*, ed. Cheshire Calhoun (New York: Oxford University Press, 2004), p. 299.

9. Examples of those who would naturalize the ethics of care are Annette Baier and Margaret Urban Walker.

10. Jean Keller, "Autonomy, Relationality, and Feminist Ethics," *Hypatia: A Journal of Feminist Philosophy* 12(2) (1997): 152–65, p. 152.

11. Marilyn Friedman, "Autonomy, Social Disruption, and Women," in *Relational Autonomy: Feminist Perspectives on Autonomy, Agency, and the Social Self*, eds. Catriona Mackenzie and Natalie Stoljar (New York: Oxford University Press, 2000), pp. 40–41.

12. See Marilyn Friedman, *Autonomy, Gender, Politics* (New York: Oxford University Press, 2003); and Marina Oshana, "Personal Autonomy and Society," *Journal of Social Philosophy* 29 (spring 1998): 81–102.

13. Meyers, "Narrative and Moral Life," p. 292.

14. For a discussion of empathy and its role in moral thinking, see Diana T. Meyers, *Subjection and Subjectivity* (New York: Routledge, 1994).

15. Lawrence Blum offers a fine set of examples in *Moral Perception and Particularity* (New York: Cambridge University Press, 1994), pp. 186–87.

16. Ibid., p. 193. On the alternative model of simulation or mimicry, see, for example, Robert M. Gordon, "Sympathy, Simulation, and the Impartial Spectator," in *Mind and Morals: Essays on Ethics and Cognitive Science*, eds. Larry May, Marilyn Friedman, and Andy Clark (Cambridge, Mass.: MIT Press, 1996).

17. Mackenzie and Stoljar, eds., *Relational Autonomy*, p. 4.

18. Diana Tietjens Meyers, "Intersectional Identity and the Authentic Self: Opposites Attract!" in *Relational Autonomy*, eds. Mackenzie and Stoljar, pp. 174–75. See also Diana T. Meyers, *Self, Society, and Personal Choice* (New York: Columbia University Press, 1989), pp. 76–91.

19. Susan J. Brison, "Relational Autonomy and Freedom of Expression," in *Relational Autonomy*, eds. MacKenzie and Stoljar, pp. 283–84.

20. Meyers, "Intersectional Identity," p. 152.

21. Daryl Koehn, *Rethinking Feminist Ethics: Care, Trust and Empathy* (London: Routledge, 1998).

22. Meyers, "Narrative and Moral Life," p. 292.

23. See, for example, Mona Harrington, *Care and Equality: Inventing a New Family Politics* (New York: Knopf, 1999); and Nancy Folbre, *The Invisible Heart: Economics and Family Values* (New York: New Press, 2001).

24. Michael Slote, *Morals from Motives* (New York: Oxford University Press, 2001), p. ix.

25. Howard J. Curzer, "Admirable Immorality, Dirty Hands, Care Ethics, Justice Ethics, and Child Sacrifice," *Ratio* 15(3) (September 2002): 227–44.

26. Ibid., p. 236.

27. On freedom as enablement or capacity, not simply noninterference, see Virginia Held, *Rights and Goods: Justifying Social Action* (Chicago: University of Chicago Press, 1989), chap. 5, "Rights to Equal Liberty." See also Martha C. Nussbaum and Jonathan Glover, eds., *Women, Culture and Development: A Study of Human Capabilities* (Oxford: Clarendon Press, 1995).

28. Annette C. Baier, *Moral Prejudices: Essays on Ethics* (Cambridge, Mass.: Harvard University Press, 1994), chaps. 6–9.

29. Annette C. Baier, "Demoralization, Trust, and the Virtues," in *Setting the Moral Compass*, ed. Calhoun, p. 177.

30. Ibid.

31. Ibid., p. 180. See also Celeste M. Friend, "Trust and the Limits of Contract," Ph.D. dissertation, City University of New York, 1995.

32. For some early thoughts, see Virginia Held, "On the Meaning of Trust," *Ethics* 78 (January 1968).

33. A related point is that in prisoner's dilemma situations, we should adopt the point of view of what "we" ought to do, or what would be better for "us," rather than the individualistic point of view of rational choice theory. See Virginia Held, "Rationality and Reasonable Cooperation," *Social Research* 44(4) (winter 1977): 708–44.

34. Baier, *Moral Prejudices*.

Chapter 4

1. See chapter 1, especially the concluding note.

2. See, for example, David Goldberg, ed., *Ethical Theory and Social Issues*, 2nd ed. (Fort Worth, Tex.: Harcourt Brace, 1995); and Steven M. Cahn and Peter Markie, eds., *Ethics: History, Theory, and Contemporary Issues*, 2nd ed. (New York: Oxford University Press, 2002).

3. See Mary Mahowald, ed., *Philosophy of Woman: Classical to Current Concepts*, 3rd ed. (Indianapolis, Ind.: Hackett, 1994).

4. See especially Genevieve Lloyd, *The Man of Reason: "Male" and "Female" in Western Philosophy* (Minneapolis: University of Minnesota Press, 1984).

5. See, for example, Sandra Harding and Merrill Hintikka, eds., *Discovering Reality: Feminist Perspectives on Epistemology, Metaphysics, Methodology and Philosophy of Science* (Dordrecht: Reidel, 1983); and Linda Alcoff and Elizabeth Potter, eds., *Feminist Epistemologies* (New York: Routledge, 1993).

6. See, for example, Elizabeth V. Spelman, *Inessential Woman: Problems of Exclusion in Feminist Thought* (Boston: Beacon Press, 1988); Patricia Hill Collins, *Black*

Feminist Thought: Knowledge, Consciousness and the Politics of Empowerment (Boston: Unwin Hyman, 1990); and Uma Narayan, *Dislocating Cultures: Identities, Traditions, and Third World Feminism* (New York: Routledge, 1997).

7. David Heyd, *Supererogation: Its Status in Ethical Theory* (New York: Cambridge University Press, 1982), p. 134.

8. John Rawls, *A Theory of Justice* (Cambridge, Mass.: Harvard University Press, 1971).

9. For argument, see Virginia Held, *Rights and Goods: Justifying Social Action* (Chicago: University of Chicago Press, 1989).

10. See Virginia Held, *Feminist Morality: Transforming Culture, Society, and Politics* (Chicago: University of Chicago Press, 1993); and Celeste M. Friend, "Trust and the Limits of Contract," Ph.D. dissertation, City University of New York, 1995.

11. See, for example, Alison M. Jaggar, *Feminist Politics and Human Nature* (Totowa, N.J.: Rowman and Allanheld, 1983); and Carol C. Gould, *Rethinking Democracy: Freedom and Social Cooperation in Politics, Economy, and Society* (Cambridge: Cambridge University Press, 1988).

12. See especially Susan Moller Okin, *Justice, Gender, and the Family* (New York: Basic Books, 1989).

13. See, for example, Marilyn Friedman, *What Are Friends For? Feminist Perspectives on Personal Relationships and Moral Theory* (Ithaca, N.Y.: Cornell University Press, 1993).

14. See, for example, Held, *Feminist Morality*; Joan C. Tronto, *Moral Boundaries: A Political Argument for an Ethic of Care* (New York: Routledge, 1993); and Rebecca Grant and Kathleen Newland, eds., *Gender and International Relations* (Bloomington: Indiana University Press, 1991).

15. Monique Deveaux, "Shifting Paradigms: Theorizing Care and Justice in Political Theory," *Hypatia: A Journal of Feminist Philosophy* 10(2) (spring 1995): 117.

16. Catharine MacKinnon, *Toward a Feminist Theory of the State* (Cambridge, Mass.: Harvard University Press, 1989), pp. 238–48.

17. Elizabeth M. Schneider, "The Dialectic of Rights and Politics: Perspectives from the Women's Movement," in *Feminist Legal Theory: Readings in Law and Gender*, eds. Katherine T. Bartlett and Rosanne Kennedy (Boulder, Colo.: Westview Press, 1989), p. 318.

18. Carol Smart, *Feminism and the Power of Law* (London: Routledge, 1989).

19. Schneider, "The Dialectic of Rights and Politics," p. 322.

20. Patricia J. Williams, *The Alchemy of Race and Rights* (Cambridge, Mass.: Harvard University Press, 1991), p. 149.

21. Frances Olsen, "Statutory Rape: A Feminist Critique of Rights Analysis," in *Feminist Legal Theory*, ed. Bartlett and Kennedy.

22. Catherine MacKinnon, *Feminism Unmodified: Discourses on Life and Law* (Cambridge, Mass.: Harvard University Press, 1987), p. 104.

23. Patricia Smith, ed., *Feminist Jurisprudence* (New York: Oxford University Press, 1993), p. 14.

24. See ibid., part IV.

25. Selma Sevenhuijsen, *Citizenship and the Ethics of Care* (London: Routledge, 1998), chap. 4.

26. See, for example, Diana T. Meyers, *Subjection and Subjectivity: Psychoanalytic Feminism and Moral Philosophy* (New York: Routledge, 1994).

27. Held, *Rights and Goods*.

28. Ibid.

29. See, for example, Kittay, *Love's Labor*; and Mary B. Mahowald, Anita Silvers, and David Wasserman, *Disability, Difference, Discrimination* (Lanham, Md.: Rowman and Littlefield, 1998).

30. Diana Tietjens Meyers, "Narrative and Moral Life," in *Setting the Moral Compass*, ed. Cheshire Calhoun (New York: Oxford University Press, 2004), p. 293.

31. Ibid.

32. Ibid.

33. For further discussion, see Virginia Held, "Moral Subjects: The Natural and the Normative," presidential address (APA Eastern Division). *Proceedings of the American Philosophical Association* (November 2002).

34. For discussion, see Michael Slote, *From Morality to Virtue* (New York: Oxford University Press, 1992); and chapter 3 in this volume.

35. See, for example, the discussions of John Keane's *Global Civil Society?* and Anne-Marie Slaughter's *A New World Order* in chapter 10 of this volume.

Chapter 5

1. Ann Cudd, Review of Virginia Held, *Feminist Morality. Philosophical Review* 104(4) (1995): 612.

2. Virginia Held, *Feminist Morality: Transforming Culture, Society, and Politics* (Chicago: University of Chicago Press, 1993), p. 213.

3. Cudd, review.

4. See Claudia Card, Review of Virginia Held, *Feminist Morality. Ethics* 105(4) (1995): 938–40.

5. See Susan Moller Okin, *Justice, Gender, and the Family* (New York: Basic Books, 1989).

6. Brian Barry, *Justice as Impartiality* (Oxford: Oxford University Press, 1995), p. 191.

7. See Annette Baier, *Moral Prejudices: Essays on Ethics* (Cambridge, Mass.: Harvard University Press, 1994).

8. Marcia Baron, "Impartiality and Friendship." *Ethics* 101(4) (July 1991): 836–57, p. 842.

9. Ibid.

10. See, for example, Jean Hampton, "Feminist Contractarianism," in *A Mind of One's Own: Feminist Essays on Reason and Objectivity*, eds. Louise Antony and Charlotte Witt (Boulder, Colo.: Westview, 1993); and Okin, *Justice, Gender, and the Family*.

11. See, for example, Claudia Card, "Gender and Moral Luck," in *Identity, Character, and Moralilty: Essays in Moral Psychology*, eds. Owen Flanagan and Amelie Oksenberg Rorty (Cambridge, Mass.: MIT Press, 1990); and Sara Ruddick, "Injustice in Families: Assault and Domination," in *Justice and Care: Essential Readings in Feminist Ethics*, ed. Virginia Held (Boulder, Colo.: Westview Press, 1995).

12. See, for example, David Gauthier, *Morals by Agreement* (Oxford: Clarendon Press, 1986).

13. See, for example, John Rawls, *Political Liberalism* (New York: Columbia University Press, 1993).

14. Robert A. Dahl, *After the Revolution* (New Haven, Conn.: Yale University Press, 1970).

15. See, for example, Diana Meyers, ed., *Feminists Rethink the Self* (Boulder, Colo.: Westview Press, 1997).

16. Gauthier, *Morals by Agreement*, p. 4.

17. Peter Vallentyne, ed., *Contractarianism and Rational Choice* (New York: Cambridge University Press, 1991), p. 4.

18. Ibid., p. 4.

19. Ibid., p. 5.

20. Jean Hampton, *Political Philosophy* (Boulder, Colo.: Westview, 1997), p. 169.

21. Cass R. Sunstein, *The Second Bill of Rights: FDR's Unfinished Revolution and Why We Need It More Than Ever* (New York: Basic Books, 2004).

22. David M. Kennedy, "Unfinished Business," *New York Times Book Review* (September 19, 2004), p. 23.

23. See, for example, Baier, *Moral Prejudices;* Virginia Held, *Rights and Goods: Justifying Social Action* (1984; Chicago: University of Chicago Press, 1989); Sibyl Schwarzenbach, "On Civic Friendship," *Ethics* 107(1) (1996): 97–128.

24. See, for example, Andrew Mason, "Political Community, Liberal-Nationalism, and the Ethics of Assimilation," *Ethics* 109(2) (January 1999): 261–86.

25. See Held, *Feminist Morality*, for further argument.

26. Nel Noddings, *Caring: A Feminine Approach to Ethics and Moral Education* (Berkeley: University of California Press, 1986), p. 47.

27. Baier, *Moral Prejudices*, pp. 25–26.

28. Martha Minow, *Making All the Difference: Inclusion, Exclusion, and American Law* (Ithaca, N.Y.: Cornell University Press, 1990).

29. Held, ed., *Justice and Care*.

30. Noddings, *Caring*, pp. 18, 112.

Chapter 6

1. J. David Velleman, "Love and Duty," paper presented at the annual meeting of the American Philosophical Association, Eastern Division, Philadelphia, Pa., December 30, 1997.

2. J. David Velleman, "Love as a Moral Emotion," *Ethics* 109(2) (January 1999): 338–74.

3. Bernard Williams, *Moral Luck: Philosophical Papers 1973–80* (Cambridge: Cambridge University Press, 1981), p. 18.

4. Velleman, "Love as a Moral Emotion," p. 342.

5. Ibid., p. 365.

6. Ibid., p. 371.

7. Ibid.

8. Ibid., p. 370.

9. Ibid., p. 361.

10. Ibid., p. 338, n.1.

11. Ibid., p. 354.

12. Ibid., p. 348, n.30; emphasis in original.

13. Thomas Hill, comment on David Velleman's "Love and Duty," delivered at the annual meeting of the American Philosophical Association, Eastern Division. Philadelphia, Pa., December 30, 1997.

14. Harry Frankfurt, comment on David Velleman's "Love and Duty," delivered at the annual meeting of the American Philosophical Association, Eastern Division, December 30, 1997.

15. See Marilyn Friedman, *What Are Friends For? Feminist Perspectives on Personal Relationships and Moral Theory* (Ithaca, N.Y.: Cornell University Press, 1993).

16. Thomas Nagel, *The Possibility of Altruism* (London: Oxford University Press, 1970).

17. Stephen Darwall, *Philosophical Ethics* (Boulder, Colo.: Westview Press, 1998), p. 226.

18. Ibid., p. 227.

19. Ibid., p. 228.

20. Martha C. Nussbaum, "The Feminist Critique of Liberalism." Lindley Lecture, University of Kansas (1997), p. 30. This lecture became chapter 2 in Nussbaum's *Sex and Social Justice* (New York: Oxford University Press, 1999).

21. Ibid.

22. Nussbaum, "The Feminist Critique of Liberalism," p. 15.

23. Friedman, *What Are Friends For?*, p. 40.

24. Ibid., p. 66.

25. Ibid., p. 59.

26. Lawrence Blum, *Moral Perception and Particularity* (New York: Cambridge University Press, 1994), p. 199.

27. Ibid., p. 200.

28. For example, Nel Noddings, *Caring: A Feminine Approach to Ethics and Moral Education* (Berkeley: University of California Press, 1986).

29. Stephen Darwall, *Impartial Reason* (Ithaca, N.Y.: Cornell University Press, 1983).

30. Annette Baier, *Moral Prejudices: Essays on Ethics* (Cambridge, Mass.: Harvard University Press, 1994), p. 26; and see chapter 1 of this volume.

31. Susan Mendus, "Some Mistakes about Impartiality," *Political Studies* 44 (1996): 319–27.

32. See Elizabeth Frazer and Nicola Lacey, *The Politics of Community: A Feminist Critique of the Liberal-Communitarian Debate* (Toronto: University of Toronto Press, 1993); and Friedman, *What Are Friends For?*

33. See, for example, Eva Feder Kittay, "Taking Dependency Seriously," *Hypatia* 10 (1995): 8–29.

34. Nussbaum, "The Feminist Critique," p. 44, n.98; emphasis added.

35. Neil MacCormick, "Justice as Impartiality: Assenting with Anti-Contractualist Reservations," *Political Studies* 44 (1996): 305–10, p. 309.

36. Mendus, "Some Mistakes about Impartiality," p. 323.

37. John Rawls, *A Theory of Justice* (Cambridge, Mass.: Harvard University Press, 1971).

38. Ronald Dworkin, *Taking Rights Seriously* (Cambridge, Mass.: Harvard University Press, 1977).

39. John Rawls, *Political Liberalism* (New York: Columbia University Press, 1993).

40. Virginia Held, *Rights and Goods. Justifying Social Action* (New York: Free Press/Macmillan, 1984); see also Robert E. Goodin, *Utilitarianism as a Public Philosophy* (Cambridge: Cambridge University Press, 1995).

41. For example, Marcia Baron, "Kantian Ethics," in *Three Methods of Ethics*, eds. Marcia W. Baron, Philip Pettit, and Michael Slote (Oxford: Blackwell, 1997).

42. For further discussion, see Virginia Held, "Access, Enablement, and the First Amendment," in *Philosophical Dimensions of the Constitution*, eds. Diana T. Meyers and Kenneth Kipnis (Boulder, Colo.: Westview Press, 1988); and Virginia Held, *Feminist Morality: Transforming Culture, Society, and Politics* (Chicago: University of Chicago Press, 1993), chap. 5.

Chapter 7

1. Robert Kuttner, *Everything for Sale: The Virtues and Limits of Markets*. A Twentieth Century Fund Book (New York: Knopf, 1998), p. 3.

2. Ibid., p. 55.

3. Paula England and Nancy Folbre, "The Cost of Caring," *Annals of the American Academy of Political and Social Science* 561 (January 1999): 39–51, p. 40.

4. Ibid., p. 46.

5. Elizabeth Anderson, "Is Women's Labor a Commodity?" *Philosophy and Public Affairs* 19(1) (winter 1990): 71–92, pp. 72–73.

6. Kuttner, *Everything for Sale*, pp. 68–69.

7. Ibid., pp. 73–74.

8. Nancy Folbre and Julie A. Nelson, "For Love or Money—Or Both?" *Journal of Economic Perspectives* 14(4) (2000): 123–40, p. 21.

9. Charles K. Wilber, ed., *Economics, Ethics, and Public Policy* (Lanham, Md.: Rowman and Littlefield, 1998), pp. 93–94.

10. Anderson, "Is Women's Labor a Commodity?" p. 73.

11. Margaret Jane Radin, *Contested Commodities: The Trouble with Trade in Sex, Children, Body Parts, and Other Things* (Cambridge, Mass.: Harvard University Press, 1996), p. 2.

12. Ibid., p. 3.

13. Richard A. Posner, *Economic Analysis of Law*, 4th ed. (Boston: Little, Brown, 1992); and Elisabeth M. Landes and Richard A. Posner, "The Economics of the Baby Shortage," *Journal of Legal Studies* 7 (1978).

14. Gary S. Becker, *The Economic Approach to Human Behavior* (Chicago: University of Chicago Press, 1976), p. 173.

15. Ibid., p. 8. See also Gary S. Becker, *A Treatise on the Family* (Cambridge, Mass.: Harvard University Press, 1981).

16. Radin, *Contested Commodities*, p. 5.

17. Jonathan Riley, "Justice under Capitalism," in *Markets and Justice*, eds. John W. Chapman and J. Roland Pennock, NOMOS 31 (New York: New York University Press, 1989), pp. 122–62, p. 125, and p. 155, n.21.

18. Kuttner, *Everything for Sale*, p. 4.

19. Ibid., p. 109.

20. Ibid., p. 86.

21. Radin, *Contested Commodities*; and Katharine Silbaugh, "Commodification and Women's Household Labor," *Yale Journal of Law and Feminism* 9(51) (1997): 81–121.

22. See, for example, Gerald Marwell and Ruth E. Ames, "Economists Free Ride, Does Anyone Else?" *Journal of Public Economics* 13 (1981): 295–310.

23. Robert H. Frank, Thomas Gilovich, and Dennis T. Regan, "Does Studying Economics Inhibit Cooperation?" *Journal of Economic Perspectives* 7(2) (1993): 159–71.

24. Robyn M. Dawes and Richard H. Thaler, "Cooperation," *Journal of Economic Perspectives* 2(3) (summer 1988): 187–97.

25. Kuttner, *Everything for Sale*, p. 158.

26. Ibid., p. 112.

27. Robin Toner, "Experts See Fix for Medicare as One Tough Proposition," *New York Times* (September 12, 2000), pp. 1 and 23.

28. Edward Wyatt, "Taking a Corporate Approach to Remaking Education," *New York Times* (January 12, 2000), p. A16.

29. Ibid.

30. Arthur Levine, "The Soul of a New University," *New York Times* (March 13, 2000), op-ed page.

31. Constance L. Hays, "Commercialism in U.S. Schools Is Examined in New Report," *New York Times* (September 14, 2000), pp. C1 and 25.

32. Steven Manning, "How Corporations Are Buying Their Way into American Classrooms," *The Nation* (September 27, 1999), pp. 11–18.

33. Immanuel Kant, *Foundations of the Metaphysics of Morals*, trans. Lewis White Beck (Indianapolis: Bobbs-Merrill, 1959), p. 429, 47.

34. See Richard Wasserstrom, *The Judicial Decision: Toward a Theory of Legal Justification* (Stanford, Calif.: Stanford University Press, 1961).

35. Virginia Held, *Rights and Goods: Justifying Social Action* (Chicago: University of Chicago Press, 1989), esp. chap. 7.

36. Radin, *Contested Commodities*, p. 30.

37. Elizabeth Anderson, *Value in Ethics and Economics* (Cambridge, Mass.: Harvard University Press, 1993), p. 170.

38. Ibid., p. 171.

39. Mary Lyndon Shanley, " 'Surrogate Mothering' and Women's Freedom: A Critique of Contracts for Human Reproduction," *Signs* 18(3) (1993): 618–39, p. 626.

40. Ibid., p. 629.

41. Juliet Ruth Guichon, "An Examination and Critique of the Contract Model of Legal Regulation of Preconception Arrangements." Ph.D. dissertation, University of Toronto, 1997.

42. See Radin, *Contested Commodities*; and David Copp, "Capitalism versus Democracy: The Marketing of Votes and the Marketing of Political Power," in *Ethics and Capitalism*, ed. John Bishop (Toronto: University of Toronto Press, 2000).

43. See chapters 12 in Held, *Rights and Goods*, and 5 in *Feminist Morality: Transforming Culture, Society, and Politics* (Chicago: University of Chicago Press, 1993). Also see Virginia Held, chapters "Access, Enablement, and the First Amendment," in *Philosophical Dimensions of the Constitution*, eds. Diana T. Meyers and Kenneth Kipnis (Boulder, Colo.: Westview Press, 1988); and "Media Culture and Democracy," in *Demokratischer Experimentalismus*, ed. Hauke Brunkhorst (Frankfurt: Surkamp Verlag, 1998).

44. John McMurtry, "Education and the Market Model," *Journal of Philosophy of Education* 25(2) (1991): 209–17, p. 214.

Chapter 8

1. Will Kymlicka and Wayne Norman, "Return of the Citizen: A Survey of Recent Work on Citizenship Theory," *Ethics* 104 (January 1994): 352–81, p. 369.

2. See David Miller, *Market, State, and Community* (Oxford: Oxford University Press, 1989).

3. See Andrew Mason, "Political Community, Liberal-Nationalism, and the Ethics of Assimilation," *Ethics* 109(2) (January 1999): 261–86.

4. John Keane, *Civil Society: Old Images, New Visions* (Stanford, Calif.: Stanford University Press, 1998), p. 4.

5. Ibid.

6. Juan J. Linz and Alfred Stepan, *Problems of Democratic Transition and Consolidation: Southern Europe, South America, and Post-Communist Europe* (Baltimore, Md.: Johns Hopkins University Press, 1996).

7. Gabriel A. Almond and Sidney Verba, *Civic Culture* (Boston: Little, Brown, 1965), p. 30.

8. Jean L. Cohen and Andrew Arato, *Civil Society and Political Theory* (Cambridge, Mass.: MIT Press, 1994), p. x.

9. Keith Tester, *Civil Society* (New York: Routledge, 1992), p. 8.

10. John A. Hall, "In Search of Civil Society," in *Civil Society: Theory, History, Comparison*, ed. John A. Hall (Cambridge: Polity Press, 1995), p. 6.

11. Keane, *Civil Society*, p. 6.

12. Hall, "In Search of Civil Society," p. 10.

13. Richard Daggar, *Civic Virtues* (New York: Oxford University Press, 1997), p. 198.

14. Ibid., p. 200.

15. Robert Kuttner, *Everything for Sale* (New York: Knopf, 1998), p. 351.

16. Ibid., p. 354.

17. Keane, *Civil Society*, p. 17.

18. Cohen and Arato, *Civil Society and Political Theory*.

19. Robert D. Putnam, *Making Democracy Work* (Princeton, N.J.: Princeton University Press, 1994).

20. Alexis de Tocqueville, *Democracy in America*, 12th ed. (New York: Vintage, 1955).

21. Putnam, *Making Democracy Work*; and Robert Putnam, "The Strange Disappearance of Civic America," *American Prospect* 24 (winter 1996): 34–49.

22. See especially John Dewey, *Democracy and Education* (New York: Macmillan, 1916), and *Experience and Education* (New York: Collier Macmillan, 1963).

23. Daggar, *Civic Virtues*.

24. See, for example, Amy Gutmann, *Democratic Education* (Princeton, N.J.: Princeton University Press, 1987); William Galston, *Liberal Purposes* (Cambridge: Cambridge University Press, 1992); Stephen Macedo, "Liberal Civic Education and Religious Fundamentalism: The Case of God v. John Rawls?" *Ethics* 108 (1995): 468–96; and Harry Brighouse, "Civic Education and Liberal Legitimacy," *Ethics* 108 (July 1998): 719–45.

25. Keane, *Civil Society*, p. 47.

26. See especially Marilyn Friedman, *What Are Friends For? Feminist Perspectives on Personal Relationships and Moral Theory* (Ithaca, N.Y.: Cornell University Press, 1993); and Virginia Held, *Feminist Morality: Transforming Culture, Society, and Politics* (Chicago: University of Chicago Press, 1993).

27. See especially Susan Moller Okin, *Justice, Gender, and the Family* (New York: Basic Books, 1989), and "Feminism and Multiculturalism: Some Tensions," *Ethics* 108 (July 1998): 661–84.

28. Joan C. Tronto, *Moral Boundaries: A Political Argument for an Ethic of Care* (New York: Routledge, 1993), p. 185.

29. Joan C. Tronto, "Care as a Political Concept," in *Revisioning the Political*, eds. Nancy J. Hirschmann and Christine Di Stefano (Boulder, Colo.: Westview Press, 1996), p. 143.

30. Ibid.

31. Ibid, p. 145.

32. See especially Kuttner, *Everything for Sale*.

33. See also Fiona Robinson, *Globalizing Care: Ethics, Feminist Theory, and International Relations* (Boulder, Colo.: Westview Press, 1999).

34. On communitarianism especially see Okin, *Justice, Gender, and the Family*, and "Feminism and Multiculturalism."

35. Virginia Held, *Rights and Goods. Justifying Social Action* (New York: Free Press/Macmillan, 1984), chap. 5.

36. Keane, *Civil Society*, p. 49.

37. Ibid., pp. 53–55.

38. See especially Okin, *Justice, Gender, and the Family*; and Martha C. Nussbaum, *Sex and Social Justice* (New York: Oxford University Press, 1999).

39. Keane, *Civil Society*, p. 34.

Chapter 9

1. Claudia Card, "Foreword," in Linda A. Bell, *Rethinking Ethics in the Midst of Violence: A Feminist Approach to Freedom* (Lanham, Md.: Rowman and Littlefield, 1993), p. xiii.

2. Ibid., p. xiv.

3. Sara Ruddick, *Maternal Thinking: Toward a Politics of Peace* (Boston: Beacon Press, 1989).

4. Ibid., p. 162.

5. Ibid., p. 163.

6. See Virginia Held, *Feminist Morality: Transforming Culture, Society, and Politics* (Chicago: University of Chicago Press, 1993), chap. 7.

7. See, for example, Deborah L. Rhode, *Justice and Gender: Sex Discrimination and the Law* (Cambridge, Mass.: Harvard University Press, 1989).

8. Carol Gilligan, *In a Different Voice: Psychological Theory and Women's Development* (Cambridge, Mass.: Harvard University Press, 1982), p. 22.

9. Annette Baier, *Moral Prejudices: Essays on Ethics* (Cambridge, Mass.: Harvard University Press, 1994), p. 237.

10. Elizabeth M. Schneider, "The Dialectic of Rights and Politics: Perspectives from the Women's Movement," *New York University Law Review* 61 (1986): 593–652, p. 318.

11. Patricia Smith, ed., *Feminist Jurisprudence* (New York: Oxford University Press, 1993), p. 3.

12. Ibid., p. 139.

13. Kimberle Crenshaw, "Demarginalizing the Intersection of Race and Sex: A Black Feminist Critique of Antidiscrimination Doctrine, Feminist Theory, and Antiracist Politics," in *Feminist Legal Theory: Readings in Law and Gender*, eds. Katherine T. Bartlett and Rosanne Kennedy (Boulder, Colo.: Westview Press, 1991).

14. Robin West, "Jurisprudence and Gender," *University of Chicago Law Review* 55 (1988): 1–72, p. 2.

15. Schneider, "The Dialectic of Rights and Politics."

16. Bartlett and Kennedy, eds., *Feminist Legal Theory*; Drucilla Cornell, *At the Heart of Freedom: Feminism, Sex, and Equality* (Princeton, N.J.: Princeton University Press, 1998).

17. Patricia Smith, "Feminist Jurisprudence: Social Change and Conceptual Evolution," *American Philosophical Association Newsletters* (spring 1995).

18. Christine Littleton, "Reconstructing Sexual Equality," *California Law Review* 75(4) (1987): 1279–337.

19. Catharine A. MacKinnon, *Feminism Unmodified: Discourses on Life and Law* (Cambridge, Mass.: Harvard University Press, 1987), p. 103.

20. Frances Olsen, "Statutory Rape: A Feminist Critique of Rights Analysis," *Texas Law Review* 63 (1984): 387–432, p. 402.

21. Ibid., p. 412.

22. Susan Estrich, "Rape," *Yale Law Journal* 95 (1987): 1087–184, p. 1114.

23. Smith, ed., *Feminist Jurisprudence*, part IV.

24. See, for example, Diana T. Meyers, "Social Exclusion, Moral Reflection, and Rights," *Law and Philosophy* 12 (1993): 217–32.

25. Selma Sevenhuijsen, *Citizenship and the Ethics of Care* (London: Routledge, 1998), chap. 4.

26. Ibid., p. 94.

27. Ibid., pp. 100, 105.

28. Ibid., p. 121.

29. For example, see Diana T. Meyers, *Self, Society and Personal Choice* (New York: Columbia University Press, 1989).

30. Patricia J. Williams, *The Alchemy of Race and Rights* (Cambridge, Mass.: Harvard University Press, 1991).

31. Ibid., p. 152.

32. Uma Narayan, "Colonialism and Its Others: Considerations on Rights and Care Discourses," *Hypatia* 10(2) (1995): 133–40.

33. See, for example, Elizabeth Frazer and Nicola Lacey, *The Politics of Community. A Feminist Critique of the Liberal-Communitarian Debate* (Toronto: University of Toronto Press, 1993).

34. For example, see Diana T. Meyers, "Rights in Collision: A Non-Punitive, Compensatory Remedy for Abusive Speech," *Law and Philosophy* 14 (1995): 203–43; and Martha Minow and Mary Lyndon Shanley, "Relational Rights and Responsibilities: Revisioning the Family in Liberal Political Theory and Law," *Hypatia* 11(1) (winter 1996): 3–29.

35. Martha Minow, *Making All the Difference: Inclusion, Exclusion, and American Law* (Ithaca, N.Y.: Cornell University Press, 1990), p. 15.

36. Ibid., p. 14.

37. Ibid., p. 268.

38. Ibid., p. 307.

39. Crenshaw, "Demarginalizing the Intersection of Race and Sex."

40. For example, see Claudia Card, "Gender and Moral Luck," in *Justice and Care: Essential Readings in Feminist Ethics*, ed. Virginia Held (Boulder, Colo.: Westview Press, 1995); and Barbara Houston, "Rescuing Womanly Virtues: Some Dangers of Moral Reclamation," in *Science, Morality and Feminist Theory*, eds. Marsha Hanen and Kai Nielsen (Calgary: University of Calgary Press, 1987).

41. Alison Jaggar, "Caring as a Feminist Practice of Moral Reason," in *Justice and Care*, ed. Held, p. 194.

42. Marilyn Friedman, *What Are Friends For? Feminist Perspectives on Personal Relationships* (Ithaca, N.Y.: Cornell University Press, 1993), p. 150.

43. See especially Susan Moller Okin, *Justice, Gender, and the Family* (New York: Basic Books, 1989).

44. See especially Sara Ruddick, "Injustice in Families: Assault and Domination," in *Justice and Care*, ed. Held.

45. Marilyn Friedman, *Autonomy, Gender, Politics* (New York: Oxford University Press, 2003).

46. See Virginia Held, *Rights and Goods. Justifying Social Action* (New York: Free Press/Macmillan, 1984).

47. Rebecca Grant and Kathleen Newland, eds., *Gender and International Relations* (Bloomington: Indiana University Press, 1993).

48. Joan B. Landes, ed., *Feminism, the Public and the Private* (New York: Oxford University Press, 1998).

49. See Joan Callahan, *Reproduction, Ethics, and the Law: Feminist Perspectives* (Bloomington: Indiana University Press, 1995); and Rosalind P. Petchesky, *Abortion and Women's Choice: The State, Sexuality, and Reproductive Freedom* (Boston: Northeastern University Press, 1985).

50. Anita Allen, *Uneasy Access: Privacy for Women in a Free Society* (Totowa, N.J.: Rowman and Littlefield, 1988).

51. Ibid.

52. Catharine A. MacKinnon, *Toward a Feminist Theory of the State* (Cambridge, Mass.: Harvard University Press, 1989), p. 179.

53. See, for example, Seyla Benhabib and Drucilla Cornell, eds., *Feminism as Critique: On the Politics of Gender* (Minneapolis: University of Minnesota Press, 1987); and Linda Nicholson, ed., *Feminism/Postmodernism* (New York: Routledge, 1990). See also Nancy Fraser, *Unruly Practices: Power, Discourse, and Gender in Contemporary Social Theory* (Minneapolis: University of Minnesota Press, 1989).

54. See, for example, Sevenhuijsen, *Citizenship and the Ethics of Care*, for discussion.

55. Nancy C. M. Hartsock, "Community/Sexuality/Gender: Rethinking Power," in *Revisioning The Political: Feminist Reconstructions of Traditional Concepts in Western Political Theory*, eds. Nancy J. Hirschmann and Christine Di Stefano (Boulder, Colo.: Westview Press, 1996), p. 42.

56. Sevenhuijsen, *Citizenship and the Ethics of Care*, p. 11.

57. Christine Di Stefano, "Feminist Political Philosophy," *APA Newsletter on Feminism and Philosophy* (spring 2000): 196–200, p. 196.

58. Nancy C. M. Hartsock, *Money, Sex, and Power: Toward a Feminist Historical Materialism* (New York: Longman, 1983).

59. Amy Allen, *The Power of Feminist Theory: Domination, Resistance, Solidarity* (Boulder, Colo.: Westview Press, 1999), p. 3.

60. Ibid.

61. See, for example, Joan C. Tronto, *Moral Boundaries: A Political Argument for an Ethic of Care* (New York: Routledge, 1993), and "Care as a Political Concept," in *Revisioning the Political*, eds. Hirschmann and Di Stefano.

62. See especially Ruddick, *Maternal Thinking*.

63. See Fiona Robinson, *Globalizing Care: Ethics, Feminist Theory, and International Affairs* (Boulder, Colo.: Westview Press, 1999); and chapter 10 in this volume.

64. Jane Mansbridge, *Beyond Adversary Democracy* (Chicago: University of Chicago Press, 1983).

65. Jane Mansbridge, "Reconstructing Democracy," in *Revisioning the Political*, eds. Hirschmann and DiStefano, p. 123.

66. For example, see Frank Cunningham, *Democratic Theory and Socialism* (Cambridge: Cambridge University Press, 1987); and Carol C. Gould, *Rethinking Democracy: Freedom and Social Cooperation in Politics, Economy, and Society* (Cambridge: Cambridge University Press, 1998).

67. See Anne Phillips, *The Politics of Presence* (Oxford: Oxford University Press, 1995); Charles Taylor, *Philosophical Arguments* (Cambridge, Mass.: Harvard University Press, 1995); and Iris Marion Young, *Justice and the Politics of Difference* (Princeton, N.J.: Princeton University Press, 1990).

68. Kathleen B. Jones, *Compassionate Authority: Democracy and the Representation of Women* (New York: Routledge, 1993).

69. See Susan Mendus, "Losing the Faith: Feminism and Democracy," in *Democracy: The Unfinished Journey*, ed. J. Dunn (Oxford: Oxford University Press, 1992); and Young, *Justice and the Politics of Difference*.

70. Held, *Feminist Morality*, chap. 5.

Chapter 10

1. See, for example, Rebecca Grant and Kathleen Newland, eds., *Gender and International Relations* (Bloomington: Indiana University Press, 1991), p. 3.

2. A few titles are: Richard Falk, *Legal Order in a Violent World* (Princeton, N.J.: Princeton University Press, 1968); Richard Wasserstrom, ed., *War and Morality* (Belmont, Calif.: Wadsworth, 1970); Virginia Held, Sidney Morgenbesser, and Thomas Nagel, eds., *Philosophy, Morality, and International Affairs* (New York: Oxford University Press, 1974); William Aiken and Hugh LaFollette, eds., *World Hunger and Moral Obligation* (Englewood Cliffs, N.J.: Prentice Hall, 1977); Michael Walzer, *Just and Unjust Wars* (New York: Basic Books, 1977); Charles R. Beitz, *Political Theory and International Relations* (Princeton, N.J.: Princeton University Press, 1979); Stanley Hoffman, *Duties beyond Borders: On the Limits and Possibilities of Ethical International Politics* (Syracuse, N.Y.: Syracuse University Press, 1981); Robert L. Holmes, *On War and Morality* (Princeton, N.J.: Princeton University Press, 1989); Steven Luper-Foy, ed., *Problems of International Justice* (Boulder, Colo.: Westview Press, 1988); and Andrew Valls, ed., *Ethics in International Affairs* (Lanham, Md.: Rowman and Littlefield, 2000).

3. See, for example, Louis Henkin, "The Use of Force: Law and U.S. Policy," in *Right v. Wrong: International Law and the Use of Force* (Council on Foreign Relations, 1989).

4. For example, see Jill Steans, *Gender and International Relations: An Introduction* (New Brunswick, N.J.: Rutgers University Press, 1998).

5. See, for example, Robert O. Keohane, "International Relations Theory: Contributions of a Feminist Standpoint," in *Gender and International Relations*, eds. R. Grant and K. Newland. See also Jim George, *Discourses of Global Politics: A Critical (Re)Introduction to International Relations* (Boulder, Colo.: Lynne Rienner, 1994).

6. See Fred Halliday, "Hidden from International Relations: Women and the International Arena," in *Gender and International Relations*, ed. Grant and Newman.

7. J. Ann Tickner, *Gender in International Relations: Feminist Perspectives on Achieving Global Security* (New York: Columbia University Press, 1992), p. 4.

8. Ibid., p. 17.

9. V. Spike Peterson and Anne Sisson Runyan, *Global Gender Issues* (Boulder, Colo.: Westview Press, 1993), p. 10.

10. Nina Bernstein, "For Americans, It's French Sissies versus German He-Men," *New York Times* (September 28, 2003), sec. 4, p. 5.

11. Peterson and Runyan, *Global Gender Issues*, p. 34.

12. See Beitz, *Political Theory and International Relations*; Onora O'Neill, *Faces of Hunger: An Essay on Poverty, Justice, and Development* (London: Allen and Unwin, 1985); and Thomas Pogge, *World Poverty and Human Rights* (Malden, Mass.: Polity Press, 2002).

13. For example, see Peter Singer, *One World: The Ethics of Globalization* (New Haven, Conn.: Yale University Press, 2002).

14. For a pluralistic view in which different values are seen as appropriately having priority in different domains, see Virginia Held, *Rights and Goods: Justifying Social Action* (Chicago: University of Chicago Press, 1989).

15. See Virginia Held, *Feminist Morality: Transforming Culture, Society, and Politics* (Chicago: University of Chicago Press, 1993), chap. 5.

16. See Margaret Jane Radin, *Contested Commodities: The Trouble with Trade in Sex, Children, Body Parts and Other Things* (Cambridge, Mass.: Harvard University Press, 1996).

17. Elizabeth Becker, "Number of Hungry Rising, U.N. Says," *New York Times* (December 8, 2004).

18. Carol C. Gould, *Globalizing Democracy and Human Rights* (New York: Cambridge University Press, 2004), p. 44.

19. Ibid., p. 46.

20. See especially Christine Di Stefano, *Configurations of Masculinity: A Feminist Perspective on Modern Political Theory* (Ithaca, N.Y.: Cornell University Press, 1991).

21. Peterson and Runyan, *Global Gender Issues*, p. 34. See, for example, Kenneth Waltz, "The Myth of National Interdependence," in *Globalism versus Realism: International Relations' Third Debate*, eds. Ray Maghroori and Bennett Ramberg (Boulder, Colo.: Westview Press, 1982).

22. Tickner, *Gender in International Relations*, p. 32.

23. For example, Hilary Charlesworth, "What Are 'Women's International Human Rights?'" in *Human Rights of Women: National and International Perspectives*, ed. Rebecca J. Cooke (Philadelphia: University of Pennsylvania Press, 1994).

24. J. Ann Tickner, *Gendering World Politics* (New York: Columbia University Press, 2001), p. 6.

25. See Tickner, *Gender in International Relations*, chap. 2.

26. The equality imagined has been not only moral but empirical—Hobbes's equal vulnerability to the sword of one's neighbor, for instance. When, on the world stage, states are imagined to be individuals, the removal from reality increases.

27. See Tickner, *Gendering World Politics*.

28. United Nations Development Programme, *Human Development Report* (New York: Oxford University Press, 1996), p. 2.

29. See Tickner, *Gendering World Politics*.

30. Peterson and Runyan, *Global Gender Issues*, pp. 92–94.

31. Sue Ellen M. Charlton, *Women in Third World Development* (Boulder, Colo.: Westview Press, 1984).

32. Peterson and Runyan, *Global Gender Issues*, pp. 94–95. See also Tickner, *Gendering World Politics*, pp. 94–95.

33. Tickner, *Gendering World Politics*, p. 77.

34. Ibid., pp. 77–78.

35. Anne Sisson Runyon, "Women in the Neoliberal 'Frame,'" in *Gender Politics in Global Governance*, eds. Mary K. Meyer and Elisabeth Prügl (Lanham, Md.: Rowman and Littlefield, 1999), pp. 215–16.

36. Ibid., p. 216

37. Emek M. Uçarer, "Trafficking in Women: Alternate Migration or Modern Slave Trade?" in *Gender Politics in Global Governance*, eds. M. Meyer and E. Prügl.

38. Halliday, "Hidden from International Relations," p. 161.

39. Peterson and Runyan, *Global Gender Issues*, pp. 161–62.

40. Chandra Mohanty, "Under Western Eyes: Feminist Scholarship and Colonial Discourse," in *Third World Women and the Politics of Feminism*, eds. Chandra Talpade Mohanty, Ann Russo, and Lourdes Torres (Bloomington: Indiana University Press, 1991), p. 56.

41. Alison M. Jaggar, "Western Feminism and Global Responsibility," in *Feminist Interventions in Ethics and Politics*, eds. Barbara S. Andrew, Jean Keller, and Lisa H. Schwartzman (Lanham, Md.: Rowman and Littlefield, 2005).

42. Ibid.

43. Ibid.

44. Natalie Brender, "Political Care and Humanitarian Response," in *Feminists Doing Ethics*, eds. Peggy DesAutels and Joanne Waugh (Lanham, Md.: Rowman and Littlefield, 2001).

45. Fiona Robinson, *Globalizing Care: Ethics, Feminist Theory, and International Affairs* (Boulder, Colo.: Westview Press, 1999), p. 7.

46. Mary K. Meyer, "Negotiating International Norms: The Inter-American Commission of Women and the Convention on Violence against Women," in *Gender Politics in Global Governance*, eds. Meyer and Prügl, p. 60.

47. Tickner, *Gendering World Politics*, p. 77.

48. See, for example, Maria Mies and Vandana Shiva, eds., *Ecofeminism* (London: Zed Books, 1993).

49. See Robinson, *Globalizing Care*, pp. 161–62.

50. See Tickner, *Gendering World Politics*, pp. 116–19, on the growth of women's activism through nongovernmental organizations.

51. Richard Falk, "The Making of Global Citizenship," in *Global Visions: Beyond the New World Order*, eds. Jeremy Brecher, John Brown Childs, and Jill Cutler (Boston: South End Press, 1993). Examples are the environmental movement and movements against the harmful effects of globalization.

52. Anne-Marie Slaughter, *A New World Order* (Princeton, N.J.: Princeton University Press, 2004).

53. Ibid., p. 3.

54. Ibid., p. 33.

55. John Keane, *Global Civil Society?* (Cambridge: Cambridge University Press, 2003).

56. Ibid., p. 18.

57. Ibid., pp. xi–xii.

58. Slaughter, *A New World Order*, p. 18.

Bibliography

Addelson, Kathryn Pyne. 1991. *Impure Thoughts: Essays on Philosophy, Feminism, and Ethics*. Philadelphia: Temple University Press.

Aiken, William and Hugh LaFollette, eds. 1977. *World Hunger and Moral Obligation*. Englewood Cliffs, N.J.: Prentice Hall.

Alcoff, Linda, and Elizabeth Potter, eds. 1993. *Feminist Epistemologies*. New York: Routledge.

Allen, Amy. 1999. *The Power of Feminist Theory: Domination, Resistance, Solidarity*. Boulder, Colo: Westview Press.

Allen, Anita. 1988. *Uneasy Access: Privacy for Women in a Free Society*. Totowa, N.J.: Rowman and Littlefield.

Almond, Gabriel A., and Sidney Verba. 1965. *Civic Culture*. Boston: Little, Brown.

Anderson, Elizabeth. 1990. "Is Women's Labor a Commodity?" *Philosophy and Public Affairs* 19(1) (winter): 71–92.

Anderson, Elizabeth. 1993. *Value in Ethics and Economics*. Cambridge, Mass.: Harvard University Press.

Andrew, Barbara S. 2001. "Angels, Rubbish Collectors, and Pursuers of Erotic Joy: The Image of the Ethical Woman," in *Feminists Doing Ethics*, ed. Peggy DesAutels and Joanne Waugh. Lanham, Md: Rowman and Littlefield.

Annas, Julia. 1995. *The Morality of Happiness*. New York: Oxford University Press.

Baier, Annette C. 1986. "Trust and Anti-Trust." *Ethics* 96:231–60.

Baier, Annette C. 1994. *Moral Prejudices: Essays on Ethics*. Cambridge, Mass.: Harvard University Press.

Baier, Annette C. 2004. "Demoralization, Trust, and the Virtues," in *Setting the Moral Compass*, ed. Cheshire Calhoun. New York: Oxford University Press.

Baron, Marcia. 1991. "Impartiality and Friendship," *Ethics* 101(4) (July): 836–37.

Baron, Marcia. 1995. *Kantian Ethics Almost without Apology*. Ithaca NY: Cornell University Press.

Baron, Marcia W., Philip Pettit, and Michael Slote, eds., 1997. *Three Methods of Ethics*. Oxford: Blackwell Press.

Barry, Brian. 1973. *The Liberal Theory of Justice*. London: Oxford University Press.

Barry, Brian. 1995. *Justice as Impartiality*. Oxford: Oxford University Press.

Bartlett, Katherine T., and Rosanne Kennedy, eds. 1989. *Feminist Legal Theory: Readings in Law and Gender*. Boulder, Colo.: Westview Press.

Becker, Gary S. 1976. *The Economic Approach to Human Behavior*. Chicago: University of Chicago Press.

Becker, Gary S. 1981. *A Treatise on the Family*. Cambridge, Mass.: Harvard University Press.

Beitz, Charles R. 1979. *Political Theory and International Relations*. Princeton, N.J.: Princeton University Press.

Bell, Linda A. 1993. *Rethinking Ethics in the Midst of Violence: A Feminist Approach to Freedom*. Lanham, Md: Rowman and Littlefield.

Benhabib, Seyla. 1992. *Situating the Self: Gender, Community, and Postmodernism in Contemporary Ethics*. New York: Routledge.

Benhabib, Seyla, and Drucilla Cornell, eds. 1987. *Feminism as Critique: On the Politics of Gender*. Minneapolis: University of Minnesota Press.

Blum, Lawrence A. 1980. *Friendship, Altruism and Morality*. London: Routledge, 1980.

Blum, Lawrence A. 1994. *Moral Perception and Particularity*. New York: Cambridge University Press.

Blustein, Jeffrey. 1991. *Care and Commitment*. New York: Oxford University Press.

Bowden, Peta. 1997. *Caring: Gender Sensitive Ethics*. London: Routledge, 1997.

Brender, Natalie. 2001. "Political Care and Humanitarian Response," in *Feminists Doing Ethics*, eds. Peggy DesAutels and Joanne Waugh. Lanham, Md.: Rowman and Littlefield.

Brighouse, Harry. 1998. "Civic Education and Liberal Legitimacy," *Ethics* 108 (July): 719–45.

Brison, Susan J. 2000. "Relational Autonomy and Freedom of Expression," in *Relational Autonomy: Feminist Perspectives on Autonomy, Agency, and the Social Self*, eds. Catriona Mackenzie and Natalie Stoljar. New York: Oxford University Press.

Bubeck, Diemut. 1995. *Care, Gender, and Justice*. Oxford: Oxford University Press.

Calhoun, Cheshire, ed. 2004. *Setting the Moral Compass*. New York: Oxford University Press.

Callahan, Joan. 1995. *Reproduction, Ethics, and the Law: Feminist Perspectives*. Bloomington: Indiana University Press.

Campbell, Richmond. 1998. *Illusions of Paradox: A Feminist Epistemology Naturalized*. Lanham, Md.: Rowman and Littlefield.

Card, Claudia. 1995. "Gender and Moral Luck," in *Justice and Care: Essential Readings in Feminist Ethics*, ed. Virginia Held. Boulder, Colo.: Westview Press.

Card, Claudia, ed. 1991. *Feminist Ethics*. Lawrence: University Press of Kansas.

Card, Claudia, ed. 1999. *On Feminist Ethics and Politics*. Lawrence: University Press of Kansas.

Charlton, Sue Ellen M. 1984. *Women in Third World Development*. Boulder, Colo.: Westview Press.

Clement, Grace. 1996. *Care, Autonomy, and Justice*. Boulder, Colo.: Westview Press.

Cohen, Jean L., and Andrew Arato. 1994. *Civil Society and Political Theory*. Cambridge, Mass.: MIT Press.

Cole, Eve Browning, and Susan Coultrap McQuin, eds. 1992. *Explorations in Feminist Ethics: Theory and Practice*. Indianapolis: Indiana University Press.

Collins, Patricia Hill. 1990. *Black Feminist Thought: Knowledge, Consciousness, and the Politics of Empowerment*. Boston: Unwin Hyman.

Cooke, Rebecca J., ed. 1994. *Human Rights of Women: National and International Perspectives*. Philadelphia: University of Pennsylvania Press.

Copp, David. 1998. "Equality, Justice, and the Basic Needs," in *Necessary Goods*, ed. Gillian Brock. Lanham, Md.: Rowman and Littlefield.

Cornell, Drucilla. 1998. *At the Heart of Freedom: Feminism, Sex, and Equality*. Princeton, N.J.: Princeton University Press.

Crenshaw, Kimberle. 1991. "Demarginalizing the Intersection of Race and Sex: A Black Feminist Critique of Antidiscrimination Doctrine, Feminist Theory, and Antiracist Politics," in *Feminist Legal Theory: Readings in Law and Gender*, eds. Katherine T. Bartlett and Rosanne Kennedy. Boulder, Colo.: Westview Press.

Cunningham, Frank. 1987. *Democratic Theory and Socialism*. Cambridge: Cambridge University Press.

Curzer, Howard J. 2002. "Admirable Immorality, Dirty Hands, Care Ethics, Justice Ethics, and Child Sacrifice." *Ratio* 15(3) (September): 227–44.

Daggar, Richard. 1997. *Civic Virtues*. New York: Oxford University Press.

Dahl, Robert A. 1970. *After the Revolution*. New Haven, Conn.: Yale University Press.

Dancy, Jonathan, ed. 1997. *Reading Parfit*. Oxford: Blackwell.

Darwall, Stephen L. 1983. *Impartial Reason*. Ithaca, N.Y.: Cornell University Press.

Darwall, Stephen. 1998. *Philosophical Ethics*. Boulder, Colo.: Westview Press.

Dawes, Robyn M., and Richard H. Thaler. 1988. "Cooperation." *Journal of Economic Perspectives* 2(3) (summer): 187–97.

DesAutels, Peggy, and Joanne Waugh, eds. 2001. *Feminists Doing Ethics*. Lanham, Md.: Rowman and Littlefield.

De Tocqueville, Alexis. 1955. *Democracy in America*, 12th ed. New York: Vintage.

Deveaux, Monique. 1995. "Shifting Paradigms: Theorizing Care and Justice in Political Theory." *Hypatia: A Journal of Feminist Philosophy* 10(2) (spring): 115–19.

Dewey, John. 1916. *Democracy and Education*. New York: Macmillan.

Dewey, John. 1963. *Experience and Education*. New York: Collier Macmillan.

Di Stefano, Christine. 1991. *Configurations of Masculinity: A Feminist Perspective on Modern Political Theory*. Ithaca, N.Y.: Cornell University Press.

Di Stefano, Christine. 2000. "Feminist Political Philosophy." *American Philosophical Association Newsletter on Feminism and Philosophy* (spring): 196–200.

Dworkin, Ronald. 1977. *Taking Rights Seriously*. Cambridge, Mass.: Harvard University Press.

England, Paula, and Nancy Folbre. 1999. "The Cost of Caring." *Annals of the American Academy of Political and Social Science*, 561 (January): 39–51.

Estrich, Susan. 1987. "Rape." *Yale Law Journal* 95: 1087–184.

Falk, Richard. 1968. *Legal Order in a Violent World*. Princeton, N.J.: Princeton University Press.

Falk, Richard. 1993. "The Making of Global Citizenship," in *Global Visions: Beyond the New World Order*, eds. Jeremy Brecher, John Brown Childs, and Jill Cutler. Boston: South End Press.

Ferguson, Ann, and Nancy Folbre. 1981. "The Unhappy Marriage of Patriarchy and Capitalism," in *Women and Revolution*, ed. Lydia Sargent. Boston: South End Press.

Fisher, Berenice, and Joan Tronto. 1990. "Toward a Feminist Theory of Caring," in *Circles of Care*, eds. E. Abel and M. Nelson. Albany: SUNY Press.

Flanagan, Owen, and Amelie Oksenberg Rorty, eds. 1992. *Identity, Character, and Morality: Essays in Moral Psychology*. Cambridge, Mass.: MIT Press.

Folbre, Nancy. 2001. *The Invisible Heart: Economics and Family Values*. New York: New Press.

Folbre, Nancy, and Julie A. Nelson. 2000. "For Love or Money—Or Both?" *Journal of Economic Perspectives* 14(4) (fall): 123–40.

Foot, Philippa. 1978. *Virtues and Vices*. Berkeley: University of California Press.

Frank, Robert A., Thomas Gilovich, and Dennis T. Regan. 1993. "Does Studying Economics Inhibit Cooperation?" *Journal of Economic Perspectives* 7(2): 159–71.

Frankfurt, Harry G. 1988. *The Importance of What We Care About*. Cambridge: Cambridge University Press.

Fraser, Nancy. 1987. "Women, Welfare and the Politics of Needs Interpretation." *Hypatia: A Journal of Feminist Philosophy* 2(1): 103–21.

Fraser, Nancy. 1989. *Unruly Practices: Power, Discourse, and Gender in Contemporary Social Theory*. Minneapolis: University of Minnesota Press.

Frazer, Elizabeth, and Nicola Lacey. 1993. *The Politics of Community: A Feminist Critique of the Liberal-Communitarian Debate*. Toronto: University of Toronto Press.

Friedman, Marilyn. 1993. *What Are Friends For? Feminist Perspectives on Personal Relationships and Moral Theory*. Ithaca, N.Y.: Cornell University Press.

Friedman, Marilyn. 2003. *Autonomy, Gender, Politics*. New York: Oxford University Press.

Friend, Celeste M. 1995. "Trust and the Limits of Contract," Ph.D. dissertation. City University of New York.

Galston, William. 1992. *Liberal Purposes*. Cambridge: Cambridge University Press.

Gauthier, David. 1986. *Morals by Agreement*. Oxford: Oxford University Press.

Gilligan, Carol. 1982. *In a Different Voice: Psychological Theory and Women's Development*. Cambridge, Mass.: Harvard University Press.

Gilligan, Carol. 1987. "Moral Orientation and Moral Development," in *Women and Moral Theory*, eds. Eva Feder Kittay and Diana T. Meyers. Lanham, Md.: Rowman and Littlefield.

Goodin, Robert E. 1985. *Protecting the Vulnerable: A Reanalysis of Our Social Responsibilities*. Chicago: University of Chicago Press.

Goodin, Robert E. 1988. *Reasons for Welfare*. Princeton, N.J.: Princeton University Press.

Goodin, Robert E. 1995. *Utilitarianism as a Public Philosophy*. Cambridge: Cambridge University Press.

Gordon, Robert M. 1996. "Sympathy, Simulation, and the Impartial Spectator," in *Mind and Morals: Essays on Ethics and Cognitive Science*, eds. Larry May, Marilyn Friedman, and Andy Clark. Cambridge, Mass.: MIT Press.

Gould, Carol C. 1988. *Rethinking Democracy: Freedom and Social Cooperation in Politics, Economy, and Society*. Cambridge: Cambridge University Press.

Gould, Carol C. 2004. *Globalizing Democracy and Human Rights*. New York: Cambridge University Press.

Grant, Rebecca, and Kathleen Newland, eds. 1991. *Gender and International Relations*. Bloomington: Indiana University Press.

Gutmann, Amy. 1987. *Democratic Education*. Princeton, N.J.: Princeton University Press.

Habermas, Jürgen. 1995. "Discourse Ethics," in Jürgen Habermas, *Moral Consciousness and Communicative Action*. Cambridge, Mass.: MIT Press.

Halfon, Mark S., and Joram C. Haber, eds. 1998. *Norms and Values: Essays on the Work of Virginia Held*. Lanham, Md.: Rowman and Littlefield.

Hall, John A., ed. 1995. *Civil Society: Theory, History, Comparison*. Cambridge: Polity Press.

Hampton, Jean. 1993. "Feminist Contractarianism," in *A Mind of One's Own: Feminist Essays on Reason and Objectivity*, eds. Louise M. Antony and Charlotte Witt. Boulder, Colo.: Westview Press.

Hampton, Jean. 1997. *Political Philosophy*. Boulder, Colo.: Westview Press.

Hanen, Marsha, and Kai Nielsen, eds. 1987. *Science, Morality and Feminist Theory*. Calgary: University of Calgary Press.

Hanigsberg, Julia E. and Sara Ruddick, eds. 1999. *Mother Troubles: Rethinking Contemporary Maternal Dilemmas*. Boston: Beacon Press.

Harding, Sandra. 1987. "The Curious Coincidence of Feminine and African Moralities," in *Women and Moral Theory*, eds. Eva Feder Kittay and Diana T. Meyers. Lanham, Md.: Rowman and Littlefield.

Harding, Sandra, and Merrill Hintikka, eds. 1983. *Discovering Reality: Feminist Perspectives on Epistemology, Metaphysics, Methodology and Philosophy of Science*. Dordrecht: Reidel.

Harrington, Mona. 1999. *Care and Equality: Inventing a New Family Politics*. New York: Knopf.

Hartsock, Nancy C. M. 1983. *Money, Sex, and Power: Toward a Feminist Historical Materialism*. New York: Longman.

Hartsock, Nancy C. M. 1996. "Community/Sexuality/Gender: Rethinking Power," in *Revisioning the Political: Feminist Reconstructions of Traditional Concepts in Western Political Theory*, eds. Nancy J. Hirschmann and Christine Di Stefano. Boulder, Colo.: Westview Press.

Hays, Constance L. 2000. "Commercialism in U.S. Schools Is Examined in New Report." *New York Times* (September 14), pp. C1 and 25.

Hekman, Susan J. 1995. *Moral Voices, Moral Selves*. University Park: University of Pennsylvania Press.

Held, Virginia. 1968. "On the Meaning of Trust." *Ethics* 78 (January).

Held, Virginia. 1977. "Rationality and Reasonable Cooperation." *Social Research* 44(4) (winter): 708–44.

Held, Virginia. [1984] 1989. *Rights and Goods: Justifying Social Action*. Chicago: University of Chicago Press.

Held, Virginia. 1988. "Access, Enablement, and the First Amendment," in *Philosophical Dimensions of the Constitution*, eds. Diana T. Meyers and Kenneth Kipnis. Boulder, Colo.: Westview Press.

Held, Virginia. 1993. *Feminist Morality: Transforming Culture, Society, and Politics*. Chicago: University of Chicago Press.

Held, Virginia. 2002. "Moral Subjects: The Natural and the Normative." Presidential address, American Philosophical Association, Eastern Division. *Proceedings and Addresses of the American Philosophical Association*. Newark, DE (November).

Held, Virginia, ed. 1995. *Justice and Care: Essential Readings in Feminist Ethics*. Boulder Colo.: Westview Press.

Held, Virginia, Sidney Morgenbesser, and Thomas Nagel, eds. 1974. *Philosophy, Morality, and International Affairs*. New York: Oxford University Press.

Henkin, Louis. 1990. *The Age of Rights*. New York: Columbia University Press.

Henkin, Louis. 1989. "The Use of Force: Law and U.S. Policy," in *Right v. Wrong: International Law and the Use of Force*. Council on Foreign Relations, 1989.

Herman, Barbara. 1993. *The Practice of Moral Judgment*. Cambridge, Mass.: Harvard University Press.

Hirschmann, Nancy J., and Christine DiStefano, eds. 1996. *Revisioning the Political: Feminist Reconstructions of Traditional Concepts in Western Political Theory*. Boulder, Colo.: Westview Press.

Hoagland, Sara Lucia. 1989. *Lesbian Ethics: Toward New Value*. Palo Alto, Calif.: Institute of Lesbian Studies.

Hobbes, Thomas. 1972. *The Citizen: Philosophical Rudiments Concerning Government and Society*, ed. B. Gert. Garden City, N.Y.: Doubleday.

Hoffman, Stanley. 1981. *Duties beyond Borders: On the Limits and Possibilities of Ethical International Politics*. Syracuse, N.Y.: Syracuse University Press.

Holmes, Robert L. 1989. *On War and Morality*. Princeton, N.J.: Princeton University Press.

Houston, Barbara. 1987. "Rescuing Womanly Virtues: Some Dangers of Moral Reclamation," in *Science, Morality and Feminist Theory*, eds. M. Hanen and K. Nielsen. Calgary: University of Calgary Press.

Hursthouse, Rosalind, Gavin Lawrence, and Warren Quinn, eds. 1998. *Virtues and Reasons: Philippa Foot and Moral Theory*. Oxford: Clarendon Press.

Jaggar, Alison M. 1983. *Feminist Politics and Human Nature*. Totowa, N.J.: Rowman and Allanheld.

Jaggar, Alison M. 1989. "Feminist Ethics: Some Issues for the Nineties." *Journal of Social Philosophy* 20: 91–107.

Jaggar, Alison M. 1995. "Caring as a Feminist Practice of Moral Reason," in *Justice and Care: Essential Readings in Feminist Ethics*, ed. Virginia Held. Boulder, Colo.: Westview Press.

Jaggar, Alison M. 2005. "Western Feminism and Global Responsibility," in *Feminist Interventions in Ethics and Politics*, eds. Barbara S. Andrew, Jean Keller, and Lisa H. Schwartzman. Lanham, Md.: Rowman and Littlefield.

Jones, Kathleen B. 1992. *Compassionate Authority: Democracy and the Representation of Women*. New York: Routledge.

Kant, Immanuel. 1959. *Foundations of the Metaphysics of Morals*, trans. Lewis White Beck. Indianapolis: Bobbs-Merrill.

Keane, John. 1998. *Civil Society: Old Images, New Visions*. Stanford, Calif.: Stanford University Press.

Keane, John, 2003. *Global Civil Society?* Cambridge: Cambridge University Press.

Keller, Jean. 1997. "Autonomy, Relationality, and Feminist Ethics." *Hypatia: A Journal of Feminist Philosophy* 12(2): 152–65.

Kittay, Eva Feder. 1995. "Taking Dependency Seriously." *Hypatia: A Journal of Feminist Philosophy*. 8–29.

Kittay, Eva Feder. 1999. *Love's Labor: Essays on Women, Equality, and Dependency*. New York: Routledge.

Kittay, Eva Feder, and Diana T. Meyers, eds. 1987. *Women and Moral Theory*. Lanham, MD: Rowman and Littlefield.

Koehn, Daryl. 1998. *Rethinking Feminist Ethics: Care, Trust and Empathy*. London: Routledge.

Kuttner, Robert. 1998. *Everything for Sale: The Virtues and Limits of Markets*. New York: Knopf.

Kymlicka, Will, and Wayne Norman. 1994. "Return of the Citizen: A Survey of Recent Work on Citizenship Theory." *Ethics* 104 (January): 352–81.

Landes, Joan B., ed. 1998. *Feminism, the Public and the Private*. New York: Oxford University Press.

Landes, Elisabeth M., and Richard A. Posner. 1978. "The Economics of the Baby Shortage." *Journal of Legal Studies* 7: 323–48.

Larrabee, Mary Jeanne, ed. 1993. *An Ethic of Care: Feminist and Interdisciplinary Perspectives.* New York: Routledge.

Levine, Arthur. 2000. "The Soul of a New University." *New York Times* (March 13), op-ed page.

Li, Chenyang. 1994. "The Confucian Concept of *Jen* and the Feminist Ethics of Care: A Comparative Study." *Hypatia: A Journal of Feminist Philosophy* 9(1): 70–89.

Li, Chenyang. 2002. "Revisiting Confucian *Jen* Ethics and Feminist Care Ethics: A Reply to Daniel Star and Lijun Yuan." *Hypatia: A Journal of Feminist Philosophy* 17(1): 130–40.

Linz, Juan J., and Alfred Stepan. 1996. *Problems of Democratic Transition and Consolidation: Southern Europe, South America, and Post-Communist Europe.* Baltimore: Johns Hopkins University Press.

Littleton, Christine. 1987. "Reconstructing Sexual Equality." *California Law Review* 75(4): 1279–337.

Lloyd, Genevieve. 1984. *The Man of Reason: "Male" and "Female" in Western Philosophy.* Minneapolis: University of Minnesota Press.

Lugones, Maria C. 1991. "On the Logic of Pluralist Feminism," in *Feminist Ethics*, ed. Claudia Card. Lawrence: University Press of Kansas.

Luper-Foy, Steven, ed. 1988. *Problems of International Justice.* Boulder, Colo.: Westview Press.

MacCormick, Neil. 1996. "Justice as Impartiality: Assenting with Anti-Contractualist Reservations." *Political Studies* 44: 305–10.

Macedo, Stephen. 1995. "Liberal Civic Education and Religious Fundamentalism: The Case of God v. John Rawls?" *Ethics* 108: 468–96.

MacIntyre, Alasdair. 1981. *After Virtue: A Study in Moral Theory.* Notre Dame, Ind.: University of Notre Dame Press.

MacIntyre, Alasdair. 1999. *Dependent Rational Animals: Why Human Beings Need the Virtues.* Peru, Ill.: Open Court.

MacIntyre, Alasdair. 1988. *Whose Justice? Which Rationality?* Notre Dame, Ind.: University of Notre Dame Press.

MacKenzie, Catriona, and Natalie Stoljar, eds. 2000. *Relational Autonomy: Feminist Perspectives on Autonomy, Agency, and the Social Self.* New York: Oxford University Press.

MacKinnon, Catharine. 1987. *Feminism Unmodified: Discourses on Life and Law.* Cambridge, Mass.: Harvard University Press.

MacKinnon, Catharine. 1989. *Toward a Feminist Theory of the State.* Cambridge, Mass.: Harvard University Press.

McLaren, Margaret A. 2001. "Feminist Ethics: Care as a Virtue," in *Feminists Doing Ethics*, ed. Peggy DesAutels and Joanne Waugh. Lanham, Md: Rowman and Littlefield.

Maghroori, Ray, and Bennett Ramberg, eds. 1982. *Globalism versus Realism: International Relations' Third Debate.* Boulder, Colo.: Westview Press.

Mahowald, Mary. 1994. *Philosophy of Woman: Classical to Current Concepts*, 3rd ed. Indianapolis, Ind.: Hackett.

Mahowald, Mary, Anita Silvers, and David Wasserman. 1998. *Disability, Difference, Discrimination.* Lanham, Md.: Rowman and Littlefield.

Manning, Rita. 1992. *Speaking from the Heart: A Feminist Perspective on Ethics.* Lanham, Md.: Rowman and Littlefield.

Manning, Steven. 1999. "How Corporations Are Buying Their Way into American Classrooms." *Nation* (September 27), pp. 11–18.

Mansbridge, Jane. 1983. *Beyond Adversary Democracy*. Chicago: University of Chicago Press.

Mansbridge, Jane. 1996. "Reconstructing Democracy," in *Revisioning the Political: Feminist Reconstructions of Traditional Concepts in Western Political Theory*, eds. Nancy Hirschmann and Christine Di Stefano. Boulder, Colo.: Westview.

Marwell, Gerald, and Ruth Ames. 1981. "Economists Free Ride, Does Anyone Else?: Experiments on the Provision of Public Goods, IV." *Journal of Public Economics*. 15, 3: 295–310.

Mason, Andrew. 1999. "Political Community, Liberal-Nationalism, and the Ethics of Assimilation," *Ethics* 109:2 (January) 261–286.

McMurtry, John. 1991. "Education and the Market Model." *Journal of Philosophy of Education* 25, 2: 209–17.

Mendus, Susan. 1996. "Some Mistakes About Impartiality," *Political Studies* XLIV: 319–327.

Mendus, Susan. 2002. *Impartiality in Moral and Political Philosophy*. Oxford: Oxford University Press.

Meyer, Mary K., and Elisabeth Prügl, eds. 1999. *Gender Politics in Global Governance*, Lanham, MD: Rowman & Littlefield.

Meyers, Diana T. 1989. *Self, Society, and Personal Choice*. New York: Columbia University Press.

Meyers, Diana Tietjens. 1994. *Subjection and Subjectivity: Psychoanalytic Feminism and Moral Philosophy*. New York: Routledge.

Meyers, Diana Tietjens. 2002. *Gender in the Mirror: Cultural Imagery and Women's Agency*. New York: Oxford University Press.

Meyers, Diana Tietjens. 2004. "Narrative and Moral Life," in Cheshire Calhoun, ed., *Setting the Moral Compass*. New York: Oxford University Press.

Meyers, Diana Tietjens, ed. 1997. *Feminists Rethink the Self*. Boulder CO: Westview Press.

Mies, Maria, and Vandana Shiva, eds. 1993. *Ecofeminism*. London: Zed Books.

Miller, David. 1989. *Market, State, and Community*. Oxford: Oxford University Press.

Minow, Martha. 1990. *Making All The Difference: Inclusion, Exclusion, and American Law*. Ithaca, NY: Cornell University Press.

Minow, Martha, and Mary Lyndon Shanley. 1996. "Relational Rights and Responsibilities: Revisioning the Family in Liberal Political Theory and Law," *Hypatia: A Journal of Feminist Philosophy*. 11:1 (Winter) 3–29.

Mohanty, Chandra Talpade, Ann Russo, and Lourdes Torres, eds. 1991. *Third World Women and The Politics of Feminism*. Bloomington: Indiana University Press.

Morgan, Kathryn Pauly. 1987. "Women and Moral Madness," in M. Hanen and K. Nielsen, eds., *Science, Morality and Feminist Theory*. Calgary: University of Calgary Press.

Nagel, Thomas. 1970. *The Possibility of Altruism*. London: Oxford University Press.

Narayan, Uma. 1997. *Dislocating Cultures: Identities, Traditions and Third World Women*. New York: Routledge.

Nelson, Hilde Lindemann. 2001. "Identity and Free Agency," in Peggy DesAutels and Joanne Waugh, eds., *Feminists Doing Ethics*. Lanham, MD: Rowman & Littlefield.

Nicholson, Linda, ed. 1990. *Feminism/Postmodernism*. New York: Routledge.

Nickel, James W. 1987. *Making Sense of Human Rights*. Berkeley: University of California Press.

Noddings, Nel. 1986. *Caring: A Feminine Approach to Ethics and Moral Education.* Berkeley: University of California Press.

Noddings, Nel. 2002. *Starting At Home: Caring and Social Policy.* Berkeley: University of California Press.

Nussbaum, Martha C. 1986. *The Fragility of Goodness.* Cambridge: Cambridge University Press.

Nussbaum, Martha C. 1999. *Sex and Social Justice.* New York: Oxford University Press.

Nussbaum, Martha C., and Jonathan Glover, eds. 1995. *Women, Culture and Development: A Study of Human Capabilities.* Oxford: Clarendon Press.

Okin, Susan Moller. 1979. *Women in Western Political Thought.* Princeton: Princeton University Press.

Okin, Susan Moller. 1989. *Justice, Gender, and the Family.* New York: Basic Books.

Okin, Susan Moller. 1998. "Feminism and Multiculturalism: Some Tensions," *Ethics* 108 (July) 661–684.

Olsen, Frances. 1984. "Statutory Rape: A Feminist Critique of Rights Analysis," *Texas Law Review* 63: 387–432.

O'Neill, Onora. 1985. *Faces of Hunger: An Essay on Poverty, Justice, and Development.* London: Allen & Unwin.

Oshana, Marina. 1998. "Personal Autonomy and Society," *Journal of Social Philosophy* XXIX, 1: 81–102.

Petchesky, Rosalind P. 1985. *Abortion and Women's Choice: The State, Sexuality, and Reproductive Freedom.* Boston: Northeastern University Press.

Peterson, V. Spike, and Anne Sisson Runyan. 1993. *Global Gender Issues.* Boulder, CO: Westview Press.

Phillips, Anne. 1995. *The Politics of Presence.* Oxford: Oxford University Press.

Pincoffs, Edmund. 1986. *Quandaries and Virtues: Against Reductivism in Ethics.* Lawrence: University Press of Kansas.

Pogge, Thomas. 2002. *World Poverty and Human Rights.* Malden, MA: Polity Press.

Posner, Richard A. 1992. *Economic Analysis of Law.* 4th ed. Boston: Little, Brown and Co.

Potter, Nancy. 2001. "Is Refusing to Forgive a Vice?" in *Feminists Doing Ethics,* ed. Peggy DesAutels and Joanne Waugh. Lanham, Md: Rowman and Littlefield.

Purdy, Laura M. 1996. *Reproducing Persons: Issues in Feminist Bioethics.* Ithaca, NY: Cornell University Press.

Putnam, Robert D. 1994. *Making Democracy Work.* Princeton: Princeton University Press.

Putnam, Robert D. 1996. "The Strange Disappearance of Civic America," *The American Prospect* 24 (Winter): 34–49.

Radin, Margaret Jane. 1996. *Contested Commodities: The Trouble with Trade in Sex, Children, Body Parts, and Other Things.* Cambridge, MA: Harvard University Press.

Rawls, John. 1971. *A Theory of Justice.* Cambridge, MA: Harvard University Press.

Rawls, John. 1993. *Political Liberalism.* New York: Columbia University Press.

Rhode, Deborah L. 1989. *Justice and Gender: Sex Discrimination and the Law.* Cambridge, MA: Harvard University Press.

Robinson, Fiona. 1999. *Globalizing Care: Ethics, Feminist Theory, and International Affairs.* Boulder CO: Westview Press.

Rorty, Amelie Oksenberg, ed. 1980. *Essays on Aristotle's Ethics.* Berkeley: University of California Press.

Ruddick, Sara. 1980. "Maternal Thinking," *Feminist Studies* 6: 342–67.

Ruddick, Sara. 1989. *Maternal Thinking: Toward a Politics of Peace*. Boston: Beacon Press.

Ruddick, Sara. 1995. "Injustice in Families: Assault and Domination," in Virginia Held, ed., *Justice and Care: Essential Readings in Feminist Ethics*. Boulder, CO: Westview Press.

Ruddick, Sara. 1998. "Care as Labor and Relationship," in Mark S. Halfon and Joram C. Haber eds., *Norms and Values: Essays on the Work of Virginia Held*. Lanham, MD: Rowman & Littlefield.

Sandel, Michael. 1982. *Liberalism and the Limits of Justice*. Cambridge: Cambridge University Press.

Schneider, Elizabeth M. 1986. "The Dialectic of Rights and Politics: Perspectives From the Women's Movement," *New York University Law Review* 61: 593–652.

Schwarzenbach, Sibyl. 1996. "On Civic Friendship," *Ethics* 107, 1: 97–128.

Sevenhuijsen, Selma. 1998. *Citizenship and The Ethics of Care: Feminist Considerations on Justice, Morality and Politics*. London: Routledge.

Shanley, Mary Lyndon. 1993. "'Surrogate Mothering' and Women's Freedom: A Critique of Contracts for Human Reproduction." *Signs* 18, 3: 618–39.

Sherwin, Susan. 1992. *No Longer Patient: Feminist Ethics and Health Care*. Philadelphia: Temple University Press.

Shue, Henry. 1980. *Basic Rights*. Princeton, N.J.: Princeton University Press.

Singer, Peter. 2002. *One World: The Ethics of Globalization*. New Haven, CT: Yale University Press..

Slaughter, Anne-Marie. 2004. *A New World Order*. Princeton, NJ: Princeton University Press.

Slote, Michael. 1983. *Goods and Virtues*. Oxford: Oxford University Press.

Slote, Michael. 1992. *From Morality to Virtue*. New York: Oxford University Press.

Slote, Michael. 2001. *Morals From Motives*. Oxford: Oxford University Press.

Smart, Carol. 1989. *Feminism and the Power of Law*. London: Routledge.

Smith, Patricia, ed. 1993. *Feminist Jurisprudence*. New York: Oxford University Press.

Smith, Patricia. 1995. "Feminist Jurisprudence: Social Change and Conceptual Evolution," *American Philosophical Association Newsletter on Feminism and Philosophy (Spring)*.

Spelman, Elizabeth V. 1988. *Inessential Woman*. Boston: Beacon Press.

Star, Daniel. 2002. "Do Confucians Really Care? A Defense of the Distinctiveness of Care Ethics: A Reply to Chenyang Li," *Hypatia: A Journal of Feminist Philosophy*. 17,1: 77–106.

Steans, Jill. 1998. *Gender and International Relations: An Introduction*. New Brunswick, NJ: Rutgers University Press.

Stocker, Michael. 1990. *Plural and Conflicting Values*. New York: Oxford University Press.

Sunstein, Cass R. 2004. *The Second Bill of Rights: FDR's Unfinished Revolution and Why We Need It More Than Ever*. New York: Basic Books.

Taylor, Charles. 1979. *Hegel and Modern Society*. Cambridge: Cambridge University Press.

Taylor, Charles. 1985. *Philosophical Papers*. Cambridge: Cambridge University Press.

Taylor, Charles. 1995. *Philosophical Arguments*. Cambridge, MA: Harvard University Press.

Tessman, Lisa. 2001. "Critical Virtue Ethics: Understanding Oppression as Morally Damaging," in *Feminists Doing Ethics*, ed. Peggy DesAutels and Joanne Waugh. Lanham, Md: Rowman and Littlefield.

Tester, Keith. 1992. *Civil Society*. New York: Routledge.

Thomson, Judith Jarvis. 2001. *Goodness and Advice: With Commentary*. Ed. Amy Gutmann. Princeton: Princeton University Press.

Tickner, J. Ann. 1992. *Gender In International Relations: Feminist Perspectives on Achieving Global Security*. New York: Columbia University Press.

Tickner, J. Ann. 2001. *Gendering World Politics*. New York: Columbia University Press.

Tong, Rosemarie. 1993. *Feminine and Feminist Ethics*. Belmont, CA: Wadsworth.

Traub, James. "This Campus is Being Simulated." *The New York Times Magazine* (Nov. 19, 2000): 88-126.

Trebilcot, Joyce, ed. 1983. *Mothering: Essays in Feminist Theory*. Totowa, NJ: Rowman & Allanheld.

Tronto, Joan C. 1993. *Moral Boundaries: A Political Argument for an Ethic of Care*. New York: Routledge.

Tronto, Joan C. 1996. "Care as a Political Concept," in Nancy J. Hirschmann and Christine Di Stefano, eds. *Revisioning the Political: Feminist Reconstructions of Traditional Concepts in Western Political Theory*. Boulder, CO: Westview Press.

Unger, Roberto Mangabeire. 1975. *Knowledge and Politics*. New York: The Free Press.

United Nations Development Programme. 1996. *Human Development Report*. New York: Oxford University Press.

Vallentyne, Peter, ed. 1991. *Contractarianism and Rational Choice*. New York: Cambridge University Press.

Valls, Andrew, ed. 2000. *Ethics in International Affairs*. Lanham, MD: Rowman & Littlefield.

Velleman, J. David. 1999. "Love as a Moral Emotion," *Ethics* 109:2 (January) 338–374.

Walker, Lawrence J. 1984. "Sex Differences in the Development of Moral Reasoning: A Critical Review," *Child Development* 55: 677–91.

Walker, Margaret Urban. 1989. "Moral Understandings: Alternative 'Epistemology' for a Feminist Ethics," *Hypatia: A Journal of Feminist Philosophy*, 4: 15–28.

Walker, Margaret Urban. 1992. "Feminism, Ethics, and the Question of Theory," *Hypatia: A Journal of Feminist Philosophy*, 7: 23–38.

Walker, Margaret Urban. 1998. *Moral Understandings: A Feminist Study in Ethics*. New York: Routledge.

Walker, Margaret Urban. 2003. *Moral Contexts*. Lanham, MD: Rowman & Littlefield.

Walker, Margaret Urban, ed. 1999. *Mother Time: Women, Aging, and Ethics*. Lanham, MD: Rowman & Littlefield.

Wallace, James D. 1978. *Virtues and Vices*. Ithaca, NY: Cornell University Press.

Walzer, Michael. 1977. *Just and Unjust Wars*. New York: Basic Books.

Wasserstrom, Richard, ed. 1970. *War and Morality*. Belmont, CA: Wadsworth Publishing Co.

West, Robin. 1988. "Jurisprudence and Gender," *University of Chicago Law Review* 55: 1-72.

White, Julie Anne. 2000. *Democracy, Justice, and The Welfare State: Reconstructing Public Care*. University Park: The Pennsylvania State Press.

Wilber, Charles K., ed. 1998. *Economics, Ethics, and Public Policy.* Lanham, MD: Rowman & Littlefield.

Willett, Cynthia. 1995. *Maternal Ethics and Other Slave Moralities.* New York: Routledge.

Williams, Bernard. 1981. *Moral Luck: Philosophical Papers 1973-80.* Cambridge: Cambridge University Press.

Williams, Bernard. 1985. *Ethics and the Limits of Philosophy.* Cambridge, MA: Harvard University Press.

Williams, Patricia J. 1991. *The Alchemy of Race and Rights.* Cambridge, MA: Harvard University Press.

Yee, Chan Sin. 2003. "The Confucian Conception of Gender in the Twenty-First Century," in Hahm Chaibong and Daniel A. Bell, eds., *Confucianism for the Modern World.* Cambridge: Cambridge University Press.

Young, Iris Marion. 1990. *Justice and the Politics of Difference.* Princeton, NJ: Princeton University Press.

Yuan, Lijun. 2002. "Ethics of Care and Concept of *Jen*: A Reply to Chenyang Li," *Hypatia: A Journal of Feminist Philosophy* 17:1, 107–129.

Index

CPSIA information can be obtained
at www.ICGtesting.com
Printed in the USA
BVHW041519281221
624965BV00003B/5